D1617447

The Making of
the Trek Conventions

The Making of
the Trek Conventions

or

How to Throw a Party for 12,000
of Your Most Intimate Friends

Joan Winston

DOUBLEDAY & COMPANY, INC., GARDEN CITY, NEW YORK   1977

To the fans:

If a picture of one of your favorites is missing, it is because we either could not reach them in time or proper arrangements could not be made.

ISBN: 0-385-13112-7
Library of Congress Catalog Card Number 77-76146
Copyright © 1977 by Joan Winston
All Rights Reserved
Printed in the United States of America
First Edition

Here is a list of all the reprinted material contained in this book:

Article from *TV Guide*—Reprinted with permission from *TV Guide* magazine. Copyright © 1972 by Triangle Publications, Inc., Radnor, Pennsylvania.

Article from New York *Daily News*—Reprinted by permission from the *Daily News,* by Anthony Burton, published by New York News, Inc. Copyright 1972 by New York News, Inc.

Article from *Variety*—Reprinted by permission from Variety, Inc., by Frank Beermann, published by Variety, Inc. Copyright 1972 by Variety, Inc.

Convention report by Devra Michele Langsam—Reprinted by permission from Poison Pen Press, No. 9. Copyright © 1972 by Poison Pen Press.

1975 trivia contest—Copyright © 1975 by Tellurian Enterprises, Inc.

The trivia contest of 1972, 1973, 1974, and for the two 1976 used by permission of Tellurian Enterprises, Inc.

Transcriptions of DeForest Kelley's broadcasts—printed through the courtesy and permission of Kaiser Broadcasting Company, WKBS-TV.

Song, "Battle Hymn of Helpers"—Copyright © 1975, Tellurian Enterprises, Inc.

Cartoons Copyright © 1976 by Phil Foglio; Song lyrics, "The Chicago Con" Copyright © 1975 by Ann Passovoy. From *The New York and Chicago Strektaculars!* published by boojums press.

Library of Congress Cataloging in Publication Data

Winston, Joan.
The making of the trek conventions.

1. Star trek. I. Title.
PN1992.77.S73W54   791.45'7

DEDICATION

This book is dedicated to many, many people, and I've probably forgotten somebody somewhere—so please forgive me:

To "The Committee," good friends and true. I couldn't have done it without them, especially: Dana Anderson (now D. Garrett Gafford), Thom Anderson, Claire Eddy, Stu Grossman, Stuart C. Hellinger, Devra Michele Langsam, Wendy Lindboe, Elyse S. Rosenstein, Steven J. Rosenstein, Louise Sachter, David Simons, Barbara Wenk, Ben Yalow, Joyce Yasner.

And a special thanks to our friends and attorneys, Sondra and Robert Harris

To all the unforgettable people who helped put "Star Trek" on the air, in front of and behind the cameras.

To ABC, and in particular Richard N. Burns and Anthony S. Farinacci, for their good wishes and understanding.

To my family, bless 'em, who didn't really understand it all, but who put up with it and loved me anyway.

To all the assistants, helpers, and fans who made the conventions possible.

To one who knows who she is and knows what I want to say— but my heart is too full.

Last, but not least, The Great Bird himself and his beautiful partner, Gene Roddenberry and Majel Barrett Roddenberry.

THANK YOU ALL.
(Whew!)

CONTENTS

The projector problem . . . The (almost) film fiasco . . . The famous carbon-arc caper . . . De Kelley makes a con call . . . Another surprise visit from Mr. Spock . . . Chekov gets mobbed . . . Uhura sings . . . Zarabeth speaks . . . Fred makes Al a Klingon . . . The printing was late . . . The Trivia Contest gets harder.

Nobody loves us . . . Everybody loves us but nobody wants us . . . We get an agent . . . We lose an agent . . . We send it to Ace . . . Fred Pohl calls Jackie . . . Everybody wants us! . . . We find a home.

The press party (They still won't go) . . . Bill Shatner and security; or, how to make Stu Hellinger cry . . . The counterfeit tickets . . . The press room panic . . . Claire's cable caper . . . Bob Lansing comes to a party and stays for the con . . . The helpers (too much of a good thing) . . . The return of the Roddenberrys . . . Bill Theiss undresses Joyce and Joan . . . Here come de judge—me! . . . The Dead Dog and Songwriting parties . . . Creative Wheelchair Wrapping 101 and 102 . . . The printing was *not* late! . . . The Trivia Contest is staggering.

College Park, Maryland . . . Detroit, Michigan . . . Chicago, Illinois . . . Boston, Massachusetts . . . Toronto, Ontario, Canada . . . Oakland, California . . . Richmond, Virginia . . . New York, New York . . . Great Gorge, New Jersey . . . Alexandria, Virginia.

The end of our five-year mission . . . The press party (So *we* leave!) . . . *Time* takes pictures . . . The Saturday-night riot . . . The Saturday-night robberies . . . The finest fans . . . The helpingest helpers . . . Meara comes *sans* Stiller . . . The Trivia Contest is overwhelming . . . The Roddenberry serenade . . . The return of DeForest Kelley . . . Jimmy

THE WHAT-IS-IT CHAPTER

A fact has been brought to my notice. I am writing a book all by myself. No Jackie, no Sondra,[1] the kid stands alone, I figure the only way to do it, my way, is to do it piece by piece, chapter by chapter. If I ever really think how many pages I'll have to write —I'd probably give up.

I admit it hasn't been easy. I have a job that I love with people I love, and it is very difficult to do a book when you are working from ten to twelve hours a day just trying to keep up with the flood of paper. Whatever time left over went to the 1976 convention. That took eleven months to put together. Some people have sneered at our working that hard—mostly those who have thought that you can put on a convention in a month or two with little or no experience. But those cons[2] always seem to fall apart. Usually because the people fall apart. Too much to do and not enough time to do it in: Slow and easy wins the race, most times. Not only do you get everything done, but you also get to know and trust each other, and that, my friends, is the main reason I'm writing this book. I have been privileged to work with a great group of people, and I'd like you to get to know them as I do.

But before we get to The Adventures of the Committee and all the fun—and we did have fun, or else why do five conventions? —I'd like to get a few things off the Winston chest. A few paragraphs up I stated that I was writing this book all by myself, which is true, up to a point. I had a lot of help from a lot of people. I also said "No, Jackie," but that's not really true. Jackie gave me invaluable advice, most of which I took. I would send Jackie a rough first draft and it would be returned, covered with red ink scrawls: "This is too long. Get to the point." "This is good." "This needs to be clarified. Clean it up." "This is funny, but it doesn't fit. Put it someplace else."

I don't know about other writers, but I have to bounce my stuff off a lot of people. To have someone able to give you constructive, lucid criticism is a priceless thing, and I must thank her here and now.

[1] Jacqueline Lichtenberg and Sondra Marshak, my coauthors on *Star Trek Lives!*

[2] Once initiated, no conventiongoer ever says the whole word again.

Elyse Rosenstein became my "irreplaceable person," especially during the last year. Whenever my memory would fail me, Elyse would always come through with the right information. I remember calling at eleven-thirty one evening and asking if she remembered whether Majel Roddenberry had arrived on Friday night or Saturday morning at the 1976 con. Without a pause, Elyse answered, "Friday night." See what I mean?

This book was written, for the most part, in longhand. I am a four-finger typist (five, if you count the thumb). Not exactly Speedy Gonzalez. At this point, I want to thank all those friends who volunteered to type for me. Some got paid, but most refused. They insisted that the opportunity to be the first to read the book was enough. Nuts, but lovable. (Well, at least they all got fed.)

To Allan Asherman, Maxine Broadwater, Heather Haven, Cynthia Levine, Elan Jane Litt, and Valerie Sussman: Thank you. I love you all.

An extra thank you to Valerie, who has become my chauffeur and, with Janet Ingber, my companion at almost all the cons I attend.

To my two secretaries—first, Andrea Romano, and now Christine Accardi—who put up with all the phone calls and general confusion when the conventions were still going on, thank you, thank you.

To Liz Barad and David Sherman, you know for what!

To all the fans who let me use their precious pictures in this book.

To Jeff Maynard, who really helped select many lovely shots from his collection. Beautiful. Also Ben Yalow, Linda Deneroff and the others.

I don't know what the policy is concerning editors, but Sharon Jarvis of Doubleday showed me the meaning of "stanch support."

And many thanks to the good Lord for blessing me with a good memory and so many good friends.

Joan Winston
New York City
January 1977

THE CAST OF "CHARACTERS"

ISAAC ASIMOV (1972, 1973, 1974, 1975, 1976)
Isaac is one of the most prolific writers around today (almost two hundred books). He writes not only science fiction (he has won the Hugo and Nebula awards), but also nonfiction and mysteries. He is a charismatic speaker, and the famous talks of Isaac about Isaac are ones we treasure. I feel he has done much to make the science in science fiction easier to understand and enjoy.

MAJEL BARRETT (1972, 1975, 1976)
Majel created the part of Nurse Christine Chapel on "Star Trek." It was a fairly thankless role, but Majel made it warm and sympathetic. She created a person and made us care what happened to her. Majel also created Lincoln Enterprises,[1] where almost anything connected with "Star Trek" can be ordered, including scripts, film clips, pictures, jewelry, etc. Her most delightful creation, however, was done with the aid and assistance of her husband, Gene. Gene, Jr., is a beautiful child and a credit to his parents.

HAL CLEMENT (1972, 1973, 1974, 1975, 1976)
My favorite story of Hal's is "Mission of Gravity," but everyone says "Needle" is his greatest. Hal also paints under the name of George Richard (the names of his two sons) and teaches school under his real name, Harry Stubbs. Our cons would not have been the same without his big grin and great good humor. And his now-classic lapel button: "Even Klingons would not smoke in an elevator."

[1] For information, send a large, double stamped, self-addressed envelope to:
Lincoln Enterprises
P. O. Box 38429
Hollywood, Calif. 90038

GORDON R. DICKSON (1976)

I met Gordy for the first time at a Lunacon (the yearly con of the New York Science Fiction Society), and he and I were guests at Rhocon I in Washington, D.C., over New Year's 1976. If it sounds as if I'm bragging, I am. He has written many books, and is most famous for his Dorsai Series. But the greatest joys at a con are the late, late shows, where good conversation and bawdy songs are carried over into the early, early shows.

JIMMY DOOHAN (1973, 1976)

Besides "Star Trek," Jimmy has appeared in over four hundred live and taped television programs, many films, and more than four thousand radio shows in the United States and Canada. Yes, he and our good captain share the same homeland. Jimmy loves the fans, and the fans return this affection tenfold. However, occasionally he will give fan security cardiac arrest by going down into the audience and shaking hands with the joyful fans. Did you know that some of Jimmy's fans call themselves "Scotties"? Logical.

PHIL FOGLIO

Phil is an up-and-coming young artist from Chicago. He has a bright, distinctive style and a marvelous sense of satire. You can always spot Phil at a con by the now famous dented black derby he always wears —and because he is so often pictured in his own work. The cartoons in this book are from a larger work called *The New York and Chicago Strektaculars!* This is a very funny pamphlet of Phil's impressions of Lisa Boynton's New York and Chicago conventions. The events illustrated here are, of course, exaggerated for satire's sake. The book is also enhanced by Ann Passovoy's delightful lyrics. It was published by boojums press which is put out by Sharon Ferraro-Short and Paula Smith, two BNFs from the Midwest. Oh, BNF means Big Name Fan, and in their case this is very true.

DAVID GERROLD (1973, 1974, 1975, 1976)

David's first television sale was also his first Hugo nomination. *The Trouble with Tribbles* made the tribble and David immortal. He has sold many scripts since then and written many books, among them an old favorite of mine, *When Harlie Was One.* David has worked as story consultant on various television shows. He was of invaluable help to us at all our conventions. Hey, David, where's the promised sequel to *Harlie?* Don't hit.

MARIETTE HARTLEY (1974)

Mariette was one of our surprise guests. She even surprised us. That's what happens when you meet some old friends on an airplane. Mariette played the character of Zarabeth in the episode *All Our Yesterdays*. She was one of the few women who had a relationship with Spock. Lucky girl.

RICHARD HOAGLAND (1974, 1975)

Dick had a horrible assignment at our 1974 con: He had to follow Leonard Nimoy. Guts, that's what it took, guts. He started with a half-filled room of fans and ended up with them wall-to-wall. He once worked for CBS as an adviser to Walter Cronkite on the Apollo flight series. Then he went to the Hayden Planetarium as the Director of Special Events. He's since gone free-lance and is writing books on the space program.

OSCAR KATZ (1972, 1973)

Oscar was the head of television production at Paramount Studios at the time of "Star Trek." He was extremely instrumental in selling the program series to NBC. He and Gene Roddenberry have been friends for many years. Oscar is now Vice President of Programming, East Coast, for the CBS Television Network. Oscar and his wife, Rose, came to our first con in 1972 and were, as they themselves said, "overwhelmed." Rose, a lovely lady, spent her last day at the con helping behind my dealer's table.

DEFOREST KELLEY (1974, 1976)

De was a marvelous guest, and the fans loved him. He was always very warm and generous with his time. He was a bit nervous at the 1974 convention because of the massive crowds (we had about twelve thousand attendees), but by the time he appeared in 1976 he was an old hand and was completely at ease. He really liked to talk with the fans on a one-to-one basis and did so whenever possible. We were especially pleased that he felt at home enough to drop in at the con suite and have a cup of coffee and sit and talk. A real gentleman and a delight.

WALTER KOENIG (1974)

Ensign Chekov would never disobey an order, especially from Captain Kirk. A lot of fans are surprised that Chekov's Russian accent is not a permanent part of Walter, which just goes to show how good an actor he is. He is now teaching at UCLA between acting, writing, and directing assignments. He collects "big little books," and if you read Chapter IV, you can see the close call he had when exiting the dealers' room one afternoon after trying to add to his collection.

ROBERT LANSING (1975)
Bob was invited to our 1975 press party by Gene and Majel Rodden-berry. He had such a good time he stayed for the whole con, appearing on panels and having a ball. Since his role as Gary Seven in *Assignment: Earth,* he has made many other TV, movie, and stage appearances. Gene has mentioned that he was going to resubmit *Assignment: Earth* to the networks. Maybe this time they'll use their brains.

MARK LENARD (1973)
Mark played two extremely diversified parts on "Star Trek." His first appearance was as the Romulan commander in *Balance of Terror.* His next was as Sarek, husband to Amanda, father of Spock. Since "Star Trek," he was a regular on "Here Comes the Brides," plus many guest shots on other shows like "Hawaii Five-O." He is attractive, tall, and extremely magnetic.

JACQUELINE LICHTENBERG (1976)
Jackie has been a professional sf writer since she sold the first story in her Sime Series to *If Magazine* in 1968. She later became interested in "Star Trek" fandom, starting the Kraith series of "Star Trek" stories which now has fifty contributors (including me) and earned her a nomination for the Best Fan Writer Hugo of 1974. After attending the Committee's 1972 con, Jackie formed the "Star Trek" Welcommittee (see Chapter IX). The 1976 con was the first time Jackie was an "official" guest at a "Star Trek" con. I'm glad it was one of ours. The sequel to her first novel, "House of Zeor," called "Unto Zeor, Forever" is to be published by Doubleday in the summer of 1978.

JEFF MAYNARD (1973, 1974, 1975)
Jeff's "Andromeda Light Show" was a tremendous success at our cons. He would work almost a whole year on each one, getting it just right, and it showed. Jeff is a professional photographer, and a lot of the pictures in this book are his. He also runs a "Star Trek" mail-order business[2] and sells his stuff at most East Coast cons, so look for his table.

---

[2] For information, send a large, stamped, self-addressed envelope to:
   New Eye Studio
   P. O. Box 10193
   Elmwood, Conn. 06110

ANNE MEARA (1976)
Anne and her husband, Jerry Stiller, are one of the best comedy teams in the business. I met Anne on the Paramount lot after visiting Bill Shatner on the "Barbary Coast" set. She had the cast and crew of "The Kate McShane Show" in hysterics with her antics. The fans welcomed her with open arms, and we were delighted that this gracious, funny lady paid us a visit.

NICHELLE NICHOLS (1974, 1976)
What can I say about Nichelle? I love her. She is kind, considerate, beautiful, talented, and smart (not necessarily in that order). A marvelous singer and dancer, we wish "Star Trek" would have made more use of those talents. If I had my druthers, she'd be the biggest superstar you ever saw. But if Hollywood is having a bad case of the dumbs, NASA isn't. Nichelle is one of their representatives, and they couldn't hardly get nobody better.

LEONARD NIMOY (1973, 1974)
Leonard was gracious enough to make a surprise visit to two of our cons. He was in town and wanted to say hello! We were very honored by his visits—he was one of the main reasons "Star Trek" was so successful. He has been doing a lot of college and theater tours lately, and I hope you will get a chance to see him. He is a fine performer and a fascinating personality.

FRED PHILLIPS (1974)
Fred did the makeup for "Star Trek"—you can blame the ears on him. He has been a master of his craft for many years. We wanted him back for an encore, but the great demand for his services prevented this return. Not only is he one of the handsomest men I ever met, but he's also a great dancer.

FREDERIK POHL (1976)
Fred came only to the press party in 1975, but we talked him into doing a panel or two for the 1976 con. Besides being an editor at Bantam Books (you can blame Star Trek Lives! on him—read Chapter V), Fred writes some of the best science fiction around. He is also a kind, sweet man, and I'm proud to be able to call him a friend.

GENE RODDENBERRY (1972, 1975, 1976)
As you can see, it took Gene two years to recover from our first con. He and Majel were an instant hit with the fans. Gene is probably the

only producer/creator in history to have his very own fan club, GRAS (Gene Roddenberry Appreciation Society). He was, for the most part, the driving force behind "Star Trek" and the "Star Trek" universe. Through his imagination and determination, Gene has given us a glimpse of the future most of us share—a vision full of hope and promise and self-realization. Thank you, Gene.

WILLIAM SHATNER (1975)

I've got to be very careful here, because everyone in fandom knows how I feel about this man. Besides being one of the handsomest men I have ever seen, he is also a superb performer. I have seen him do drama, comedy, farce, and the classics and excel in each. He has done over five hundred shows here and in Canada. Bill has worked steadily since "Star Trek" in television, movies, and summer theater. His recent forty-five-college tour was an immense success and left everyone clamoring for more. We must thank Gene for his perception and taste in casting Bill as our Captain Kirk. I don't think anyone else could have made him as real and as human.

GEORGE TAKEI (1973, 1974, 1975, 1976)

As you see, George put up with us for four years. The D'Artagnan of the *Enterprise* has a master's degree in theater from UCLA. His wanderlust has taken him into the Rocky Mountains, the Alaskan Panhandle, Baja California, and Europe. Active in local politics, George sits on the Transportation Board of Los Angeles County. A true, gentle man with a great sense of humor. However, we think it's best to keep all fencing foils out of reach.

WILLIAM WARE THEISS (1975, 1976)

"Star Trek" was Bill's first assignment as costume designer. As of February 1977 he has been nominated for an Academy Award for his work on *Bound for Glory*. We are all very, very proud. It was Bill's fertile imagination that added so much to the realism and believability of the "Star Trek" universe. Those fabulous "Look, Ma, no hardly anything" costumes were worth tuning in for. Bill is also an excellent speaker and makes any panel he graces shine.

HOWARD WEINSTEIN (1976)

Howie made his first professional sale at the age of nineteen, and his animated episode *Pirates of Orion* is well known to "Star Trek" fans. He does both pro and fan articles and is currently working on a situation comedy for television. For better or worse, he has become part of our group, and we enjoy his company very much—especially when he brings his guitar (he sings a mean folksong).

THE "COMMITTEE"

ANDERSON, DANA L. F. (1973, 1974, 1975, 1976)
Free-lance artist and writer
ANDERSON, THOM (1973, 1974, 1975, 1976)
Convention consultant
ASHERMAN, ALLAN (1972)
Free-lance editor and artist
BODNER, RENÉE (1973, 1974)
Film production
EDDY, CLAIRE (1976)
Undergraduate, political science and medieval history
GOTTESMAN, REGINA (1972)
Library co-ordinator for Avon Products, Inc.
GROSSMAN, STU (1975, 1976)
Comic book-store owner
HELLINGER, STUART (1972, 1973, 1974, 1975, 1976)
Advertising production manager, Hearst Publications
LANGSAM, DEBORAH (1972, 1973, 1974)
Duke University, working on doctorate in biology
LANGSAM, DEVRA (1972, 1973, 1974, 1975, 1976)
Children's librarian
LINDBOE, WENDY (1975)
Computer Data Corporation, chasing satellites
ROSENSTEIN, ELYSE PINES (1972, 1973, 1974, 1975, 1976)
Nova Enterprises[1]
ROSENSTEIN, STEVEN (1972, 1973, 1974, 1975, 1976)
Computer and software development, Grumman Aerospace Corporation

[1] For catalogs, send inquiries and two stamps to:
Nova Enterprises
P. O. Box 149
Parkville Station
Brooklyn, N.Y. 11204

SACHTER, LOUISE (1975)
  Graduate student, Greek and Romance languages
SALMAS, EILEEN BECKER (1972)
  Free-lance instructor, film production
SCHUSTER, ALBERT (1972, 1973, 1974)
  Printer and convention dealer
SIMONS, DAVID (1974, 1975, 1976)
  Convention dealer
WENK, BARBARA (1974, 1975, 1976)
  Library branch manager
WILSON, MAUREEN (1973)
  President, Gene Roddenberry Appreciation Society
WINSTON, JOAN (1972, 1973, 1974, 1975, 1976)
  Manager, contracts, administration, ABC Television
YALOW, BENJAMIN (1974, 1975, 1976)
  Computer programer
YASNER, JOYCE (1972, 1973, 1974, 1975, 1976)
  Free-lance editor

CHAPTER 1

A FOLLOW-UP ON THE FIRST CONVENTION;
OR,
WHAT HAVE WE GOTTEN OURSELVES INTO?

We did it. Our January 1972 convention did it. We lit the fuse, and fandom burst into flame.

Up until that time, "Star Trek" fandom had been underground. Fans here and there all over the country, printing their fan magazines, holding club meetings, and each thinking they were the only ones. Isolated fans in Essex Junction, Vermont, were hiding their love for "Star Trek" because they had no one else to share it with—thinking they were alone.

The publicity our convention received appeared in hundreds of papers all over the United States and around the world. Thousands and thousands of fans discovered a most marvelous fact:

They were *not* alone.

The one that started it all was a trade publication with a circulation of about fifty thousand. That's not so much, you might say, how could that matter? Well, this publication just happened to be *Variety*, the famous bible of show business. And anybody who is somebody in television, films, radio, or the theater reads *Variety*.

I can't claim the credit for this coup—that belongs to Bob Newgard, then a Paramount vice president. It was his idea to call *Variety* and set up an interview. Here are some excerpts from that front-page (I know, I couldn't believe it either!) article. Special thanks to the publisher, Syd Silverman.

"STAR TREK" CONCLAVE IN N.Y. LOOMS AS MIX OF CAMPY SET AND SCI-FI BUFFS[1]

BY FRANK BEERMANN

"How quickly they forget" is not a statement that can be made about fans of NBC-TV's old series "Star Trek." The demise of the sci-fi skein in 1969 brought some bitter attacks on the network, mostly from high school and college students, but it was off the schedule that fall, nevertheless. It has continued in syndication, of course, and even now is airing in 100 or so markets in the U.S. and more than 70 overseas.

And now the first convention of "Star Trek" fans is about to be held in New York. So far there is an advance registration of over 700 and 1,500–2,000 are expected to show up for the bash which will run this weekend (Jan. 21–23) at the Statler-Hilton.

When Al Schuster, a New York printer and sci-fi buff, decided that what the world needs now is a "Star Trek Con," he and associates Joan Winston and Elyse Pines thought that maybe they could attract about 300 or 400 to the event, but it seems to have snowballed in this era of quick nostalgia.

According to Miss Winston, who in her normal down-to-earth life is Coordinator for Business Affairs for the east coast at CBS-TV, she became involved because she once submitted an outline for a "Star Trek" episode and knew creator and exec producer Gene Roddenberry and others involved in the production—besides being a great fan of the show.

Oscar Katz's Role

Roddenberry will be at the convention along with Oscar Katz, now a programming veep at CBS, who as exec producer at Desilu originally sold the show to NBC. Isaac Asimov, the sci-fi writer, will be another guest. He will talk about "The Original Mr. Spock," a character whose change after the first two years of the series distressed many aficianados.

And Paramount TV (which acquired rights to the series when it bought the Desilu studios) is providing the convention with 15 episodes to show visitors. They'll also have a blooper reel, which Miss Winston giggles, "may be pretty dirty," but presumably will be

[1] Reprinted by permission from *Variety*, published by Variety, Inc. Article by Frank Beermann, Copyright 1972 by Variety, Inc.

shown late enough at night to be missed by younger conventioneers.

William Shatner, star of the series won't be there—he's busy
making a picture in Hollywood. But he'll provide some competition
for the convention. A film of his for TV, "The People," will appear
on ABC-TV in primetime during the convention. Shatner said he was
sorry about that when contacted but it was too late to reschedule
the pic. That may lose some of the visitors for an hour-and-a-half,
for many of the tourists are strictly Shatner buffs and many of them
are from Canada, his home country.

A "Camp" Meeting

But the entire focus won't be on "Star Trek." The affair is taking
on some elements of a "camp" meeting. Among the attractions will
be a Trading Post, consisting of huckster tables. (The Trading Post
was one of the areas on the U.S.S. Enterprise, the "Star Trek" space
ship, after which the convention site is roughly designed). The
tables in that area go for $15 each and some of the hucksters will
have as many as four. Their wares will consist of old comic books,
Big Little books and such memorabilia as code rings from old radio
serials and the like.

It sounds as though there may be a profit after it's all over, but
Miss Winston doubts it. She points out, expenses have been high,
even though Schuster himself has given them a very good deal on
the large amount of printing required.

If there is a profit, though, Miss Winston said Schuster will get
most of it. The rest will be shared by herself, Miss Pines and others
who have devoted large amounts of time to the project. But, she
adds, no one is expecting to retire on the proceeds.[2]

Vote For Revival

The whole thing is being done with such good will, according to
Miss Winston, that, NBC program chief Mort Werner has also been
invited, although he participated in "Star Trek's" demise. But, the
inviting letter assures him, no one is mad at him for taking it off.
The letter went out late and the organizer are still awaiting an
answer.

So there won't be a surfeit of profits, what's in it for all? Well,
there's love and nostalgia and, if enough interest is sparked, Miss
Winston says, Paramount may very well look to sell a new "Star
Trek" series to a network.

[2] I received $92.46 as my share of the profits. JW.

And that's a consummation devoutly to be desired by a Star
Trekker with an ounce of space dust in his veins.

Variety appears, except for special editions, every Wednesday,
and this piece was in the January 19, 1972, issue, just before the
convention weekend. That Wednesday I got a call from the New
York *Daily News* (its weekday circulation is over five million):
"Would you mind if a reporter and photographer showed up on
Friday?" I didn't think we'd mind too much.

A picture appeared with the January 22 article they did showing huge crowds surrounding the registration table with Elyse
Rosenstein taking money, giving out tickets, and answering questions—all at the same time. It was only fitting that she be in the
middle of all this because she thought up the whole idea in the
first place. That'll teach her.

A GALAXY OF KIDS DIG STARDUST[3]

BY ANTHONY BURTON

If you don't already know it, Star Trek Lives! Captain Kirk and
that redoubtable Vulcan, Mr. Spock, and Bones are still hurtling
around the galaxy on the starship Enterprise, powered by the admiration of fans still besotted by the old TV show.

Hundreds upon hundreds of kids proved it yesterday when they
descended on the Statler Hilton for the first Star Trek convention,
chattering eagerly about the exploits of their space heroes.

Organizer Al Schuster had expected about 500 to attend the convention. But, four hours before it was officially due to start, he
looked around at the mob scene on the 18th floor and said: "It's
wild. We're going to have at least 3,000 people here. They're coming in from all over, Arizona, California, Canada. There's a whole
busload from Toronto."

At Least 30 Star Trek Clubs

It was the first full-scale appearance of the Star Trek subculture
that has grown up around a show now seen only in reruns. Schuster
said he knew of at least 30 Star Trek clubs around the country.

"The fans are mostly high school and college kids," he said, "al-

---

[3] Reprinted by permission from the *Daily News*, by Anthony Burton, published by New York News, Inc. Copyright 1972 by New York News, Inc.

though some people in their mid-30s are bananas about the show. And here's a letter from an 8-year-old in Brooklyn who digs it."

Registration at the three-day convention cost the star-struck youngsters $3.50 a head. If 3,000 show, Schuster and his committee will clear about $5,000 profit.

"It's no rip-off," said Schuster, 31, a printer. "I'm more of a science fiction buff than a Star Trek fan, and I wanted to demonstrate that I can hold a successful convention because I'm bidding for the right to hold an international science fiction convention here. I had no idea this would be such a hit."

He said that girl fans were particularly fascinated by the emotionless Mr. Spock because he was so cool. But Diane Saunders, 22, of Brooklyn said: "It's the stories, not the characters, that get me."

Sees Shades of 'Hamlet'

"I see a lot of parallels with 'Hamlet' . . . violence, action and human conflict. I've seen some episodes half a dozen times. It's like reading a good book more than once."

For their $3.50, the conventioneers get films of the Enterprise's adventures, talks, a costume ball, an art show, a guest of honor, Gene Roddenberry, who conceived the program, and a book of photographs of characters.

"Actually," Schuster commented, "some of these people are a bit insane on the subject."

The way they were coming into the Statler Hilton yesterday, it would have taken at least the Klingons, Kirk's villainous enemies, to stop them.

How about that? They even did some research and knew about Klingons. Of course, "Star Trek" *was* running five days a week on Channel 11 (WPIX) in New York at the time. (And Channel 11 is owned by the *Daily News.*)

By the way, we charged a membership fee of $2.50 prior to the con and $3.50 at the door. Them days are gone forever. . . .

Thursday and I got a call from *TV Guide. TV Guide!* (Circulation forty-four million!) See what I mean about the importance of *Variety? TV Guide* was sending Bill Marsano and his family to cover the con. Bill was on vacation, and it was the only way he would come. Could he see me on Saturday? I thought I could manage that. *TV Guide! Oy vey!* What if nobody came? Not to worry—we expected eight hundred and got over three thousand.

GROKKING[4] MR. SPOCK[5]
or
May You Never Find a
Tribble in Your Chicken Soup

BY WILLIAM MARSANO

All over the country today, people are wearing *"Star Trek* Lives" T-shirts, pasting *Star Trek* bumper stickers on their cars and maybe, for all I know, falling on their knees before graven images of Mr. Spock.

Why? Well, it's because, back at the end of January, *Star Trek's* fanatic band of fans held their first national convention—nearly three years after the series was shot out of orbit by NBC.

Star Trek's fans, loyal as always and more numerous than ever, easily filled and overfilled an entire floor of New York's Statler-Hilton hotel.

The convention started early Friday morning, Jan. 21, when a mob of *Star Trek* fans (known as Trekkies) showed up several hours early, just to be sure they didn't miss anything. Good thing they did, too: the NASA display, described as packed in "several cartons," arrived in several *crates* totaling more than two tons. Early Trekkies willingly fell to work assembling the one-third-scale models of the Apollo spacecraft and lunar module, and propping up the real, full-size space suit. By afternoon, when the convention was to have just begun, it was already in full cacophonous swing, a condition that prevailed without letup all weekend.

By early Saturday, the crowd had swollen to 2000—500 more than had been expected. Trekkies had trekked in from as far away as Canada and California. They listened reverently to speeches by members of *Star Trek's* production team and wandered ceaselessly through the displays of nostalgia and handicrafts: oil portraits of *Star Trek* heroes, handmade space-creature dolls, home-stitched *Star Trek* uniforms and models of outer-space hardware, including the *Star Trek* phaser, a kind of ray gun that, one Trekkie told us, could do anything from stun a victim to "disassemble its molecules" so they will rattle around like a bunch of loose nickels.

The main action was in the Trading Post, which was bursting

[4] Grok—to dig without letup.
[5] Reprinted by permission from *TV Guide*R magazine, the March 25, 1972, edition, Copyright © 1972 by Triangle Publications, Inc., Radnor, Pennsylvania.

with nostalgia dealers and small knots of Trekkies surging about with eyes glazed and elbows flailing. There we met Joan Winston, a CBS business coordinator and one of the convention's, or "con's," organizers. Joan told us that the whole project "started, very slowly, back in April of last year. Then the next thing I knew, I was drafted to take charge of the Trading Post and the NASA exhibit— and now we have *this*."

"This" was the polite bedlam that surrounded us, a crowd now estimated at 2400 and doing feverish business in the Trading Post. Most of the items offered related to *Star Trek*, and many of them focused on Mr. Spock, *Star Trek's* most popular hero. The selection ranged from Spock wooden nickels and lapel buttons proclaiming "I Grok Mr. Spock" to Spock prints, Spock calendars ($1 each) and handmade Spock plaster busts for $11.99. There were also *Star Trek* publicity photographs and tape recordings, scripts to be auctioned, individual frames of *Star Trek* scenes rescued from the cutting-room floor and snapshots of the series taken off TV sets.

More general items included old science-fiction magazines (fetching up to $30), movie posters, books, comics, cartoon panels, ray guns (one mint-condition 1934 Buck Rogers model was tagged at $85), a 4-inch tarantula embedded in plastic ($25) and a Knights of Columbus sword.

Also: large numbers of "fanzines" or "zines"—magazines and newsletters published and written by fans. These serve as an underground communications network for fans, who are a tightly knit group, and as a vanity press for hopeful science-fiction writers and artists. (Wave-of-the-Future note: most of the zines we saw were produced by women.)

Most Trekkies are in the junior high school-to-college age group, but there is one, weaned on *Star Trek* reruns (seen on 120 stations in the U.S.), who is only 3, and another who is 92. And there are several *levels* of Trekism. Some are simply blindly devoted to the series; mere Trekkieboppers as it were. But others have absorbed the series into their very beings; they are able to recite long stretches of *Star Trek* episodes verbatim, often mix *Star Trek* words into their speech and presumably did well on the *Star Trek* Trivia Questionnaire given to each conventioneer. (Sample question: "What was the name of the Andorian in 'Journey to Babel'? A: Gav, B: Thelev, C: Garth." Give up? The answer is Thelev, you big dummy.)

Michael Spence, a quiet, nattily dressed Princeton student, explained some favorite Trekkie phrases. "Most common," he said, "are insults and compliments. A *Denebian slime devil* is a terrible thing to be called, and there's always *tribble*, a nice but pesky creature that multiplies every few hours. You might say, 'May you find a tribble in your chicken soup.' for example. Vulcans—Spock's people—have a traditional benediction, 'Peace and long life,' and the response is 'Live long and prosper.' The only Vulcan compliment I know is one I've never learned how to pronounce; it's a cross between clearing your throat and strangling. Like this: *glabegk enkov.* If a Vulcan compliments you, that stands for quite a lot."

We ran into Shirley Gerstel of Paramount Television, which had provided 15 *Star Trek* episodes to be screened at the convention. "The calls and letters that come into my office are tremendous," she told us. "I keep passing them on to the West Coast. I never thought that *Star Trek* would come back, but now there's a rumor that Paramount might start making it again."

That, indeed, was the convention's principal rumor; it passed from one Trekkie to another, electrifying them. We asked Gene Roddenberry, *Star Trek's* executive producer and creator, and the convention's guest of honor, about the rumor of *Star Trek's* return.

"I didn't think it was possible six months ago," he said a little dazedly, "but after seeing the enthusiasm here I'm beginning to change my mind. It is possible to do it from my standpoint. We had such a family group on the show that it's totally different for us. We still meet and drink together, and we're all still friends, so for this show it *is* possible." (Someone else added darkly that the *Green Acres* crew did *not* still meet and drink together.)

Roddenberry explained *Star Trek's* special appeal, which is, according to him and all of the Trekkies we spoke to, entirely unrelated to the shallow glamour of rockets, ray guns and such.

"The world is violent and unhappy," Roddenberry said, "and it's ridiculous to have it as it is. That's what youth has been saying for the past dozen years, and that's what *Star Trek* stood for. Youth is looking today at things like the violence in Northern Ireland and saying, 'My God! How is such a thing possible in the 20th century?' So they dig a show that says we're not only going to have to love each other as Catholics and Jews, blacks and whites, but that if we go into space we're going to have to learn to relate to things that may look like giant slugs."

The sentiments may seem unlikely, but ring true: the conventioneers were an ecumenical group, a thoroughly mixed bag of blacks, whites, Puerto Ricans and Orientals, old and young, men and women, in suits and in rags. And it is fondly remembered that when the Russians, who put the first man in space, scolded *Star Trek* for having no Russian characters, Roddenberry promptly acknowledged the omission and installed Ensign Chekov in the series.

Saturday evening produced the convention's unusual costume ball, which featured no music and no dancing—just a simple stage for the viewing and judging of the costumed contestants. Notable creatures and characters from *Star Trek* (and elsewhere) were represented. Shouts and applause greeted the Klingon ambassador; a hybrid tribble; the Vulcan warrior queen; Bele from the planet Cheron; Pi, the intergalactic Piper; an Empath (a creature able to rid one of pain); a Starfleet Academy cadet modeling a Terran (earthling, to you) formal gown; Al Capone (from a *Star Trek* episode set in the 1930s); the ambassador from Horombus IV; Count Dracula, from nowhere in particular; and a handful of little girls about 7 years old, some of whom were Mr. Spock and one of whom said she was "a Mudd woman. That's like a robot, but I forget where from." Her mother didn't remember either.

After the ball, there was a blooper film of fluffs, pratfalls, practical jokes and hilariously unprintable incidents on the *Star Trek* set. Then *Star Trek* episodes were shown until 1 or 2 A.M., nobody remembers exactly.

By Sunday, the final day, the pace still had not slowed. A large crowd gathered to hear Isaac Asimov, science-fiction guru and the author of more than 100 books on a multitude of subjects, speak about Mr. Spock. Asimov, by the way, is also a Dinosaur—an esteemed member of the First Fandom, the elite group of early science-fiction fans. And a richly entertaining speaker.

At lunch time, the convention registered its 3000th Trekkie. Then the organizers gave up; they stopped counting and let everyone else in free. More *Star Trek* episodes were shown until late afternoon, when the convention finally ended.

The crowd, exhausted but happy, filtered out of the hotel, lingering here and there like guests reluctant to leave a successful party. "*Star Trek* lives!" one Trekkie called out to us in passing. "May the great bird of the galaxy come to roost on your planet!" we yelled back.

Great article, right? Right. I even got a mention. That was when we started getting all those letters. I got them addressed to CBS. Lovely letters. I adore getting letters, but I *hate* answering them. I am a phone phreak, and Ma Bell will attest to that—my bills make merry reading. Calls to fans all over the country to find out about conventions, fan clubs, fanzines, and do some plain "Star Trek" talk.

All of this was very exciting then, as I had not been in fandom that long. Actually, I had only discovered there was such a thing as "fandom" through a fluke.

In January 1969 I visited the set of "Star Trek" and got to meet all sorts of people, not just the cast and crew. One of the people was a young girl by the name of Paula Crist. She was an officer of both the Leonard Nimoy and William Shatner fan clubs. Paula very sweetly became my "wheels" for the time I was to remain in Los Angeles. I am a typical New Yorker: I don't drive —at all.

Partially to repay her for this favor and partially because I wanted to see her again, I invited her to visit with me in New York. The Friday night she was to arrive she was to call me from the airport and I would come and pick her up and we would take the bus back to my apartment. Well, I decided to surprise her and meet the plane. Don't *ever* do that. I waited by the luggage pickup, and she never showed up. She had immediately gone to a phone and tried to call me—as she was supposed to do.

I gave up waiting and had them check the passenger list and, sure enough, she had been on the flight. I then had them page her—several times. As luck would have it, those were exactly the times Paula picked to try my apartment—just one more time. It was a real comedy of errors, but the best was yet to come.

I finally gave up and went home. I was afraid to call her parents in Sacramento because I didn't want to worry them, so I worried. Finally by Sunday I was a quivering mass of hysteria, so I called Mr. and Mrs. Crist. It seems Paula had called them and told them what had happened and she was staying with a girl named Eileen Becker. (Eileen was a most fervent Spock fan at that time, and she and Paula had corresponded.) I called Eileen's house, and her parents told me that Paula was now staying with someone by the name of Elyse Pines. I tried Elyse's home, but there was no answer.

I kept calling till finally, at two in the morning, Elyse answered the phone. They had been showing Paula the sights and had just gotten home.

Paula got on the phone, and I got the whole adventure. When I didn't answer the phone she got shook and called Eileen, who came to pick her up at the airport. She stayed with the Beckers for one night and then went to visit Elyse, whom she had also written to. All the while she had been trying to call me, but with no answer. We discovered she had my old number and not my new one, which I was sure I had sent her, but by that time I wasn't sure of anything. Anyway, Paula finally came to stay with me, and Eileen and Elyse came up to visit. You can see that the legend of "Star Trek" fans' kindness and generosity is not just a legend.

After Paula left I still kept up the friendship with Elyse and Eileen. One day they asked me a very fateful question: "Are you going to Philcon?" I then asked them a question that was to change my entire life. "What's a Philcon?"

Philcon is the annual convention of the Philadelphia Science Fiction Society. A few hundred sf fans get together and talk and have great parties. Philcon 1970 was my very first convention. It was there that I met David Gerrold for the first time. Elyse knew him, and he stopped by our dealer's table. Oh yes, we shared a dealer's table. We sold pictures, film clips, articles, and other little goodies. This was way before anyone ever heard of licenses or anything like that. I made thirty dollars and was hooked!

My next convention was Lunacon, the annual science-fiction convention held in New York City—after which Elyse called on that never-to-be-forgotten day and said, "Hey, why don't we have a little 'Star Trek' convention?" She had been with Devra Langsam, and Devra thought it was a good idea. Let me introduce you to Devra.

I'm sure most of you at this time know about fanzines. Devra Langsam, one of our hard-working crew was editor of *Spockanalia*, the very first "Star Trek" zine and still one of the best. She now puts out, intermittently, *Masiform D*. But besides editing, Devra writes. Here is a short piece she wrote on the 1972 convention for family and friends who wanted to know "what happened." Ruth Berman, a friend of Devra's, reprinted it in her excellent zine, *T-Negative*.

STAR TREK CONVENTION[6]

or

What Would I Have Done for Aggravation
if I Hadn't Been Helping Run a Convention?

BY DEVRA MICHELE LANGSAM

When Elyse Pines suggested that it might be fun to have a
STcon,[7] I heartily agreed and imagined an attendance of 250.
Kindred lunatics Al Schuster, Eileen Becker, Joan Winston, my
cousin Debbie Langsam, Joyce Yasner, Regina Gottesman, Stu
Hellinger, Steve Rosenstein and Allan Asherman gathered, and we
organized for a "nice little con." The enthusiastic response en-
couraged us . . . an advance registration of 300 should mean at-
tendence of 600. . . . Advance registration hit 600 about the time
we received confirmation of Dorothy Fontana's appearance as a
guest speaker. We started talking about a superwonderful attend-
ence of 1200 when Gene Roddenberry and Majel Barrett said that
they'd be able to come, too.

As con time came closer and closer, I got more and more nervous.
The front-page article in *Variety* really shook me—I visualized
hordes of people milling about—but I took comfort in the fact that
the total Lunacon registration is usually double the advance registration—and our advance was only 800. Just to be on the safe side,
though, we decided to prepare for 2,000.

Wednesday night, January 19, I picked up Maureen Wilson at
Port Authority Bus Terminal. Thursday, after a restful half night
of sleep, we began to run off 2,000 copies of various con things,
like two-page questionnaire forms. (It takes a helluva lot longer to
do 2,000 than it does to print 500!) At 2:00 P.M. we zithered out
to the airport to pick up Bjo Trimble and Richard Arnold, who
had come in from California and St. Louis, respectively. (This
should have been a warning to us, or something.) After depositing
them at the hotel, we battled traffic homeward, where we gulped
down omelettes and ran off the rest of the con things. Joyce Yasner,
as she helped with the paper cutter, remarked, "You know, if the
man from the funny farm came to take us away, there'd be absolutely nothing we could say in our defense."

[6] Reprinted by permission from Poison Pen Press, No. 9. Copyright © 1972
by Poison Pen Press.
[7] Fan shorthand, obviously, for Star Trek convention.

This truthful comment proved added incentive. We got the printing done and finally came to rest at the hotel, for the fourth time,
around 11 P.M.

The room clerk began things suitably by asking if we were from
STcon, saying he knew I was because of my pointed ears. Maureen,
previously abandoned at the hotel with our baggage and all the
mimeo paper, had already coerced Judith Brownlee, Carrie Peake,
and Steve Barnes into doing some collating. Asked how she'd
identified them as helpful types, Maureen said, "I stood in the
lobby looking hopeless until I spotted people with idics, so I asked
if they'd like to help—PU-LEEZE!" Settled in our room, we staggered up to the con suite, planning to continue collating, stapling,
not to mention stuffing. In the hall, we ran into a man who was
wandering around saying, "Where the hell is 1051?" Since he bore
a remarkable resemblance to Gene Roddenberry, we took him with
us, and the collating gave way to a mildly wild party, with Roddenberry and Majel and several very nice people interested in discussing the practicalities of space travel. Not having eaten in a long
time, we devoured some cold french fries that were sitting around.
Yeech! During one of our periodic attempts to locate Bjo (who'd
gone out to dine with Charlie and Dean Brown[8] in upper God's
country), we missed seeing the private run of the bloopers. This
was the leitmotiv of the con—Maureen missing the bloopers. We did
manage to stay awake long anough to watch "The Cage." It was
my first viewing of the complete show, and I must say it's probably
one of the best ST episodes ever filmed, even when seen at 2:30
A.M.

Friday, first official day of the con. Cursing vigorously, we dragged
ourselves out of bed at 9:30 A.M. and went for breakfast.[9] Then
Maureen and I walked twelve blocks looking for a branch of my
bank. There not being any, we started back, stopping to buy a
gross of pencils and some extra masking tape. When we got back
to the hotel, Judith gave me a postsolstice present—a photo entitled
"All right, Captain, put it back into your pants." (Copies will be
furnished to those idiots who help with next year's art show.)

Meanwhile, back at the hotel, the mobs were gathering. Due to
the hotel's error, some people thought the con was opening at 8 A.M.,
whereas in reality it was supposed to begin at 2 P.M. By ten-thirty,
the vestibule was frothing with people, while the registration files
were somewhere vague and indistinct, the head of the art show had

[8] They are the editors of an excellent Hugo-winning fanzine called *Locus*.
[9] Hah! At least *you* had breakfast! I had to make do with half a cup of
cold coffee. JW.

not shown, there was no way to open the curtains in the art show room, *and* the hangings we were to use hadn't been nailed together. Every time I walked out of the art show room, I was accosted by dozens of people waving money at me, while my cousin Debbie bobbled hopefully around the back of the mob urging people to go have coffee, have lunch, make a phone call—only go away and come back *later.*

After gnashing their teeth for a while (the boards that the hotel was to lend us for the art show never materialized either), Maureen and Bjo pitched in, tieing back the curtain with random bits of string and trying to get the show organized. I pegged up some of the art on the insulating board meant to display STXmas cards and old *Spockanalia* art ("In case there's not enough art to make a nice show . . ."). Periodically someone would poke a head in and ask, "When is the art show opening?," and we would all scream, "*Go Away!*" Two wonderful girls, Fran and Pat, asked if they could help. We exiled them to the con suite, where they cheerfully stuffed about six hundred envelopes until we could find room to hang the rest of the art. Somewhere along the line, Richard Arnold produced *food!* (wonderful man that he is), and eventually registration opened. Every now and then I would plow my way out to the front desk by screaming "Committee! Committee coming through!" (a suicidal admission, under the circumstances) and remark on the people packing the lobby from wall to wall. We finally got Judith and Pat Kelly to buy us some pegboard, and hung art madly on all available surfaces.

At 3 P.M., they sent me to organize the slide show (another of those leftovers that hadn't gotten done the day before). Barbara Wenk and I got that set, but then snafued on working the tape recorder. Finally, by something a little short of a miracle, Judith and I taped the show narrations and hauled everything upstairs,[10] only to find out the screen wasn't ready. Feeling vaguely like a plump Christian before a Roman lion-feeding, we rushed around setting up—would you believe a ten-foot movie screen that *snaps* into place? Gene Roddenberry, who'd come up to view the unbelievable mob scene, opened the con with a nice, improvised speech. Debbie introduced him simply as "The man who gave us 'Star Trek,'" and the audience gave him a standing ovation. After his speech, there was a mass movement to follow Gene out, which we forestalled hastily by appeals of "Please don't mob Mr. Rodden-

[10] Just to straighten out your sense of direction, the con was being held in the top floor of the hotel, the Pentop Suite. So we had to go UP to get to the con and DOWN to get to our rooms and the street. Got it?

berry" and assurances that he would be available for autographs later. Fortunately, people sat down again.

After rescuing GR from the fans, we actually got started more or less on time. Aside from having to share a chair with Elyse as she worked the slides, while Judith ran the tape recorder under the table, everything went quite well. Mary Schaub's tribble poem was the hit of the show.

Next we collected chairs and water; and Sherna Comerford, Debbie (my cousin), Joyce, and I were on a fan panel, "How *Not* to Write an ST Story, or Don't Make Him Say That!" We followed our formal talk with questions from the floor. Ken Scher very helpfully walked around with one of the hand mikes so that questions could be heard. The audience seemed to be quite interested, and I enjoyed the panel very much.

The art show having finally been thrown together, we then went to the hotel's Mayflower coffee shop for dinner, with Bjo, Richard Arnold and Daphne Hamilton, and a cast of thousands.[11]

After dinner, I helped at registration for a while. Then we kidnaped Hal Clement into room 411 and talked until about 3 A.M. (We knew we'd be all right exposing Hal to this, since he'd unflinchingly—or should I say unblushingly—entered our room earlier, when there was a dirty naked picture of Spock taped to the lampshade.) The evening was highlighted by a dramatic reading of "Star Dregs," with Sherna Comerford as announcer—a marathon part.

Somewhere during the evening I offered to help Hal load his slides into the projector, rashly promising to deliver it to him at 9:30 A.M. Bjo lured him away to breakfast with the slide tray, while I pulled myself together. I was all set to follow them when Joan Winston called from the con suite. "Ya gotta get up here and stuff!" she wailed[12] (We had run out of prepared packets about six-thirty the night before.) Somehow room service doesn't seem quite so glamorous over a mound of unfilled manila envelopes.

Eventually Hal got back from breakfast and we got the projector sorted out. I heard his speech only because I was running the slides again. (The only program items I saw were the ones I worked on, since I was too nervous and runaround to sit down even when I didn't have to work.)

There were mass autograph sessions with Gene Roddenberry and Majel Barrett, the running of which I was happy to avoid, since

[11] *That* was one I made. JW.
[12] Right on. I did a lot of wailing at that convention. JW.

they looked like the last great land run of the frontier. I escaped to
the con suite to find out that we had run out of membership cards.
While my Aunt Dorothy (Debbie's mother) and her sisters Bea
and Dinah collated and stapled stray copies of the fanzine list, I
cut up bright pink index cards, and Maureen wrote "STCon" on
them. Roberta Hendler went out in an unavailing search for more
pink index cards (leaving her sister Vivian to stuff with us), so
the last three hundred people to register got little blue slips of
paper with a gold star on them.

One of the weirder things about this con was the food. Either
there was none, or their was a surfeit. Thursday I had 1½ real
meals topped off by the aforementioned cold french fries and red
wine. Saturday I had 4 meals, including Maureen's sandwich, since
her roomservicetakesforever hamburger had arrived at the same
time as her delayed lunch. *Then* we had a formal dinner (where
Elyse was officially named "The Screaming Yellow Zonker"[13]), from
which we left in haste to set up the Costume Ball. Once again, the
wall-to-wall people presented a slight problem, which I assisted
with by prowling up and down narking "Get Out of the aisle!" We
had 78 costumes, quite a good number[14], including a beautiful
nasty Klingon, two Rigellian bloodworms, a tribble, and some
purple ambassadors. Someone asked me what my costume was (a
black hot-pants evening gown), and I said, "I'm a Committee member; I'm insane,"[15] and then went hopping down the aisle on one
foot.

The Costume Ball was made particularly notable by some weird
lady who wandered across the stage and took the mike away from
Debbie just as she was beginning to introduce Bjo (serving as one
of the judges). The weird lady asked "Zelda Firkin" or "Esther
Aster" or somebody like that to come to registration. Debbie'd just
resumed the intro when someone, presumably Zelda or Esther or
whoever, stumbled onto the stage, walked across, and then off
again. Then the Esther or whoever walked *back* across the stage,
still carrying her oversized shopping bag. As Debbie later explained
to Bjo, "We were trying for six interruptions, but we had to make
do with only three."

---

13 Don't you remember, Devra? I was the official namer. JW.
14 In later cons we were to have over 200! The purple ambassadors were
the Basta sisters, and Joyce had worn her Surak costume and was upset
because *TV Guide* had called her a Vulcan warrior queen. It had only
taken her about three months to crochet the darn thing.
15 This became something of a tradition—Devra doing her "crazy Committee member" bit.

Once again, Maureen missed seeing the bloopers, since we were down in the bar with a few friends and some Committe types. GR stopped over to say hello and bought our drinks. Afterward, we lured our friends up to a party in the infamous 411, where we drank "pon farrs" (warm tomato juice, cayenne pepper, vodka, a green cherry, and a slice of cucumber—symbolic of something or other) and listened to an obscene ST tape. Our friends had to leave at 10 A.M. Sunday to catch a plane, and we did our best to keep them up until then, giving up at 4 A.M., when our eyelids gummed shut.

Sunday we dragged ourselves up for the final stint. While Isaac Asimov spoke, I helped at registration, where people were still pouring in as a result of the TV news coverage Saturday night. The big item on my day was the art auction, which ran in competition with the bloopers—naturally, Maureen missed them again. I got a beautiful piece by C. Lee Healy called "Prince of Darkness." We were very pleased with the art show, which despite little or no advance publicity got some really fine art.

After the auction, I was in the Schuyler Room when a reporter from WBAI came looking for Committee members to interview. Al (co-ordinator) Schuster, Steve Rosenstein, and I had a pleasant time talking to her. We managed to get in some good words about the great people who'd helped out, and the generally lovable nature of ST fans in toto.

By 5:00 P.M. it was all over but the clean-up, repacking the NASA exhibit, the filing, the book-keeping, finding some food. . . . At 6 P.M., three guys came in, looking for the convention.

After we'd carted all the leftover items up to the con suite, we gathered up the Denver people and went out for a slightly drunken Chinese meal. Deciding we were too tired to go home, we moved down to the con suite, sat around, and talked. Joyce, with great good sense, called her father and went to sleep in her own bed. The rest of us (not counting Maureen, who flaked out about 11 P.M.) had a little dessert in the coffee shop (Richard had coffee and pickles. Ugh!) until it was time to see Bjo off for her 1 A.M. bus to the airport. Then Barbara Wenk and I talked until about 6 A.M.

We were able to fit all our belongings into a taxi late Monday—the three of us, four suitcases, one carton of paper, two cartons of God-knows-what, and a cardboard model of the transporter panel, not to mention the partridge in the pear tree.

Now that it's over, it's still kind of hard to believe. Did we really have more than three thousand people sign up or come? Were all those strangers really so helpful and understanding? Did they really thank us for letting them help? Are we really planning *another* (to a muted chorus of "You must be crazy") next year?

Sigh.

In parting, a very special thank you to all those good-natured, generous people who helped at the art show, registration, stuffing, collating, and stapling; Renée Bodner, Paul Algava, Richard Arnold, Thom Anderson, Dana Friese, those guys from Princeton who helped set up the NASA things, Liam, DJ, Bjo Trimble, and Maureen Wilson, and most of all, all those people whose names I've forgotten or don't know. Thank you all so much.

Thank you, Devra and Ruth. That gives you another side of the first convention.

My own version of that first convention became Chapter Three of the book *Star Trek Lives!*, which I titled: "I Should Never Have Answered the Phone. . . ." It contained many of the adventures—and misadventures—chronicled in the previously quoted articles and some personal stories that happened to me in my official capacity as publicity chairperson.

The most interesting—and most heart-thumping—was the NASA exhibit. I had requested a "little" display. Instead they sent a one-third mock-up of the lunar module, a one-third-size-mock-up of the LEM, a full-size genuine space suit and 18 illustrated light panels, weighing forty-two hundred pounds and shipped in seven crates nine by ten by six feet. And they sent it early.

The shipper's usual storage charge was $10 per hundred weight—per day. My mind boggled at a storage fee of $1,260—the Committee would be in hock for years! It took a lot of fancy phonework before the problem was solved and I could breathe again.

Well, despite well-meaning and sound advice from friends and relatives after the hard work and near crises of the first convention, we decided to have another. Obviously, we were all masochists. But perhaps one of the reasons for this decision lay in something quite nice that happened on the last day of the con. A delegation of fans presented the Committee with a yard-wide piece of paper with a thousand or so signatures on it that said: "To the Star Trek Con Committee, Thank You."

"STAR TREK" TRIVIA CONTEST QUESTIONNAIRE
"STAR TREK" CONVENTION, 1972

Prize: "Star Trek" poster

Winner will be determined on bases of accuracy and time of submission. The earliest correct questionnaire will be considered the winner. Should no one correctly answer all questions, the earliest questionnaire with the greatest number of correct answers will be considered the winner.[16]

1. What was the name of the other starship in *The Doomsday Machine?*
   A. *Potemkin* B. *Constellation* C. *Intrepid*
2. What test did Spock botch in *The Immunity Syndrome?*
   A. Acetylcholine test B. Robbiani Dermaloptic test C. Hydrocelphalic test
3. What type of sword did Scotty use in *Day of the Dove?*
   A. Jaggers B. Foil C. Claymore
4. What was the name of the actor who played in two "Star Trek" episodes?
   A. William Campbell B. William Schallert C. Whit Bissell
5. Mara was the wife of ——.
   A. Kor B. Kang C. Koloth
6. What made Spock uncomfortable in *The Apple?*
   A. The pretty yeoman B. Vaal C. The band of flowers
7. In *Mirror, Mirror,* what was the alternate sick bay turned into?
   A. A circus B. A torture chamber C. A gambling den
8. The M-5 was invented by ——.
   A. Cochrane B. Roykirk C. Daystrom
9. Who played the captain's yeoman in *The Cage?*
   A. Majel Barrett B. Andrea Drumm C. Sally Kellerman
10. A pill was used instead of a hypospray injection in ——.
    A. *The Cage* B. *Where No Man Has Gone Before* C. *The Naked Time*
11. Name the inhabitants of the planet in *Mirror, Mirror.*
    A. Melkots B. Iotians C. Halkans
12. What was the name of the Andorian in *Journey to Babel?*
    A. Gav B. Thelev C. Garth

[16] This was also how all the subsequent winners were judged.

13. The name of the original medicine man in *The Paradise Syndrome* was ——.
   A. Salesh   B. Koloth   C. Kaweena

14. What was the name of the Vulcan starship that was destroyed in *The Immunity Syndrome?*
   A. *Lexington*   B. *Exeter*   C. *Intrepid*

15. Which *Enterprise* line officer did not attend the Academy?
   A. Scotty   B. Sulu   C. Chekov

16. What was the full name of the lieutenant in *Who Mourns for Adonais?*
   A. Carolyn Parrish   B. Carolyn Barrows   C. Carolyn Palomas

17. The gunman whose clothes were appropriated by Kirk in *A Piece of the Action* was ——.
   A. Kracko   B. Kalo   C. Oxmyx

18. The name of the arena in *The Gamesters of Triskelion* was ——.
   A. The Triad   B. The Exercise Area   C. Combat Area

19. The real inventor of Nomad was ——.
   A. Cochrane   B. Daystrom   C. Roykirk

20. Captain Kirk's nephew is ——.
   A. Peter   B. Sam   C. John

21. Gary Seven's assistant in *Assignment: Earth* was ——.
   A. Roberta Lincoln   B. Isis   C. Beta 5 Computer

22. The name of Deela's boyfriend in *Wink of an Eye* was ——.
   A. Rojan   B. Raal   C. Kalo

23. The original title for *The Way to Eden* was ——.
   A. *Joanna*   B. *Eden*   C. *Voyage to Eden*

24. The original title for *The Paradise Syndrome* was ——.
   A. *The Paleface*   B. *Paradise*   C. Same as now

25. McCoy named his empath ——.
   A. Jewel   B. Gem   C. Ruby

CHAPTER II

MASOCHISTS, INC., RIDES AGAIN;
OR,
HE SAYS *WHO* MIGHT BE COMING?
(The 1973 International "Star Trek" Convention, February 16– 19, 1973, the Commodore Hotel, New York, New York)

POCKET PROGRAM
THE 1973 INTERNATIONAL "STAR TREK"
CONVENTION

Friday, February 16, 1973

3:00 P.M.	"Warp"
4:00	Len Wein
5:00	Slide shows
6:00	Dinner break
7:30	"Andromeda Light Show"
8:30–2:00 A.M.	Evening films

Saturday, February 17, 1973

11:00 A.M.	Hal Clement
12:00 Noon	George Takei
1:00 P.M.	Lunch break
2:00	James Doohan
3:00	Oscar Katz: "Genesis II"
4:00	"Star Trek" writers' panel:
	D. C. Fontana
	David Gerrold
5:00	Dinner break
7:30–2:00 A.M.	Evening films

Sunday, February 18, 1973

11:00 A.M.	Brunch (food, special prizes, award, speakers)

2:00 P.M.	Auction, Art Show
3:00	General auction
4:00	Isaac Asimov
5:00	Dinner break
7:15	Costume call—prejudging
8:30	Costume call

Monday, February 19, 1973

10:00 A.M.	Auction, Art Show
11:00	David Gerrold
12:00	D. C. Fontana
1:00	Lunch break
2:00	Panel discussion:
	D. C. Fontana
	James Doohan
	George Takei
4:00	Convention ends

EXHIBITS

Friday
Dealers' room opens 2:00 P.M., closes 7:30 P.M.

Saturday
Dealers' room opens 10:00 A.M., closes 7:30 P.M.
Art Show and Fanzine Exhibit opens 11:00 A.M.,
  closes 7:30 P.M.

Sunday
Dealers' room, Art Show, and Fanzine Exhibit
opens 10:00 A.M., closes 7:30 P.M.

Monday
Dealers' room, Art Show, and Fanzine Exhibit
opens 10:00 A.M.
Dealers' room closes 4:00 P.M.
Fanzine Exhibit closes 2:00 P.M.
Art Show closes 1:30 P.M.
  Please pick up your art.

Films will be shown daily in the west ballroom
during most programing hours.

HOTEL COMMODORE - GRAND BALLROOM FLOOR

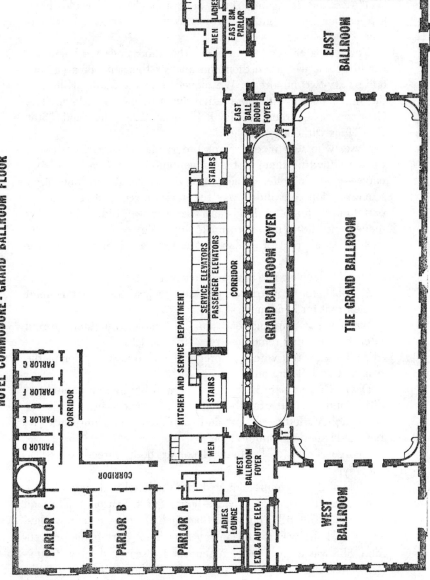

Rendering By Lowell Patton

Well, we did it again. You'd have thought we would have learned our lesson, but no, we ran another "Star Trek" convention.

We were a bit better prepared this time since we knew we would get between five thousand and six thousand fans (actual tally: sixty-two hundred). We moved from the Statler-Hilton to the much larger and more expansive Commodore Hotel. The Commodore ballroom could hold over three thousand "Star Trek" fans without groaning.

Elyse, who was in charge of programing, had written to all the stars inviting them to the convention. I admit we were very naïve—we didn't offer money, mostly because, at that time, other science-fiction cons didn't pay the guests a fee, just some transportation, hotel, and food—also because we didn't have any money and didn't expect to make any. The 1972 con had given each of us a profit of $92.46—not exactly a minimum wage for eight months' work.

We did receive some answers, however.

Al spoke to Leonard Nimoy, and he just could not commit himself that far in advance.

We never got an answer from Bill Shatner, but then he said later that he didn't remember receiving our letter.

Walter Koenig's wife was pregnant and due just prior to the con. So that left him out.

David Gerrold said he could come and became an annual tradition, and one of the family along with Hal and Isaac.

De Kelley's letter got lost and didn't reach him until after he had made another commitment.

George Takei and Jimmy Doohan both agreed to come. Hooray!

Most of the Committee moved into the hotel two nights before the convention opened. I had a house guest, Sharon Emily, and didn't move in till Thursday. Sharon had come in a few days early, and she was to stay in my apartment during the convention. She was a great help. Whenever I discovered I had forgotten something (which was pretty often) she would bring it the next day. Thank heaven for Sharon.

Jackie, Sondra, and I shared a room. Jackie wasn't arriving until Saturday night—she is an orthodox Jew and spent Friday and Saturday at home. It was simpler that way. Sondra arrived Thursday afternoon and we checked into the hotel—or at least we tried. The bellboy took us to our room, but it seemed that someone, or rather two someones, were already occupying that particular room. From the glimpse we got, it was rather small and dark. How would we fit three people into a room that size?

I called the manager, and he apologized and got us another room. It was not on the con floor, but would we make do? Oh boy, would we make do. It was twice the size of the other and light and airy. The extra bed took hardly any room at all.

After getting settled, we dashed up to the convention suite to see what we could do—stuff envelopes, handle the phones, etc. We found out that Al was still at the printer's doing the Trivia Contest. There would be no stuffing tonight. But boy, would there be stuffing tomorrow.

(The Trivia Contest was a devilish invention of Elyse's. She did the first one for the 1972 convention, and Linda Deneroff was the winner. After that, Elyse and Linda would put their little heads together and, along with questions submitted by fans fill their fiendish quotas. The questions were not easy to start with, and by 1974 anyone who took the test seriously would be sure to bring a copy of Bjo Trimble's *Concordance*[1] to help get over the rough spots. Sometimes the tests were marked at the con and the winner announced then and there; at other times Elyse would lug them home and the winner would find out by mail. I took the test *once* and got a magnificent 68 per cent! Aaarrgh.)

What was taking place was a photo session. I was talking a mile a minute—as usual—when I suddenly realized that the two gentlemen the cameras were focused on were Jimmy Doohan and George Takei. I got a big hug and kiss from each, and we settled down to a gabfest. They are truly charming and delightful.

One of my most poignant memories of that evening is meeting a lovely young girl from Hawaii named Roberta. One night prior to the convention, I was sitting at home when I got a long-distance call from, of all places, Hawaii. It was a gentleman whose daughter was coming to our convention, and he wanted to make

[1] This was the original fan publication, not the later Ballantine edition.

sure she had a membership. She loved the show, and as a matter of fact he was talking to me because "Star Trek" was on and she would not leave the TV set. I told him I would make sure she had a ticket. And I did.

We had a contest at the convention with a prize for the fan who had come from the farthest away. It was between Roberta and a young girl from Germany. Someone had a small map of the world in his address book. We measured the distances from New York with a ruler, and Hawaii won by an inch and a half. Roberta won.

Because she had traveled so far, I made sure she met George and Jimmy that evening. She was a slim blond girl with glasses, shy, but at that moment glowing with happiness. I saw her at various times during the convention but did not get much of a chance to talk with her again. However, I would see her in the midst of crowds talking and laughing with other fans.

Roberta sent me a lovely note along with two "Star Trek" sketches several weeks later as a thank you for making the con so memorable. I thought again how sweet she was.

A few months later I learned through fans that she had died of leukemia. No one at the con knew that she was ill. The trip to New York and the convention was her family's last gift to her, the thing she wanted most in all the world. How glad I am that she had a good time, and how I wish I had spent more time with her. I can still see her face, so happy and excited—full of joy and enthusiasm.

FRIDAY, FEBRUARY 16, 1973

Al, poor baby, had finally finished the printing of the Trivia Contest and Costume Ball instructions, etc., at about two o'clock that morning. We squeezed about a dozen people into the minuscule living room of the con suite to stuff. Stuff what, you say? The forty-four-page program book, the Trivia Contest, the Light Show flier—well, you get the idea.

Elyse was a bit upset. She had worked for weeks with Linda Deneroff on the questions for our fiendish Trivia Contest. Oh, it was ready all right. But red ink on bright yellow paper? When she asked Al why, he said he'd had a lot of red ink and a lot of yellow paper.

"Well, I just hope no one goes blind!" Elyse replied.

So there we were, stuffing everything into these slippery, slithery, plastic shopping bags with Mr. Spock's picture on them—elbows and knees jabbing and poking portions of your neighbor's anatomy (watch that, buster). It was very hectic. That set the tone for the entire convention: hectic.

A for-instance: At ten o'clock the programing books were still at the binder's. And they had to be ransomed (we did not as yet have our current triple AAA rating for making good on bills) from the nice gentlemen at the bindery. So Ben Yalow and Dave Simons got a certified check from the bank and arranged for the books to be delivered that afternoon. But to make sure that we had some for the opening of the con, they each sat with one of these humongous boxes containing hundreds of books on their laps for the long cab ride back to the hotel.

Another for-instance, with Ben: While we were stuffing in the living room, Ben had his own set-up in the bathroom. You read right, friend, *bathroom*. He had worked it out this way: Two girls were in the tub, back to back collating with stuff piled on the edge of the tub, while another helper collated on the sink and another collated *under* the sink and one on the john and one huddled on the floor slipping the whole muddle into the shopping bags. Ben, have you ever stuffed college freshmen into Volkswagens?

The previous year the hotel had double-crossed us and told everyone the con opened at 8:00 A.M. This year we made sure they were aware that we did not open till 2:00 P.M. We put it in letters of fire on their foreheads. Well, not exactly, but we did use some strong language.

I was in charge of the press room and the film program, but I continued stuffing till I got a call from the ballroom floor that the press were looking for me. I decided I'd better get down to the press room and get things organized. Famous last words! It was the old beloved bedlam again, with a little chaos on the side. The lines for registration were stretching down into the mezzanine (we were on the ballroom floor!), but everyone was extremely patient and well-behaved. They either pulled out books or began deep philosophical conversations with their neighbors in line. ST folk are nice.

Most of the fans had come to the con because they had received our progress reports. The progress reports had been manually addressed and sorted in Zip Code order, all ten thousand of them, by the Committee and some helpers. This was done in a space of fourth months, on weekends, working sometimes till the sun rose over Al's printing presses.

I walked into the press room and found that nothing had been set up. It looked like New Year's had taken place five minutes before I walked through the door. I called the hotel's Banquet Department, and they said they would take care of it right away. Well, almost right away. Like two calls and forty-five minutes later. I thought I might as well look for Debbie and see if she had the forms for the press room.

I managed to fight my way through the mob to registration, where Debbie Langsam and Renée Bodner were running things. Al was again at the printer's. So what else is new? Renée was handling registration with the help of our trusty (and he was, too) treasurer, Thom Anderson. Debbie was co-ordinating like mad and actually making some headway. A great organizer, that girl. She had my press passes and release forms and some of my people who had been looking for me.

My yeomen (I refuse to call my people gofers) were fantastic. Loyal, true-blue, Kung Fu experts—just perfect. I made Ellen Schlakman my chief yeoman, and her sister Carol, Germaine Best, Lauren Grey, Helene Kaplan, Ruth Schoenberger, and Marty Tannenbaum were the rest of my able crew. When the press started pouring in, we decided we'd do the work now and get organized later. Actually, it worked out very well. Of course, I did feel a little funny when I talked to a man for fifteen minutes, then found out he was from Time, Inc.!

Only because I'm nosy, I left my group for a few moments (my assistant Ellen laughs hysterically every time I say "a few minutes") and made the rounds of the convention. I walked into the Windsor Ballroom complex, the three rooms of which contained the art show, the dealers' room, and a display area. There was a huge sign on the art room door, "KEEP OUT—THIS MEANS YOU." So I walked in. Devra Langsam was busily put-

Hi diddle diddle, a poster and a pair of rubber ears.

The crowd's stampeding down the hall to rip the stars to pieces small

To keep as souvenirs.

Gene Roddenberry in a moment of repose at the 1972 con. (*Benjamin M. Yalow*)

Majel Barrett Roddenberry listening entranced to one of Gene's speeches. *(Benjamin M. Yalow)*

James Doohan making his first appearance at a "Star Trek" convention, here at the 1972 con. Don't you just love his beard? *(Jeff Maynard)*

A grinning George Takei during his first appearance at the same convention. *(Jeff Maynard)*

ting up the easels she and her father had built for the paintings, while Maureen Wilson and Joyce Yasner were making bid sheets over in the corner. They got quite a bit of help, which they richly deserved, but were most fortunate in having Barbara Wenk on hand. I will tell you why in a minute.

Meanwhile, when Devra discovered that the "KEEP OUT—THIS MEANS YOU" sign was not working, she got a fabulous idea. She made a new sign. This one said *"KROYKAH!"*[2]—and you know, it worked! When it was finally removed later in the day, the crowds of buyers and browsers streamed inside.

I made a mental note to return in time for the art auction. There was an absolutely gorgeous portrait of Kirk in oil by Roz Oberdiech Ludwig that I had to have—I mean I *had* to have it.

I walked across the hall to the display area, where Art Brumaghim and Mike McMaster, two guys from Poughkeepsie, were putting together their two-year project: a full-scale model of the *Enterprise* bridge. (It was gorgeous, but it was in pieces all over the floor.) When the boys finally had put it all together, they went out for a celebratory Coke. Later they made back their expenses by taking Polaroid pictures of fans seated on the bridge for a nominal fee.

But the boys had to eat, and one day they left the room alone, with the doors closed and signs all over the place saying "CLOSED," "KEEP OUT." Sometime later, in the Art Show room, Barbara Wenk heard this enormous *thewump!* She looked out to see a forest of fans trampling all over the bridge model. She raced across the hall and threw herself across the doorway screaming, politely, for the fans to leave the room. Oddly enough, they left, and Barbara kept guard on the door until the guys came back. There was much talk of having a medal struck off in her honor!

I tried to walk into the dealers' room, but there was our old friend chaos again. Dealers were not even set up, and they were already selling. What were they selling? David Gerrold was there with all his books and loads and loads of tribbles. There were pictures of Kirk and Spock and McCoy and Scotty and Sulu and Nurse Chapel and Uhura. And the U.S.S. *Enterprise* in any size, shape, or form you could think of, and a few you

[2] *Kroykah!* is Vulcan for Stop!

couldn't or wouldn't. Of course, if you wanted to see a crocheted *Enterprise* or a Klingon ship you would have to go to the Art Show.

As I glanced around I noticed things hanging on the walls. Like posters and signs. On the newly, very expensively repapered walls. As I remembered our last meeting with the banquet manager, Ray Pospicil,[3] he was quite emphatic about *nothing*, and I mean *nothing*, being put on his beautiful new flocked wallpaper.

I saw Phil Seuling, whom Al had put in charge of the dealers' room. Phil was not on the Committee. He ran some very successful cons of his own during the year and was handling the dealers' room as a favor to Al. I told him what I believed was the understanding with the hotel. Phil was very busy setting up the room and answering questions from the other dealers. He told me, not too politely, to mind my own business. *He* was in charge. I found Debbie who found Al who told Phil that I had been quite right and the stuff had to come off the walls. I steered clear of Phil for the rest of the day. I must admit that he did not hold a grudge, and we still say "Hi" at cons.

That was the last time I was to see the dealers' room until just before the close of the con on Monday. Luckily for me, Sondra, Jackie, Regina Gottesman, Sharon Emily, and assorted lovely fans helped out at my table. Sondra, especially, was a salesperson par excellence.

The press room was really crowded now—everyone had jumped in and was taking down names, checking credentials, and giving out press passes. In passing registration, I saw that the lines had lengthened and were now down to the main floor! Renée looked as though defenestration would be her favorite diversion. Debbie was just getting into an elevator with Ray, and I heard her say, plaintively, "What *else* did Al forget to do?" Ah, yes.

The "Star Trek" Light Show, a brilliant collage done by Jeff Maynard, was to start off our Friday evening program, and then we were showing films. *Films!* The films were still in my office at

---

[3] Ray ended up becoming our "Beloved Popsicle" because the Committee couldn't pronounce "Pospicil." He didn't seem to mind at all.

CBS. Good grief, which is what I would have if those films did not arrive on time. Grabbing a big, strapping lad who turned out to be James Minter from Columbia University, I hustled the two of us into a cab.

It is usually frowned upon to remove films and such from the CBS building without twenty passes and a letter from Paley. Thank God the security personnel at CBS knew me, because both of us staggered out of the building under a layer of "Star Trek" films.

I think we have a pretty good security system at the conventions. When not in use, the films are kept in the hotel vault. During use, a fan's arms are wrapped around them and not unwrapped until they are actually put on the projector. At times even the projectionist has problems. Those kids cling!

The films. This section should really be about the projectors. I don't remember where we rented them from, or if we borrowed them, but they gave us a lot of trouble—a lot of the time. Friday night was one of those times. One projector had already broken down, and we were using our spare. We had another one lined up for the weekend, but it was all the way out in Brooklyn. So, every time the dratted thing broke down, I would go into my song and dance. One time I explained how a TV pilot got on the air. The next time I told them some odd things that went into putting on a convention. The third time I told them something of my visit to the "Star Trek" set. They were very patient and gave poor Mike Tarr, our projectionist, time to fix things again.

By the time the last film was on we were winding it by hand. I would stand behind the projector and bat the reel around keeping, or trying to keep, an even pressure on the reel. Ever do that for forty minutes? Don't. You get very pooped. But we *refused* to announce another malfunction.

Earlier in the evening I had put on a "Man from U.N.C.L.E." episode called *The Strigas Affair*. The main guest star was Bill Shatner, and one of the featured players was Leonard Nimoy! I thought the fans would get a kick out of seeing them together in something other than "Star Trek." Boy, was I wrong! All they wanted was "Star Trek," and why were we taking up precious time with this?

After the con, I returned the episode to the nice gentleman at MGM. I told him it was much enjoyed. And it was—by me and the Committee, who sneaked away from their posts to watch.

The only other non-"Star Trek" films at the convention that we played with success were *Silent Running* and a "Sixth Sense" episode written by D. C. Fontana.

After the films were over that night—morning would be more exact, since it was 2:00 A.M.—Al, Debbie, and the projectionist, Mike Tarr, and I adjourned to the con suite. We wanted to set up the film schedule for Saturday.

Al said we could use the East Ballroom as well as the West Ballroom. I wondered about this, since the East Ballroom had been badly water-damaged some weeks prior to the convention. But Al said Ray said it was all right, so I didn't worry.

We juggled times and episodes between the two ballrooms till 4:00 A.M. Suddenly Al just lay down on the floor, closed his big blue eyes, twitched a few times, and went to sleep right in front of us. He had been up more than thirty hours straight. We watched with a kind of numbed fascination for a few moments. At that point I felt a few twitches coming on myself and left to go to bed.

I crept into the room, trying not to make any noise, but the blankety-blank bathroom door would squeak every time I opened and closed it. I tried not to awaken Sondra, and if I did, she was sweet enough not to mention it.

SATURDAY, FEBRUARY 17, 1973

The registration lines were not as bad this day. They were steady, but not the huge crowds of yesterday. The ladies from the Convention and Visitors' Bureau really appreciated that.

I, however, did not appreciate the phone call I got from Helene that morning. It was then that I found out we lacked the East Ballroom. Since Al had said we "had" the East Ballroom, I told Helene we had it, and that was that. Unfortunately, she did not mention that the person who had told her of our lack was the banquet manager, Ray Pospicil. I rushed downstairs and walked into World War III: At least it would have been, if Ray were not such a doll. We cleared up the misunderstanding and changed the film schedule—again. Sigh.

I was told that Hal Clement had enchanted one and all with his speech on astronomy. I think it may have been all those "Star Trek" asides that spiced his speech.

Our next speaker was George Takei, and he always does a beautiful job. The fans make no bones about being able to listen to those golden tones for hours and hours. And they would, too, if we would permit it. This time, however, it was a very, very special occasion indeed. It was the first time that any of the stars of the show had ever been seen at a convention.

George is an extremely erudite man; he has his master's degree in theater from UCLA. He's also very well-spoken—rarely at a loss for words. I can't quote his entire speech, but I remember him talking about the massive support "Star Trek" received from its fans—how optimistic the show was—how they united with a common purpose and a common goal. He held everyone in the palm of his hand.

Jimmy Doohan was on next, and what a charmer this man is. Everyone asked him to do the Scotty burrrr that set all the female fans acquiver. Every other question was about the engines and matter-antimatter drive.[4]

Elyse suggested I introduce the next guest. It was Oscar Katz, vice president of programing, East Coast, for CBS. He had brought slides from Gene's then-new project, "Genesis II." Oscar gave a short introduction and then an explanation of each of the slides. It was very well done, and the fans could not wait to see the show. (If you remember, it was not picked up as a series and we were all very disappointed.)

D. C. Fontana and David Gerrold were on next with a writers' panel.

I wish I could have been in the ballroom to see them. I would like to say now that many times when I describe a panel or an event I am giving someone else's point of view. I, unfortunately, was unable to attend much of the programing at the conventions. However, I believe it is important that you receive a well-

---

[4] Jimmy's standard answer was "You first have to understand the Principle of Concupicity." Don't bother to look it up—it doesn't exist.

rounded feel of the convention activities. I will try to mention the name of whoever had the adventure or saw the panel. Most of the programing information was obtained from Elyse, bless her 5′1″ heart.

On the surface the con must have appeared to be running like an expensive digital timepiece. Behind the scenes, however, we would fly from chaos to catastrophe (Committee coming through! Okay, what's the problem?) and back again. We were told later that people swore our feet never touched the ground as we warped from one section of the convention floor to the other.

I walked into the press room and was surrounded by my crew. I had been taking care of a large problem in the West Ballroom, and the helper I had sent back with that message must have delivered it to Garcia, because he sure as Hades hadn't delivered it to Ellen.

In my absence the press room had had its first major catastrophe. George had not showed up for his three-o'clock press conference, and no one could find him. Ellen had taken command (you see why she was my chief yeoman) and had sent search parties throughout the hotel and Grand Central Station looking for him.

The helpers were still scattered to the four winds an hour later when Ellen got a call from the con suite. It was George. It seemed he thought his press interview was for the next day and had just discovered that he had his schedule turned to the wrong page.

When he entered the room, Ellen sent Carol and Helene to round up the patient press. She then told George to stand on *that spot* and not move! Ellen said later that she'd thought of gluing his shoes to the floor, but that he'd probably have walked around in his socks.

Strangely enough, that very afternoon a gentleman from the New York *Times* told me he thought our press room was one of the most professionally run he'd ever come across.

"I really think it's a great idea to not only have separate interviews with all the guests, but to have a schedule listed so one can plan one's time effectively."

I must apologize for not remembering the gentleman's name, but I will never forget his words.

With me wearing two hats, so to speak (press and films), Ellen had to be able to take charge. She did so in a very efficient manner. It has always been my belief, with both Ellen and later Mike Weisel, who became my film assistant, that when I am not available my assistants *are me!* Whatever orders they give, whatever decisions they make, I will back them to the hilt. I trust them both implicitly, and they have never given me cause for regret.

The Committee dinner was planned for 8:00 P.M. I raced up at 7:30 P.M. to discover that Jackie Lichtenberg had arrived; her friend, Judy Thomases, had driven her in. Jackie was also coming to the dinner, since Oscar Katz couldn't make it, and she was considered a celebrity of sorts due to her famous "Kraith" series. (This is the Lichtenberg version of "Star Trek," her own concept, and she has a stable of about fifty writers, including myself, writing stories based upon Jackie's impressions of the characters. It's really good, and you can write to the "Star Trek" Welcommittee (see Chapter IX) on where and how to get it.

As I quickly showered and dressed, Sondra walked in, frazzled from her day of dealing. Sharon Emily was with her, also pooped. I felt guilty because they were working my table, selling my pictures, articles, and stuff. But they said they enjoyed talking to all the fans and had had a really good time. I remembered all the cons where I had seen nothing of the convention *but* the dealers' room and I'd had a ball. I didn't feel quite so guilty anymore.

We finally got to the Club Suite. I don't really drink very much, but I managed to get a glass of goodness just before we went into dinner. Jackie, who is kosher, didn't eat anything but the fruit cup and dessert, so Steve, who was sitting next to her, got double portions of everything else. Need I say he did not object?

The minute we spotted the huge basket of rolls in the middle of the table a cry went up:

"Bald Tribbles!!!"

I can't remember who did the actual christening, but David was delighted. This was the first moment of relaxation the Committee had known in days, and suddenly the air was filled with rolls—most of them aimed at David. He's young and fast and eluded most of them. The main culprit was Stu Hellinger. A mean man with a roll.

After dinner we went down to the Art Show room in the Windsor Complex. I followed the judges around and found myself bidding on about a dozen different paintings and sketches of Kirk. There were two in particular that caught my eye. One was the oil painting I mentioned earlier, and the other was a sketch by Karen Flanery.

(I have a gorgeous pen-and-ink drawing of Shatner by Karen hanging on my living room wall. It was a gift from a dear friend, Joyce Muskat. Yup. The author of one of my favorite episodes, *The Empath.* She had sent me the picture as a birthday present, and it is one of my most treasured possessions.)

The judges were most fascinated by the work of a very young friend of mine, Jennifer Reid. I had first met Jen through another friend, Adrienne LeVine. I was doing my thing behind our convention registration table at Phil Seuling's Annual Comicon over the July 4 weekend in 1972. Adrienne came to visit and introduced me to Jen. Jen was very interested in the programing and had brought her tape recorder to record the speeches and panels. Now, this was not your baby cassette recorder—this was a huge Sony reel-to-reel with two humongous speakers on a wooden platform with wheels. When Jennifer wanted a recording, she was not one to do things by half measures.

She asked if I would do her the favor of keeping the recorder behind the table so she would be free to roam around minus encumbrances. I said that it was no problem, and outside of an occasional glance to make sure no one walked off with it, it was no trouble at all. A few hours later, Adrienne and Jen came back. Jen thanked me and we talked for a while, and then they left.

I forgot all about this until a few weeks later, when I received a mailing tube in the post. It was a glorious portrait of Kirk with eyes that seemed to follow you around the room. I wrote and thanked her profusely. Just think, if I ever do her a *real* favor, she'll probably send me a marble bust!

Back to the Art Show. It was practically a unanimous decision —Jen won Best of Show! Most of her work at this time was of Spock. Spock as Pharaoh, Spock as Lancelot, Spock as Tristan. All beautifully rendered in pen and ink. Everyone was overwhelmed. I mentioned to Betty Ballantine (yes, Ballantine Books) that I had a sketch by Jennifer.

"You're very lucky," she said. "Hold onto it. It will really be worth something someday."

As if I would ever part with it.

I almost forgot. We could not get into the Art Show right away, since the room was locked and we had to get the key. So we took George, Jimmy, D.C., David, and the other guests to see the bridge display. They all just stopped dead and stared. Then George took his position at the helm, Jimmy sat in the command chair, and Dorothy took Chekov's place—didn't that make a great shot?

We all took turns getting our picture taken in the captain's chair. Jeff had his equipment with him, as had Ben, and they took turns taking group shots of the guests and the Committee. What a marvelous souvenir. (See the one Jeff took of Jimmy and George.)

SUNDAY, FEBRUARY 18, 1973

I would have dearly loved to have slept a bit late this morning, but we got the news the night before that Leonard Nimoy was coming. He had called Al to say he was in town and would like to pay us a visit. Ohboyohboyohboyohboy!!

I washed and dressed doublequick in order to set up everything in the press room before the brunch at 11:00 A.M. Leonard was due at about 2:00 P.M. Just as I was putting down my hairbrush and picking up my purse, Jackie casually mentioned that she and a group of "Kraith" admirers were holding their very first get-together that afternoon—at two o'clock!

I stopped in midstride. If I tell her, the Committee may kill me—but if I don't, I'm sure she'll kill me.

I told her. And swore her to secrecy. Also Sondra. As I left the room, I really felt sorry for them. Sondra would have to talk to hundreds of people in the dealers' room and not be able to tell a soul about the huge surprise package due at 2:00 P.M. I'm sure that her blood pressure jumped ten degrees as every hour passed. I know mine did.

Poor Jackie. She ran around frantically trying to find everyone to cancel the meeting and getting everyone royally mad at her, mostly because she couldn't think of a reason why she was canceling the meeting. Of course, after Leonard left, she explained everything. Then they got even more upset. Why hadn't she told them that he was coming? She explained that she had given me her word, and all was forgiven.

Who says women can't keep a secret? Out of the then thirteen members of the Committee, only four were male! I mean, it shows to go—some of us didn't even tell each other.

Later in the afternoon, when the shouts and shrieks filtered into the Art Show room, Devra turned to Joyce and said, "I didn't want to tell you before because I thought you'd get too excited (Joyce is a fervent Spock fan), but Leonard's here."

Joyce grinned. "Yes, I know. I heard about it last night."

Then they closed the Art Show and cowered behind the closed doors as the room shook from the fans thudding by.

More about that later. Let's get back to the Brunch That Almost Didn't Happen. As I mentioned before, the East Ballroom was off-limits because of water damage. We had sold several hundred tickets to the brunch, and there was no way that everyone would fit into the West Ballroom. After much pleading, begging, and sobbing, the hotel let us use it on a limited basis. That meant no tables underneath the flaky northeast corner. Okay, okay, fine.

No one took into consideration, however, the natural draft conditions in the room. It became a game as all conversation would stop and we'd watch a particularly large piece of curling paint flutter down. Bets would be made on whose table it would land on. At one point, David (who was our emcee, and very good indeed) saw one land in Isaac Asimov's soup.

"Eat, Isaac, eat. A little calcium never hurt anybody."

At another time, a huge piece broke off and floated halfway around the room before it settled down, completely covering one table. It's a good thing they were between courses. The waiters had to clear off the whole table. They were not happy about it, either.

While the ceiling fell and David and Isaac traded witticisms, the Committee tried to control their collective stomachs and remain calm. We and the guests were seated on a dais along the east side of the ballroom. I was seated next to Jimmy, which was delightful. At least it was delightful the few moments I spent in my seat. He just couldn't get over the convention and the fans.

"I'm having such a marvelous time. I'm getting a high on all the love and affection. This has been an absolutely fabulous three days."

Well, if you want the truth, Jimmy is pretty fabulous, too. Oops, I had to leave. I had to get the blooper reel from Dorothy's room. We would never leave it in the film room. It was always taken back upstairs after each showing.

I got back to my seat just in time to leap up again and go get another surprise guest. *Bravo,* a German magazine, had run a "Star Trek" essay contest, and the first prize was a visit to New York and our convention! How about that? The winner was a young girl (please don't embarrass me and ask her name), whom David introduced to the audience. He said she must have come from the farthest distance, but we told him about Roberta, and she was introduced from the audience. Everyone applauded and cheered. It proved that "Star Trek" was an international phenomenon as well as a national one.

Before my next leave of absence, I was able to enjoy the Battle of Isaac and the Waiters. There had not been room on the dais for all of our guests, and Isaac and Hal had said they would rather sit at a table with some of the fans. They had the table right in front of the podium. That made it easier for David and Isaac to trade insults—in a very friendly way, of course. There seemed to be some confusion, however, in the waiters' minds; apparently each one thought the other was taking care of that table, so that it was not served until Isaac caught a flying waiter's sleeve and pointedly indicated his empty fruit cup. Since everyone else was on their main course, Isaac had cause for pique. This caused the waiters to go into a huddle, and the one with the short straw served their table. That's why Isaac was eating his soup (cold) while everyone else was eating their ice cream (melted). I'm sorry, Commodore, but it was not one of your greater meals.

Still chortling, I wended my way to the ballroom to retrieve the blooper and make sure they had *Silent Running* scheduled. That was a coup of mine. I had seen the picture at a private screening and just loved it. I fell in love with the drones, Huey and Dewey. It also had some beautiful songs, and Thom and

Dana had played "Hymn to the Sun" at their wedding. Through Oscar and Rose Katz I had met Diane Lampert and her husband, Fred Stewart. Diane had written the lyrics and Peter Schickele had written and conducted the music for the movie. I had called Fred and he had called Doug Trumbull, one of the producers of *Silent Running*, and that is how we got a print to show at the convention. Convoluted—but nice. Anyway, the picture would run until about two o'clock, just when Leonard was due to make his appearance. Perfect.

My next stop was the press room. There was a lull, the eye of the storm, so to speak, and Ellen, Carol, Germaine, Helene, and Marty were discussing the current rumors.

1. Leonard Nimoy was coming.
2. Leonard Nimoy was *not* coming.
3. Bill Shatner was coming.
4. Bill Shatner was *not* coming.
5. The sky was falling.

I told them *numero uno* was the winner, *but* they could not tell anyone—not even their dearest friend—and they couldn't make any noise, either. Have you ever seen silent pandemonium?

I got back to the brunch just in time to be introduced to the fans. All the rest of the guests and Committee had been introduced, and they were taking bets on whether I would make it back in time. I made it.

The Committee was very tense (try terrified, that's a good word). Al, Stu, Thom, several large helpers, and the security guards were waiting at a side door for Leonard. I had gone into the darkened West Ballroom, where *City on the Edge of Forever* was running, to clear a path. Since it was lunchtime, the room wasn't too crowded. I shifted chairs so no one, especially that particular someone, would trip. I got a few strange looks, but that was all. (I can hear a few of my dear friends saying, "But you *are* strange, Joan.")

Our surprise package was brought up by the service elevator and through the kitchen. Actually, that sounds much too simple —it happened more like this:

Al, Thom Anderson, Stu Hellinger, Ben (again), Dave, and a few very *large* helpers loitered around the mezzanine lobby trying to look inconspicuous. This is not easy, since these people are usually too busy racing hither and yon to gather into a group for any length of time. Occasionally some fan would look up curiously but would finally go away because he knew that if he asked any questions he would probably be killed.

Everyone would take turns eyeballing all the approaching cabs. Finally: jackpot! Leonard Nimoy and his lovely wife, Sandi, were whisked into the hotel and immediately surrounded. He was wearing, among other things, a tan raincoat and a warm, beautiful smile. The couple was hurried down the hall to the waiting elevator, with everyone taking turns telling Mr. N—politely, of course—to please keep his six-foot-one-inch-tall head *down!*

As they walked they could see one or two fans look up toward them and then stand slack-jawed. They had seen and, ohmighod, recognized our illustrious guest. This was really no problem—it just looked as if a sudden paralysis had overtaken a certain portion of the people in the lobby. When our group was about fifteen feet from the elevator, a crackling cry of SPPPPOOOOOCCCCCK! split the heretofore quiet Commodore air. Mr. and Mrs. Nimoy were politely but frantically rushed into the waiting elevator as the thunder of equally frantic feet began to be heard. When they reached the ballroom floor, they sped down to the darkened West Ballroom, which I had just cleared, and arrived pale and breathless. Just as the door was closed, the first wild-eyed fans reached the top of the stairs. (See Chapter VI for a similar William Shatner adventure.)

Steve Hartman was a member of the security squad that fateful year, when Leonard Nimoy was scheduled to make an *un*scheduled appearance. Steve was stationed in the huge foyer outside the main ballroom. One of the helpers ran up to tell Steve that Phil Seuling had made his now-famous announcement in the dealers' room.

Steve quickly started to position helpers at each of the doors leading into the ballroom. Suddenly the now familiar sound of thundering feet reached his ears. Whoops. He noticed an unguarded door and headed across the foyer toward an unbusy (how could there be such a thing?) helper just as the wall of frantic fans hit! There is nothing on this green earth that will prevent a loyal Spock fan from seeing his favorite—a mere body in the way doesn't count at all, as Steve discovered.

As the dust settled, his prone form was found in the middle of the foyer with a dozen footprints scattered over his heretofore pristine T-shirt. As he dazedly got to his feet, Claire Eddy walked over and explained what had happened. Steve's only comment was a bemused, "Oh, that's nice!"

So you want to be a helper at a "Star Trek" convention, huh?

Jimmy was already in the ballroom with George. He was going to introduce our guest. We brought Leonard through the now empty West Ballroom into the main ballroom; he was to wait behind the movie screen until Jimmy finished his introduction. The film was still running and had about five more minutes to go. Those five minutes were not to be seen that afternoon. Some sharp-eyed fans had seen us bring Leonard in, and the cry of Spoooocccck! tore through the Commodore corridors.

Both Stu Grossman (then a dealer, now a member of the Committee) and Shirley Maiewski (also a dealer and now chairperson of the "Star Trek" Welcommittee) told me this one.

They were both working behind tables in the dealers' room. It was jammed. The fans were buying everything and anything in sight. They were selling everything but the chairs behind the tables, and they could have sold those, too—if they had said Jimmy or George had sat in them.

Just then Phil Seuling raced into the room. Ponytail flying, he leaped on a chair behind one of his tables and in his clear, far-reaching baritone shouted, "Spock is here! He's in the main ballroom right now!"

Within the wiggle of a pointed ear, the room was empty. The dealers turned to look dazedly at each other and then at the suddenly depopulated room—the room that had just been filled to the gunnels with madly buying fans. Then all eyes went to Phil. If looks could kill, Phil would have been very sick that day.

At that moment the Committee wasn't feeling too hotsy-totsy either. The fans were pouring into the ballroom, and all we could do was thank the powers-that-be that the fire marshals or the hotel people weren't there. It seemed as if the entire attendance of six thousand was trying to get into the room.

We stood onstage ready to lock arms in a good cause. My life started to flash before my eyes. (Surely I had done more than that?) Jimmy started to make the announcement. Have you ever seen about four thousand people rise and surge forward? Toward you? Extremely unsettling.

Jimmy saved the day—and our lives. "If you take one more step, our guest will leave without making an appearance." Four thousand fans turned into a lot of Lot's wives.

Leonard walked onto the stage to a huge roar and standing ovation. He was visibly moved. He gave a short but lovely speech. He said that everyone connected with the show deserved credit. He had loved working with all the cast and crew, and the whole three years had been a beautiful experience. The fans hung on every word.

And then, because we had planned it for twelve hours, we got him safely out of the room and into the press room. Except those of us guarding the arts and crafts, the Committee got to meet him, and he was gracious enough to say that he remembered me from my visit to the "Star Trek" set. We found his wife, Sandi, to be as charming and gracious as he.

We introduced the little girl from Germany to him, and she gave him an award from *Bravo* magazine for being the most popular television star in Germany. (Bill had come in second.)

Leonard was taken out through the kitchen again but, by some mistake, led through the lobby to get a cab. (No dear, you did not see Mr. Spock in the lobby—that was a Fig Newton of your imagination.) A flock of fans came out of the Howard Johnson's across from the hotel just as the Nimoys got into a cab. They spotted him, and a somehow familiar shriek of "Spoooccck!" split the icy Forty-second Street air. The cab took off with four fearless fans clinging to it like leeches, as two trucks and a crosstown bus slewed across the icy street, trying not to hit the hysterical fans.

At this point, the Committee was holding hands, screaming and jumping up and down in the three-degree cold. "We did it! We got him in and out of the con, and he's still alive!!"

The fans in the hotel would not believe that Leonard had left. They even cased the ladies' room. Some of them started yelling for "Captain Kirk." We tried to explain that Bill was working on a picture in California, but they would not take "No" for an answer. We finally said we were letting him down on a rope from the balcony. Do you know, four thousand fans looked up?

It would have been a marvelous time to collapse, but the convention was still going on—so back to work. Oops, I had completely forgotten that the art auction was taking place. My pictures. The press room was quiet then, so I ran downstairs.

I was too late for Karen's sketch; that had already been sold. Blast. But the oil painting of Kirk was due to come up soon. I went over to Devra and explained that I did not want to be away from the press room for too long, and could she please put that picture up next? Devra is a doll and said she would. Al was doing the auctioneering and doing a good job, too.

I was not the only one who wanted that portrait, no siree. The bidding was hot and heavy. When the bidding reached seventy-five dollars I told the girl bidding against me that I had two hundred dollars in my bag and was quite prepared to spend all of it for the picture. I know that was kinda mean, but I wanted that painting. I got it for seventy-five dollars. I gave Devra the money, got my receipt, and ran back to the press room with my prize. Everybody oohed and aahed, and some of them even drooled a bit. Roz does good work. The painting now hangs in my living room for one and all to admire. Don't touch, just admire.

Isaac was on at 4:00 P.M., and the room was jammed. Isaac talked for about sixty seconds on "Star Trek" and then about an hour on Isaac, but everyone ate it up. He is a witty, charming man, and I am proud to be allowed to call him "Isaac."

We closed the press room at five o'clock, and I went upstairs to try to take a short nap. I was pooped. It had been a long day, and I had had only about four hours' sleep the night before. I had been dozing for about a half hour when Jackie and Sharon walked in.

A few days prior to the convention, Jackie and Sondra had come over to the apartment. Sharon had altered one of Sondra's pantsuit tops to make a costume for Jackie. She was going as T'Pring. I did her hair, then I made her up, and it was like working with virgin territory. Jackie does *not* wear makeup. She feels applying it takes up precious time that could better be spent on writing. Listen, I would go without makeup myself if someone would guarantee that I would write like Jackie.

Sharon had also made a costume for herself. It was a representation of a dress a Vulcan ambassador's wife might wear—a black chiffon overdress with a black crepe sheath underneath. It was just lovely. She and Jackie hurried down to the prejudging, and Sondra and I got dressed. I wasn't leaving right away, though. Bill was on a "Mannix" show that night, and I didn't want to miss it. I might as well have, since the television reception in the hotel left much to be desired, and there were about twenty-four Bills on the screen instead of one.

Sondra had given me the money from the dealers' table, and since there had been a robbery the night before (a dealer's room had been robbed), I put it in the safest place I could think of. No, not the hotel lock box. That would have been too simple. I divided up the five-, ten-, and twenty-dollar bills and stuffed each cup of my bra. That night Raquel Welch had nothing on me.

I wore that night, for the first time, the Kirk shirt my friend Alice Parker had made for me. It was a copy of the wrap-around shirt Kirk wore in *Enemy Within*. It really looked good, especially with my treasure chest underneath.

The costumes were absolutely fantastic. I thought they were worthy of a World Science Fiction Convention. One in particular caught everyone's eye. He described himself as a "Transporter Malfunction." He came onstage blasting carbon dioxide into the air, with dead tree branches, a huge turtle carapace, a deer's antlers, large stalks of gladioli and other strange assorted paraphernalia festooning his body. Of course, he won first prize.

This was Dana's first time as co-ordinator of the Costume Ball, and she did a beautiful job. Everything ran like clockwork. Allan Asherman was her announcer, and that also became a tradition.

We were to have another surprise guest. Mark Lenard was in town, and he is a favorite of Devra's. Being quick-witted, she called his hotel and invited him to pay us a visit. Maureen Wilson also wanted to see him since she was organizer and president of his fan club.

"Do you think they'll remember me?" he asked. "I made only two appearances on the show."

"They'll remember you, I promise."

When he arrived in the ballroom, he was immediately surrounded by a dozen or so perceptive females. Mr. Lenard is a magnetic male—very much like Sarek, the part he played in *Journey to Babel.*

Devra, not wanting her surprise mussed, used the now famous "Langsam Lunge." This consists of a firm arm slashing through the air like a rapier accompanied by a loud voice saying, "Committee coming through, Committee coming through!" It really works. Of course, it helps if you are five-nine and have sharp elbows. She whisked him backstage, and Allan made the announcement.

"We have a surprise guest tonight. But it's *not* William Shatner," he quickly added. The collective intake of breath from the excited audience almost swept Allan from the stage, but grabbing hold of the podium and before the audience could get actively hysterical, he hurriedly announced, "Spock's father, Sarek!"

There was a standing ovation as Mr. Lenard walked onto the stage. Little did he realize that playing that one part would make him immortal—in the minds of "Star Trek" fans, anyway. He made a very short speech thanking everyone for their kind welcome and became one of the judges, joining Oscar Katz, Isaac Asimov, Hal Clement, David Gerrold, and Jim Steranko (a famous comic-book artist). The first line of his speech was a beauty: "I understand my illustrious son was here this afternoon." A lovely, wry wit.

After the ball was over . . . dum-de-diddy-dum . . . Where was I? Oh yes. Mark graciously agreed to sign autographs for the fans. They lined up ten deep outside the press room, and he signed and signed and signed.

The press cornered me outside and asked for some interviews. I fought my way through the crowd—you know, that "Langsam Lunge" really works—and asked Mr. Lenard if he was agreeable. He looked up, raised a Sarek-like eyebrow, and said, "Maybe later."

Unfortunately, the press decided not to wait and took off. Unfortunate for them, that is. It's not often an actor puts his fans before the press, and I thought it was a lovely gesture.

By the way, if you thought you saw Dracula stalking the halls

that night, it was just Stu Hellinger in the cape Eileen Becker
had made for him. Weird. But then the whole Committee is
kinda weird at times. Like Devra doing her imitation of a Committee member and hopping across the stage on one foot. See
what I mean?

MONDAY, FEBRUARY 19, 1973

In case I hadn't mentioned it, we were selling daily tickets to
the con as well as four-dayers. You should have seen the faces on
the fans when they discovered who had been at the con on Sunday. Talk about disappointed! They had serious thoughts of
hara-kiri, with some defenestration on the side.

After the art auction (I had already gotten my stuff, so I didn't
get to this one), David Gerrold was scheduled for the main
ballroom. His speech was a very good one, as they usually are,
but a little different. The title was: "Support Your Local Writer."
He explained what the writer does and "though we tend to think
that the actors make up all those clever little things by themselves, it is the writer who put the words in their mouths. The
actor's skill comes from taking the writer's lines and bringing
them to life as well as finding things in them. It is a team effort."

David felt very strongly about this, and I think he gave the audience something to ponder.

At this point the Committee was feeling the effects of little
food and less sleep. As a matter of fact, we were all a bit frayed
around the edges. By the time the last event was on, we just
wanted it to be over so we could relax.

Jackie and Sondra were getting material for *Star Trek Lives!*
and wanted interviews with George and Jimmy. We invited
them up to our room when the con closed. Jackie had gotten up
early that morning (she *always* gets up early; I'm a sybarite and
love to sleep late) and raided one of the neighborhood delica-
tessens and brought back all sort of munchies. They were to
come in handy now.

Jackie and Sondra had their trusty tape recorder going, and
George was answering questions. All my kids were listening, fascinated. The door was open, and before we knew it, ever so
gradually, we found the convention Dead Dog Party taking
place in our room.

I must have sent Lauren Grey down to the Grand Central Deli for sodas and stuff a dozen times. There was one problem: They did not stock Pepsi-Cola. Most of the Committee, especially Al, loved Pepsi. So I grabbed some helpers and brought back a half-dozen six-packs.

We could hear the party when we got off the elevator. As we rounded the corner leading into our corridor, we stopped in shock. There were fans sitting on the floor, in the hallway, drinking sodas and talking for as far as the eye could see. When we finally reached the room, we could barely squeeze inside.

There was George still giving Jackie and Sondra their interview. A kid with a Polaroid was taking pictures. Each bed had at least ten bodies sprawled on them. The floor was an ocean of arms, legs, potato chips, and cola cans.

We were greeted with great affection and quickly denuded of the Pepsi. I managed to secrete a couple of cans in the john tank —I went for them, didn't I? After most of the fans left and we had put all the empty soda cans out in the hall in plastic bags (to be instantly retrieved by Devra for recycling purposes), someone suggested dinner. Good thinking!

We checked around, and most of our guests seemed to have left for parts unknown. But we found George and set out for Mama Leone's. Down in the lobby I grabbed Ray Pospicil, the banquet manager. He had been so helpful all during the con, even taken a room there so he would be on twenty-four-hour call, that he deserved dinner, too.

Someone had called the restaurant, so they had a big table set up for us when we arrived. We got our drink and dinner orders in and settled down to a happy gabfest. Al and Debbie were seated at one end of the table and Ray and I at the other, with the rest of the Committee and George seated along the sides. Ray told me all about the Banquet Department, and I told him about television. He had a great fund of weird hotel happenings to relate, and I had a ball.

Al had ordered a bottle of special wine to go with dessert, and the wine was really delicious. We passed it around the table, and by the time it got back to Al (who, being the polite host, had not taken any), the bottle was empty. We all had a fit of giggles at the expression on his face.

But he was very cool—he just ordered another bottle. That was when we still thought we had made some money from the con. That, also, was one of the reasons we were having this celebration dinner. It was not until after we paid all the bills that we discovered we were about eight hundred dollars in the hole. Oh that hotel bill. It seems most of the people had not told the hotel they were with our convention, so *they* did not receive the special room rate and *we* did not get their rooms credited to our room count. That added $$$ to our bill. Sigh. (Of course, we all had to kick in extra $$$ to pay that.)

But that discovery was much later, and we could still enjoy our dinner. After dinner we decided to walk back to the hotel, since it was an absolutely gorgeous evening. Somehow Dana and I ended up walking with George. We started to walk in step, and I told them a little story:

I had been out on the town with some friends, and we had decided to make a night of it. We had gone to the theater, dinner, and dancing. We finished the evening by dancing up Fifth Avenue at 4:30 A.M.

George laughed and said, "Well, it's not four-thirty and it's Park Avenue, not Fifth. . . ."

To the surprise of everyone walking normally behind us, we started to sing "We're Off to See the Wizard" and did high kicks and "Off to Buffalos" down Park Avenue. Dana and I were very disconcerted to find that George could kick higher than we could! When we got to the echoing caverns of Grand Central Station, we switched to (shades of *Naked Time* and Lieutenant Riley) "I'll Take You Home Again, Kathleen." But we were on key. I think.

We got back to the hotel, said our farewells, and sleepily fell into bed. We said our real good-byes the next day as we packed and headed for home. Sondra was to stay with me for a while before returning to Baton Rouge, and we caught a cab to my apartment. Sharon had left it neat as a pin—a state it was not used to at all.

Elyse woke me up the next afternoon to set up the date for the first meeting to plan the 1974 convention. On that note, I went back to bed.

58   THE MAKING OF THE TREK CONVENTIONS

"STAR TREK" TRIVIA CONTEST QUESTIONNAIRE
INTERNATIONAL "STAR TREK" CONVENTION, 1973

1. What is the name of Chekov's imaginary brother from *Day of the Dove?*
   A. Igor   B. Piotr   C. Sergei
2. Who was originally chosen to play the lead role in "Star Trek"?
   A. William Shatner   B. Martin Landau   C. Jeffrey Hunter
3. What is the serial number of the *Galileo?*
   A. NCC-1071/1   B. NCC-1701/7   C. NCC-1701/1
4. What is the title of the first "Star Trek" episode aired?
   A. *Man Trap*   B. *Where No Man Has Gone Before*
   C. *The Cage*
5. What actor turned down the role of Mr. Spock?
   A. Martin Landau   B. Lawrence Montaigne   C. Mark Lenard
6. What are the names of the four (4) starships besides the *Enterprise* that appeared in *The Ultimate Computer?*
   A. *Lexington, Excalibur, Hood, Intrepid*   B. *Hood, Potemkin, Excalibur, Defiant*   C. *Potemkin, Hood, Lexington, Excalibur*
7. What general order is the noninterference, "Prime Directive"?
   A. General Order No. 1   B. General Order No. 4   C. General Order No. 7
8. What is Yeoman Rand's room number?
   A. 5C46   B. 4C36   C. 3C46
9. What type of currency was used in *The Gamesters of Triskelion?*
   A. Dinars   B. Quatloos   C. Dollars
10. In what way did Kirk cause the other starships to back off in *The Ultimate Computer?*
    A. By leaving the *Enterprise's* shields down   B. By pleading with them   C. By outrunning them
11. What were the cave dwellers in *The Cloud Minders* called?
    A. Halkans   B. Troglytes   C. Thralls
12. What metal makes up the protective shields of the Earth outposts located along the Neutral Zone?
    A. Neutronium   B. Lead   C. Cast rodinium
13. What Vulcan word means "stop," and is never disobeyed?
    A. *Kroykah*   B. *Tal-shaya*   C. *Troykah*

14. What chemical is Spock's blood based on?
    A. Nickel   B. Copper   C. Iron

15. What size is an explosion created by the short-circuiting of a starship's matter-antimatter engines?
    A. 97.835 megatons   B. 97.835 begatons   C. 97.835 kilotons

16. What was the Doomsday Machine's hull composed of?
    A. Cast rodinium   B. Black diamond   C. Neutronium

17. What was the name of the floating city in *The Cloud Minders?*
    A. Ardana   B. Argelius   C. Stratos

18. What was Kahn a product of?
    A. Selective breeding   B. Mental conditioning   C. Gene surgery

19. With what did Kirk fight the spores of Omicron Ceti III?
    A. Subsonic sound   B. Emotion   C. Acetylcholine

20. What type of radiation flooded the colonists in *This Side of Paradise?*
    A. Berthold rays   B. Gamma rays   C. Zeenite rays

21. In *Charlie X,* Charlie is very much attracted to the captain's ———.
    A. Communications officer   B. Yeoman   C. Engineer

22. In *Dagger of the Mind,* the new machine that was created leaves one's mind ———.
    A. Burned out   B. Frozen   C. Blank

23. What did Kirk use against Balok to save his ship?
    A. A new weapon   B. A corbomite laser   C. A bluff

24. What play did the Karidian Players perform aboard the *Enterprise?*
    A. *Macbeth*   B. *Hamlet*   C. *Julius Caesar*

25. Who was apparently killed by the White Knight?
    A. Spock   B. Sulu   C. McCoy

26. Trelane was in actuality———.
    A. A small boy   B. An omnipotent being   C. A disguised alien

27. Kahn's people in the *Botany Bay* left Earth in ———.
    A. 1990   B. 1996   C. 1998

28. Shaun Geoffrey Christopher will lead the first mission to ———.
    A. Saturn   B. Jupiter   C. Alpha Centauri

29. In *Operation: Annihilate!* Spock is rendered temporarily ———.
    A. Blind   B. Deaf   C. Dumb

30. Harry Mudd's wife's name is ———.
    A. Irma   B. Adirna   C. Stella
31. In *The City on the Edge of Forever*, McCoy is accidentally injected with ———.
    A. Cordrazine   B. Benjisidrine   C. Stokaline
32. What did McCoy leave on Iotia?
    A. Thermal concrete   B. Communicator   C. Medikit
33. It thought it was in love with Kirk.
    A. The ship's computer   B. A tribble   C. The "Companion"
34. Loki was ———.
    A. Black on the right side   B. Black on the left side
    C. Neither of the above
35. Which of the following is *not* a starship?
    A. *Hood*   B. *Constitution*   C. *Kongo*
36. While on shore leave on the planet Argelius, Lieutenant Commander Scott ———.
    A. Murdered three girls   B. Saw a white rabbit   C. Spent the entire time reviewing technical journals
37. The final command in the *Enterprise* destruct sequence is ———.
    A. Code Zero-Zero-Zero-Destruct   B. Code Zero-Destruct-Zero-Zero   C. Code Zero-Zero-Destruct-Zero
38. What mineral does the Federation get from Ardana?
    A. Zeenite   B. Dilithium   C. Rytalin
39. What is the name of the dairy on the milk truck in *The City on the Edge of Forever?*
    A. Fountain   B. Widen   C. Westheimer
40. In *The City on the Edge of Forever*, what time did McCoy arrive in New York City?
    A. 10 A.M.   B. 6 P.M.   C. 2 A.M.
41. In which episode is Starbase 200 mentioned?
    A. *The Alternative Factor*   B. *Court-martial*   C. *The Menagerie*
42. Which of the following is *not* a quotation from Shakespeare?
    A. *Dagger of the Mind*   B. *All Our Yesterdays*   C. *Who Mourns for Adonais?*
43. Who was ship's surgeon under Captain Pike?
    A. Dr. Boyce   B. Dr. McCoy   C. Dr. M'Benga
44. What incident gave Dr. McCoy cause to believe he could cure a rainy day?
    A. Identifying and curing the disease on Miri's world
    B. Patching up the horta   C. Saving Sarek's life

Nichelle Nichols addressing the 1974 Convention, with David Gerrold beside her. *(Jeff Maynard)*

Isaac Asimov and Gene Roddenberry at their first meeting at the 1972 convention. Gene's tie was a present from his fan club president, Maureen Wilson.

David Gerrold holding one of his famous tribbles as he sits in the command chair of the *Enterprise* bridge mock-up at the 1973 con. *(Jeff Maynard)*

James Doohan and George Takei taking up familiar positions on the bridge mock-up during the same con. *(Jeff Maynard)*

That year's surprise guest, Mark Lenard, who played Spock's father in *Amok Time*, signing autographs for a crowd of appreciative fans. *(Benjamin M. Yalow)*

Joan Winston and Oscar Katz introducing the "Genesis II" slide show at the 1973 con. *(Jeff Maynard)*

45. Who is Petri?
    A. Thelev's aide   B. A lawgiver   C. The Elaasian ambassador

46. How old is Sarek?
    A. 130   B. 102   C. 72

47. What was Marlena's job?
    A. Chemist   B. Computer specialist   C. Sociologist

48. What was the purpose of the Babel conference?
    A. To settle the conflict on Altair VI   B. To debate the admission of Coridan to the Federation   C. To consider the action against the Orions

49. On what deck is Kirk's cabin?
    A. 4   B. 5   C. 6

50. In what episode besides *The Corbomite Maneuver* was corbomite mentioned?
    A. *The* Enterprise *Incident*   B. *The Tholian Web*   C. *The Deadly Years*

51. Who didn't believe in little green men?
    A. Captain John Christopher   B. Colonel Fellini   C. Air Police sergeant

52. How old were Spock and T'Pring when they were promised to each other?
    A. 5   B. 7   C. 12

53. What name did Kirk use when disguised as a citizen of Organia?
    A. Tharn   B. Barona   C. Bilar

54. Where was Zephram Cochrane born?
    A. Alpha Centauri   B. Earth   C. Mars

55. Where did Scott keep his prized bottle of old scotch whisky?
    A. Under his bed   B. Behind an ornamental shield   C. In an antique helmet

56. What office did Mara hold on Kang's ship?
    A. Weapons officer   B. Science officer   C. Communications officer

57. Where in the *Enterprise* is the auxiliary control room?
    A. Engineering   B. Deck 11   C. The central computer banks

58. Which of the following is a Klingon nerve gas?
    A. Benjisidrine   B. Stokaline   C. Theragin

59. In what episode was Captain Kirk missing his command insignia?
    A. *Charlie X*   B. *The Naked Time*   C. *The Enemy Within*

60. Spock's pulse rate is ———.
    A. 242   B. 72   C. 392

61. McCoy once told Captain Kirk his medical history. Until the
    spores restored them, McCoy ——.
    A. Had his tonsils out and once broke two ribs   B. Had his
    tonsils and appendix out   C. Had his appendix out and
    once broke two ribs

62. In *The Cage*, Captain Pike's horse is named ——.
    A. Twister   B. Prince   C. Tango

63. Who called Spock a pointy-eared thinking machine?
    A. Captain Kirk   B. Mr. Spock   C. Harry Mudd

64. Which group of three (3) starships have all been destroyed?
    A. *Constellation, Farragut, Defiant*   B. *Lexington, Intrepid,
    Yorktown*   C. *Potemkin, Exeter, Excalibur*

65. General Order 7 is ——.
    A. An order to destroy a planet in two hours   B. The death
    penalty for visiting Talos IV   C. The noninterference di-
    rective

66. The serial number of the U.S.S. *Constellation* is
    A. NCC-1701   B. NCC-1371   C. NCC-1071

67. What was the name of the second pilot?
    A. *Man Trap*   B. *Where No Man Has Gone Before*
    C. *The Cage*

68. In which episode does Spock briefly go blind?
    A. *The Alternative Factor*   B. *Errand of Mercy*   C. *Oper-
    ation: Annihilate!*

69. In *For the World Is Hollow and I Have Touched the Sky*,
    what is the name of the high priestess?
    A. Natira   B. Rayna   C. Zarabeth

70. What is Chekov's first name?
    A. Pavel   B. Ivan   C. Piotr

71. What was the name of Nurse Chapel's fiancé?
    A. Andrew Korby   B. Roger Korby   C. Roger Andrews

72. What was the full name of Captain Kirk's brother?
    A. George James Kirk   B. George Samuel Kirk   C. Sam-
    uel George Kirk

73. What was the name of Flint's ward?
    A. Julia   B. Rayna   C. Droxine

74. What was the name of the baby high chief in *Friday's Child*?
    A. James Leonard Akaar   B. Akaar James Leonard
    C. Leonard James Akaar

75. What is the length of the *Enterprise*?
    A. 947 ft.   B. 632 ft.   C. 826 ft.

76. The phaser rifle appeared in only one episode. Which one?
    A. *The Menagerie*   B. *Operation: Annihilate!*   C. *Where
    No Man Has Gone Before*

77. What is the name of the Tholian commander?
   A. Balok   B. Loskene   C. Yarnek
78. What was Kirk's reply to Scotty's coded remark in *Whom Gods Destroy?*
   A. Queen to King's level one   B. King to Queen's level one   C. Queen to Queen's level one
79. Which of the following was *not* destroyed?
   A. The *Intrepid*   B. The *Yorktown*   C. The *Valiant*
80. What was the name of the disease that McCoy contracted in *For the World Is Hollow and I Have Touched the Sky?*
   A. Xenopolycythemia   B. Rigelian fever   C. Vegan chorio-meningitis
81. Who invented the M-5 computer?
   A. Dr. Crater   B. Dr. Daystrom   C. Dr. Lester
82. How many attendants carried T'Pau's litter?
   A. 2   B. 4   C. 6
83. What planet was at war with Eminiar VII?
   A. Elas   B. Ariannus   C. Vendikar
84. How long has the Vulcan peace existed on Spock's home planet?
   A. 600 years   B. 1,000 years   C. 2,000 years
85. Who was Kirk's Indian rival for Miramanee?
   A. Salish   B. Cochise   C. Kommack
86. What starship vanished into interspace with Kirk aboard?
   A. *Intrepid*   B. *Valiant*   C. *Defiant*
87. What card game is played on Beta Antares 4?
   A. Poker   B. Fabrini   C. Fizzbin
88. What is a Vulcan method of execution?
   A. *Tol-shaya*   B. Death by hanging   C. *Lirpa*
89. What was mined on Janus 6?
   A. Zeenite   B. Dilithium Crystals   C. Pergium
90. What was the actual charge against Kirk in *Court-martial?*
   A. Culpable negligence   B. First-degree murder   C. Man-slaughter

MIX 'N' MATCH: Indicate the letter that corresponds with the episode in which each character appeared

91. Nancy Hedford   A. *Wolf in the Fold*
                    B. *This Side of Paradise*
92. Zora   C. *Journey to Babel*
                    D. *Friday's Child*
93. Korob   E. *Savage Curtain*
                    F. *I, Mudd*

94. Shras   G. *The Alternative Factor*
                         H. *Errand of Mercy*
95. Eleen   I. *Metamorphosis*
                         J. *The Doomsday Machine*
96. Cloud William   K. *Catspaw*
                         L. *What Are Little Girls Made Of?*
97. Droxine   M. *Tomorrow Is Yesterday*
                         N. *Dagger of the Mind*
98. Stella   O. *The Omega Glory*
                         P. *The Paradise Syndrome*
99. Ayelborne   R. *Elaan of Troyius*
                         S. *The Cloud Minders*
100. Lazarus   T. *Return of the Archons*

CHAPTER III

ON WRITING A BOOK;
OR,
BEWITCHED, BOTHERED, AND BEFUDDLED

The 1973 convention had been over for just a few weeks when something happened that changed my whole life. I was in the bank in the CBS Building and met an old friend, Dick Burns. Dick and I had worked together before at CBS. He was now vice president of the Contracts Department at ABC.

I congratulated him on his new job, and as we walked out of the bank, we talked. He told me that one of his people was leaving. "If I ever thought you'd leave CBS I'd offer you the job," he said.

I had been restless for some time, so I turned to him and grinned, "Make me an offer." And he did.

It was a full executive position rather than the administrative job I had at CBS. It was also for more money, which was nice. But what really appealed to me was the faith he displayed in my capabilities.

I went up to my boss at CBS and told him of my offer. He was nice enough to say he was shook. I had had a very good relationship with him, but he was a little bit of a male chauvinist, and in my opinion, I don't think he felt women could do as good a job as men in certain areas.

This was in March, and I was in for a very difficult three months. Dick wanted me, but ABC had other ideas. They felt, and rightly, I guess, that the job should be filled from within the company. Fine. But this job was not one that could be learned in a few days or even weeks. I had many years of experience plus many contacts within the industry.

Dick very honestly interviewed everyone they sent to him. But if they were qualified in one area, they were not qualified in another. After two months of this I was a nervous wreck!

Dick had given me a start date of June 18, and that was only three weeks away. I had wanted to spend some time in Baton Rouge with Sondra. I was going to write my " 'Star Trek' Set" chapter for *Star Trek Lives!* (you'll read more about this later). I had planned to spend two weeks with her but had to give CBS two weeks' notice. So with my heart in my mouth and with my fingers and toes crossed (yes, it is very hard to walk that way), I limped into my immediate superior's office and gave notice. Then I walked into the john and got royally sick. What was I doing? Suppose the job didn't come through? I thought of all the department stores my monthly payments kept in business, and I shuddered.

I phoned Sondra and told her when I was coming down. "One week!"

"You promised me two!"

"Actually its ten days," I stammered, "I'll just have to type fast." Good luck. We both knew that typing was not my speed. (Oops, sorry.)

The only person at CBS who knew of my foolhardiness was Ginny Frey. She was marvelous and gave me moral support at every opportunity. And there were many. I had half expected a small party or something, since I had been with CBS for a good long time. But Ginny said they didn't really have enough time to plan one and would have it after I left. I sure hoped they invited me.

We were riding down in the elevator the Tuesday of my last week with my boss and his vice president. He, the vice president, turned to me and said, "Gee, Joan, if I don't get to see you at the party on Thursday, we'll have a drink together before you leave." As this sunk in, Ginny poked him in the ribs and my boss kicked him in the shins. He suddenly turned red. I turned to Ginny, who was even redder, and asked, "What party?" At this point the elevator doors opened and my boss and the vice president erupted into the CBS lobby. As Ginny tried to scuttle away, I grabbed her arm. One look into my eyes and she told me all.

It was supposed to be a surprise. She was to take me into the restaurant next door to CBS Thursday night for a drink. Everyone was going to leap out of the walls and yell "SURPRISE!" Well, I would have had a SURPRISE! for them. I was planning to work late Thursday night to clean up the last of the debris on my desk. Now I had two days' warning and plunged in with a will—with Ginny's help, of course. Since she was going to be my replacement, it worked out well for both of us. Thursday afternoon Dick called me at the office. ABC had finally okayed my papers, and I had a job! Hooray! I could go to the party with a happy heart.

Was that a party? That was party! Now you're going have to bear with me, because I'm gonna brag a little. I had a president, fourteen vice presidents, and about two dozen directors and associate directors plus their secretaries. I was speechless—which, if you know ol' motormouth at all, was something to see.

There was one VP in attendance who surprised one and all. I had invited Dick, since I wanted everyone to meet him. My VP walked up to Dick and said, "Okay, we've got an outfielder, two first basemen, and a catcher. What else are you offering?" Dick looked very serious, "How about four pairs of sneakers and three pair of laces?" VP pursed his lips, "Throw in the other pair of laces and you've got a deal."

That set the tone for the whole party. Delightful daffiness.

I had loved CBS, but there comes a time in one's life when it's time to move on. It was a happy-sad time. And did I know what time it was! My going-away gift was a gorgeous digital desk clock in chrome and rosewood. I didn't dare leave it in my office, since it was too much of a temptation. It is on the bookcase in my living-writing room and gives me quiet joy every time I look at it.

Party time was over, and I left for New Orleans. Sondra and her husband, Alan, picked me up at the airport. When we got to their lovely home, the first thing Sondra showed me was the *Enterprise* model Alan had done hanging from the ceiling over the couch. I felt instantly at home. Alan went to bed, but Sondra and I stayed up talking for hours and hours and hours. That was to happen almost every evening of my stay, and I must admit it was great.

The next morning Sondra took me into the study, pointed to the typewriter and blank sheets of paper, and said, "Write." I wrote.

I typed about five pages a day, because most of my time was spent staring into space. I was trying to dredge up the memories of all those fantastic days I'd spent visiting on the "Star Trek" set just before the program was canceled. As I wrote, more and more things began to come back to me. I have an excellent memory, when I put my mind to it, especially when it concerns events that mean a great deal to me. Those six days were a once-in-a-lifetime experience. From all the letters and comments I've received, many fans seemed to be able to feel the joy and enchantment I felt. I couldn't ask for a greater compliment.

With Sondra's help, the chapter was finished. It was time for me to head home to my new job. Well, I thought the chapter was finished, but it was to be rewritten about a half-dozen times before it reached the publisher.

Back in New York I settled quickly into my new job—which was just as well, since the Committee was in the middle of planning the 1974 convention. This was to be a biggie. We had made a deal with the Americana Hotel, which had the second-largest ballroom in the city. The largest was the New York Hilton, which we could in no way afford. Yes, Virginia, you do have to pay the hotel to use their space, and what you pay them is usually a lot. We were planning for about ten thousand people, and I think we got more than we bargained for.

We had sent out our first group of fliers with information about the convention, and memberships were starting to drift in, for which we gave thanks, since we had lost money on the 1973 con, and we each had to contribute fifty dollars to pay for the fliers, postage, and printing costs. Some cons save a bit from the profits of the previous convention (hah!) or else have someone finance them. With us it was a Committee project.

Elyse and Steve were doing the progress report that year. I had done it for the previous conventions with their help, but my job at ABC was taking up more and more of my time. However, I was still doing the program book and was diligently looking for new pictures and blooper shots. The fans really seemed to get a kick out of the latter.

Sondra and Jackie were not idle during this period. They were finishing all the other chapters of *Star Trek Lives!* I get many letters from fans telling me how much they have enjoyed those chapters. I had nothing to do with them. They are all the work of my coauthors, and they deserve all the praise. They've earned it.

Back to the con. I was delighted to learn from Elyse that we were going to have DeForest Kelley. Dorothy Fontana and David Gerrold were coming again, and so was George Takei. We were also lucky enough to get Nichelle Nichols and Walter Koenig. As I said before, it was going to be a biggie! The make-up man from "Star Trek," Fred Phillips, agreed to come late in November, and with our regulars, Hal Clement and Isaac Asimov, our guest list was complete.

We had decided to have our first press party and were really excited. I got a list of all the major media in New York plus United Press International and the Associated Press. We would send out the invitations about ten days prior to the convention. I had never thrown a party for the press before, but I figured if you mixed them with large quantities of celebrities, liquor, and food, the party should take care of itself. It turned out I was right.

While I was doing my thing, the rest of the Committee was doing theirs. The Americana gave some people problems. Poor Devra had to figure out a way to hang square pictures in a round room. The Princess Ballroom was to be used for the art show and, boy, was it round. But Steve Rosenstein was having a good time with all the electrical equipment. They had a professional set-up for the lights and sound stystem, and a huge movie screen that let down from the ceiling. This was a tremendous relief to Steve, whose main memory of the 1973 convention was putting up the movie screen and taking down the movie screen and putting up the movie screen and taking down, you get the idea.

You can see the results of all that energy in the next chapter.

CHAPTER IV

STRAITJACKETS ARE IN,
AND I'LL HAVE MINE IN PALE BLUE, PLEASE;
OR,
"STAR TREK" MEETS THE FIRE MARSHALS
(The 1974 International "Star Trek" Convention, February 15–18, 1974, the Americana Hotel, New York, New York)

POCKET PROGRAM
THE 1974 INTERNATIONAL "STAR TREK"
CONVENTION

Friday, February 15, 1974

2:00 P.M.– 7:00 P.M.	Registration	Foyer
2:00 P.M.– 7:00 P.M.	Dealers' room open	Royal Ballroom
3:00 P.M.– 6:00 P.M.	Films	Imperial Ballroom
7:30 P.M.	"Star Trek" anthology	Imperial Ballroom
8:30 P.M.– 2:00 A.M.	Films	Imperial Ballroom

Saturday, February 16, 1974

10:00 A.M.– 7:00 P.M.	Registration	Foyer
10:00 A.M.– 7:00 P.M.	Dealers' room	Royal Ballroom
10:00 A.M.– 6:00 P.M.	Art Show	Princess Ballroom
10:00 A.M.– 6:00 P.M.	Exhibits	Versaille Terrace
11:00 A.M.	"Star Trek" (animation)	Channel 4 WNBC-TV
12:00 NOON	Dorothy C. Fontana	Imperial Ballroom
1:00 P.M.	Walter Koenig	Imperial Ballroom
2:00 P.M.	Lunch	
3:00 P.M.	DeForest Kelley	Imperial Ballroom
4:00 P.M.	Hal Clement	Imperial Ballroom
5:00 P.M.	David Gerrold	Imperial Ballroom

| 6:00 P.M. | Dinner | |
| 8:00 P.M.– 2:00 A.M. | Films | Imperial Ballroom |

Sunday, February 17, 1974

10:00 A.M.– 7:00 P.M.	Registration	Foyer
10:00 A.M.– 7:00 P.M.	Dealers' room	Royal Ballroom
10:00 A.M.– 6:00 P.M.	Art Show	Princess Ballroom
10:00 A.M.– 6:00 P.M.	Exhibits	Versaille Terrace
10:00 A.M.	Art Show Auction No. 1	Imperial Ballroom
11:00 A.M.	Nichelle Nichols	Imperial Ballroom
12:00 NOON	Lunch	
2:00 P.M.	Isaac Asimov	Imperial Ballroom
3:00 P.M.	Fred Phillips (make-up)	Imperial Ballroom
5:00 P.M.	Dinner	
7:15 P.M.	Costume Prejudging	Versaille Ballroom
8:30 P.M.	Costume call	Imperial Ballroom
12:00 P.M.– 2:00 A.M.	Films	

Monday, February 18, 1974

10:00 A.M.– 3:00 P.M.	Registration	Foyer
10:00 A.M.– 4:00 P.M.	Dealers' room	Royal
10:00 A.M.–12:00 NOON	Art Show	Princess Ballroom
10:00 A.M.–12:00 NOON	Exhibits	Versaille Terrace
11:00 A.M.	Art Auction No. 2 (general auction)	Imperial Ballroom
12:00 NOON	Panel discussion: Nichelle Nichols Walter Koenig DeForest Kelley George Takei	Imperial Ballroom
1:00 P.M.	Lunch	
2:00 P.M.	George Takei	Imperial Ballroom
3:00 P.M.	Panel Discussion: Dorothy C. Fontana David Gerrold Fred Phillips	
4:00 P.M.	Convention ends	

THURSDAY, FEBRUARY 14, 1974

Most of the Committee had moved into the Americana Hotel on the previous evening, but I had to finish an important report, so I wasn't going to the hotel till today. It was not a good day for me to start a convention. I had to be at the hotel by 4:30 P.M. to set up for the press party (our first) at 6:30 P.M. And there I sat, in the throes of a gall bladder attack!

At 3:45 P.M. I was in my office, my nose on my knees, trying frantically (you know, you're right, I always seem to be frantic) to finish that special report for the Powers-that-be at ABC. Would I make it? You bet your big, red rubber ball I made it! Handing Andrea, my harassed secretary, the many scrawled sheets to decipher, I rushed off. And then rushed right back—to remind her that she and Bob Golub had promised to bring the "Star Trek" episodes with them to the party. Bob is one of the program attorneys in my department and a "Star Trek" fan. An intelligent and charming man. He had also volunteered to act as the bartender at the party.

I met Jackie, the one and only Lichtenberg (creator of the Kraith Series, who has been a Hugo nominee for Best Fan Writer; she hates to be called "Jackie" and only out of love tolerates it from her incorrigible Joanie) at the reception desk of the hotel. (Whew!) It seems there was a mix-up about the room reservations. This was to be the usual rather than the unusual thing that weekend. I had only made the reservation, in writing, three times. The matter was taken care of, and I finally made it to my room on the forty-ninth floor.

I was sharing the room with Sondra's mother, Mrs. Anna Hassan. She is one of the sweetest ladies in the galaxy, and I love her. She helped me unpack and insisted I lie down for a while.

Since Elyse had been kind enough to get most of the munchies for the party, and Sharon Emily was bringing the rest of the stuff, I could relax for a few moments. I took some medication and lay down on the bed to let it take effect. I was having the operation a week after the convention and couldn't wait. I remember Jackie saying to me, "What are you having out after next year's con, Joanie?" Well, there wasn't much more they could take.

I was horizontal for about ten minutes when a rap on the door announced Shirley Maiewski and Daphne Hamilton from Massachusetts to say hello. Sondra's mother, Anna, explained my "condition" to Shirley and Daph. They said they'd see me later and left. That was Thursday. I *think* I saw them at a party in Daphne's room on Saturday night, but I couldn't swear to it. So much for getting together with old friends. Sigh.

The next knock was Debbie Langsam and Renée Bodner. Debbie was assistant chairman, and when you couldn't find Al you could scream at her—only you didn't, because she's too nice. Renée was in charge of registration, and a very harrowing job that is, too.

Al was going to be late with the truck (so what else was new?), and the truck had the liquor for the party in it. Aha. Oh, oh. Money was handed to Dave Simons, who corralled some helpers and made a sortie to the vodka vendor across the street.

After a quick shower (I had given up trying to get some rest) I trundled down to the con suite where the press party was to take place. Our own beloved bedlam again.

Let's see: liquor, glasses, napkins, soda, bottle opener—what was missing? Ice, you idiot! Linda Deneroff lugged back a ten-pound bag, and we were in business. Almost. As Sharon Emily unpacked all the goodies, I noticed that one major goodie was missing: the cheese to go with those boxes and boxes of crackers. Stuffing some bills into Sharon Black's hands, I sent her on her way with cries of "Cheddar, Swiss, Gouda, bleu cheese . . ." echoing after her.

We had just sliced the last salami when the first guests arrived. Among them were Bob Golub and my secretary, Andrea Romano. They had brought the films and several shopping bags containing press room supplies, more plastic glasses, and the three first chapters of *Star Trek Lives!* These last were put against the wall near the door of the con suite.

(A few days later, Jackie asked for the chapters, since she wanted to read something from one. That's when the hysteria started. The only shopping bags in my room had some plastic glasses and party stuff in them. The one for the press room was *in* the press room. We instigated a search. No one seemed to have seen the shopping bag after the press party. Had it been, *gulp*, tossed out with the trash? Had someone walked off with it by mistake, as a joke? We were getting desperate. All the originals and the copies I had made were in that bag. We had all our notes—but to start all over again . . .)

Finally, a helper remembered a shopping bag she had put in the closet of the room that Devra, Joyce, and Barbara were sharing. She had been putting some other stuff from the con suite in there and tossed that in, too. Neither of them had known whose bag it was, and each assumed it belonged to the other. They had been so busy with the con that they hadn't had time to peek inside the bag. They finally did as they were packing to go home.

The shopping bag and its contents at our feet, Jackie, Sondra, and I compared new gray hairs. I won.

Now that the salami is sliced, let's get back to the party. There were about fifty people there, among them representatives from the Associated Press, United Press International, *TV Guide*, ABC, CBS, WPIX, Columbia Pictures, United Artists, and the *National Star*. And our "Star Trek" guests who . . . well, that's a story, too.

We wanted to pick up De Kelley, George Takei, and Nichelle Nichols, who were coming in on a 4:00 P.M. flight arriving at Kennedy Airport. It was the time of the gasoline shortage; you must remember that. The only way we could get a full tank of gas was to rent the car surrounding it, soooo, we contacted a local rent-a-car, and they promised us a *full-sized* four-door sedan with a *full* tank of gas. When we called to confirm that the car was available, they said, "Sure!" Our welcoming contingent raced over, and suddenly the answer was "No!" We would have to wait "a few minutes." The phrase was to echo in our ears for the next forty minutes. We kept looking at the clock and dying a little.

The car finally arrived: it was not a full-sized one, and it had only half a tank of gas—enough, we hoped, to get our contingent and the far-from-fresh-looking chariot to the airport. By the time we pulled to the curb at the terminal, we had been running on fumes for the past ten minutes and praying a lot.

De, Nichelle, and George arrived on the same plane, Elyse's famous planning again. Also on the flight was Zarabeth, I mean Mariette Hartley, looking fabulous. She was visiting friends in New York and met our group on the plane. Not thinking too clearly, our stalwart twosome, Ben Yalow and Stu Hellinger, invited her to share our car. De and Mariette were tallest, so they shared the front seat with Stu. George, Nichelle, and Ben shared the back seat with the leftover luggage. However, before the trek back to New York, they had to get gas. There was one station at JFK dispensing gas—with an eyedropper, it's true— but they had to have gas. So they got in line with all the other cars and waited and waited, all scrunched up in that little car. But our stars are a good-natured crew and joked through the long wait. It was then that Ben and Stu invited Mariette to the party that night, but she was unable to attend. But she said that she would be delighted to speak at the con the next day. Our first "coup."

The salami was giving out, and where were our guests? It was now 7:30 P.M. There was a flurry at the door. DeForest Kelley had arrived. He looked around as I came up to him and sighed in relief.

"Joan, thank God, a familiar face."

A quick hug, then he proceeded to charm the bejebers out of everyone in the room. It is amazing how different a party looks when you are floating three feet off the floor. A truly charming, gentle man.

The next charmer par excellence was George Takei. Within moments the entire Committee—female contingent—had rushed up, and you could barely see George as we exchanged warm greetings and hugs and kisses. (This was one of the side benefits of being on the Committee.) He had been a great hit the year before, and because he had helped us contact the guests for this year's con, he had been made an honorary member of the Committee.

Suddenly the room lit up and this beautiful ebony doll walked in. Nichelle Nichols is not more than five-two, but her personality is seven-eight. More lovely than we remembered; every man in the room had her surrounded in seconds. She has a fantastic wit and an even more fantastic fund of stories—most of which cannot be printed here.

The press dragged them off, one by one, for interviews. They used what would be Al's room during the convention but was now the Pepsi-Cola warehouse. I think Al takes it intravenously. The press also asked where Walter Koenig was, and they were told that he was not due in till the next afternoon. They were quite disappointed.

I had just poured the last of the scotch when our wandering heroes arrived (Remember them?) Al, Eli Friedman, and Nick Pappas had all the paraphernalia from the truck loaded onto huge dollies and were bringing it into the suite. We got a gaggle of helpers to unload, and listened to their tale of woe. They had been stuck in the Holland Tunnel for hours because of an accident and were exhausted.

The helpers quickly unloaded the boxes and there, just in time, was the liquor. The party was supposed to be from 6:00 to 8:00 P.M.; it was now 9:30 P.M., and no one showed any signs of leaving. It finally broke up at 10:30 P.M. when Al announced he would like to take a shower. Since he was using the con suite as his living quarters during the con and was pooped from his foray into New Jersey, he had a good point.

Our guests went to their rooms, and we policed the area. I had brought, thank heavens, those huge plastic garbage bags. Next time I think we will bring an electric broom. Cracker crumbs are hard to pick up with fingers that have had three drinks.

As the Committee sprawled around the suite in various attitudes of tired, someone brought up the subject of food. Food. Hey, that's right. None of us had had the chance to eat since lunch, and it was now 11:00 P.M. So, in typical Committee fashion, we had a meeting, mostly trying to think of places that would be open and willing to take eighteen foodless fiends.

We ended up at the hotel coffee shop. They may never recover from the con. Fans eat at the oddest hours, and we were some of the oddest fans you might ever meet.

After dinner we decided to run some episodes in the con suite. I had my 16mm projector at the hotel as a back-up in case the rentals pooped. As we set up I realized that something was missing. Good Lord, I had forgotten to pack the sound system! Dave Simons, Eli Friedman, and Manny Mouriño took a cab over to my apartment and found it. That is so easy to say if you haven't seen my apartment. Pack Rats Anonymous has selected it as the Nest of the Year. The boys finally returned, and we saw *Naked Time*. I'm sure that if any of the guests had picked that moment to peek into the con suite they would have had the lot of us carted away. It was as if we knew that we would never get the time to see these films once the con opened. And were we right.

FRIDAY, FEBRUARY 15, 1974

This is the press room?! Well, yes, but at the moment Renée was using it. All her helpers were putting the membership cards together for the opening of registration at 2:00 P.M. We could have it later this afternoon for the press.

Leaving my squad of helpers to clean up around the edges, I went back upstairs to check on the films. Oh, lucky timing. Steve and Wally, the projectionist, were surrounded by Camera Mart equipment, looking a bit bewildered. It seemed that Wally knew Bell & Howell and RCA projectors backward, forward and inside out, but the Eiki, no. Aha, I did know Eikis, owning one, and proceeded to explain its intricate workings to Wally and Steve, and talked myself into a four-hour session in the "Black Hole of Calcutta."

Wally, some helpers, and I lugged the projector and films down to the projection booth. It was very quaint, about the size of a large elevator which, strangely enough, was what it was. Once we had loaded everything into it, Wally pressed a button, and we started to descend from the fourth floor down through the ceiling of the Imperial Ballroom, fifty-five feet above the floor.

Hello dere.

Wally connected the projector after inserting the three hundred-arc bulb. Boy, would that ever put a picture on the screen. Only it didn't. Good grief, a dud bulb! Good ol' Camera Mart.

I climbed out of the booth and called Camera Mart. Don't you love the easy, calm way I said that? I climbed out the booth . . . What happened was I had hysterics, *then* I climbed a seven-foot steel ladder set into the wall, clinging fearfully to Wally, and then grabbed onto an itty-bitty steel bar and clawed some holes in the wall as I bent into a pretzel trying to clear a foot-wide extension of the ceiling, cursing my brand-new slacks and high heels as I went.

Okay, Camera Mart, what's with the projector that's costing us
$$$ a day? The power pack? What power pack? The one up on
the forty-ninth floor in the closet. That's what power pack.

It was one of those days.

Mike Weisel, who was to become my film assistant, and irre-
placeable in this area, and his friend John Moroney helped me
carry it back to the booth.

Oh drat! I had to climb back down!

Okay, Hotel Americana, now you know where all those gouges
in the wall came from: my frantic fingernails searching madly
for purchase as Wally grabbed each foot and tried to place it on
the ladder. I wonder if the con's three-hundred-thousand-dollar
liability insurance covered this.

By the end of the con I was going up and down that ladder
like a monkey (no cracks). Goes to show, one can get used to
anything.

Suddenly Elyse disappeared. Jeff Maynard had tried to regis-
ter for his room and had been told that he would have to pay for
it—in advance. Now, Jeff was one of our guests, a nonpaying
guest. His "Light Show" was a great favorite with the fans, and
we were paying for his room as a courtesy. Elyse tried to explain
this to the desk manager but could not get through. She finally
asked if any other guests were not on their list of "convention
guests." The desk manager handed her his list, and she quickly
spotted three names—missing! Jeff's, Hal Clement's, and Walter
Koenig's!

Elyse marched up to the banquet manager's office in high
dudgeon (and high voice, too). She wasn't known as the Scream-
ing Yellow Zonker for nothin', kiddo. The manager quailed as her
piercing soprano sent a crystal vase to its "maker." He quickly
produced his list to show her that the three names were not on it.

"I am not interested in your list; where is the one that *I* gave
you?"

He pawed frantically through the file and finally ten minutes
later came up with the list of guests that Elyse had sent him
eight weeks prior to the convention. There were the three names.

"Aha!" said Elyse.

"Oho!" said Jeff.

"Uh-oh!" said the manager.

Sweeping up the shards of his vase, he promised to rectify the error. You betcha.

On one of my press room checking forays, I noticed the huge crowd building up. Where there had been dozens there were now hundreds and hundreds. And it was only 11:00 A.M. I ran into Renée and Al, and suggested opening registration early.

"We said it would open at two, and that's when the booths and the ladies from the convention bureau are due to arrive," said Renée.

"But what if they're late or something? I mean the crowds are really getting big. Can't we open now so the fans won't have to wait so long?"

Nope, 2:00 P.M. was set, and that was that.

I remember Dana telling me when we had over three thousand on line at 1:00 P.M. and she approached Al to open up early. His reply: "Oh, it's not that bad."

And when someone had the inspiration to play "Star Trek" tapes to calm the huge crowd, Al gave the same comment: "Oh, it's not that bad." Al, ask Barbara and Dana and Ben. It was that bad.

Ask David Gerrold. He went down into the bowels of the lower levels of the Americana on Saturday and told stories and answered questions for almost two hours. Ask Isaac Asimov—he was there, too. What do you do for people like this? A life-saving certificate? A pint of blood?

Meanwhile, Ben's brilliant, analytical computer mind was figuring out the best way to line up the fans to make the most efficient use of the available space. Our official photographer suddenly found himself in charge of crowd control!

Barbara Wenk was hauled bodily out of the Art Show and set up at the end of the long, long line with a large piece of posterboard attached to a long tube that stated, "This is the end of the line." There were several occasions during that day when Barbara thought the very same thing.

We were only going to show films till five, but decided to continue till registration closed—whenever that was. I went down to the dais in the ballroom, introduced myself, and told them the film schedule for the con. Since I had the blooper reel scheduled every few hours, the crowd was ecstatic. Whew.

Back to the press room. Ellen Schlakman, my assistant, her sister Carol, and Ruth Schoenberg were the only ones there; everyone else, including our newest addition, Allyson Whitfield, had been grabbed for crowd control. I found out that was the order of the day; everyone was minus most of their helpers.

The press had been asking for me, De had been asking for me. Where had I been? I took them to the window overlooking the ballroom and pointed. The projection booth seemed very small and far away. I felt myself regarded with awe. You betcha.

Because of the condition of the press room, no interviews were set up until the next day. I wasn't going to think about that now because I was finally going to go to the john. No, I wasn't either. Suddenly, I remembered I hadn't checked the huckster room. I had promised Paramount that we would make sure all the people selling "Star Trek" stuff knew about getting a license from Paramount. I circled the huge room, asking my questions and giving copies of Paramount's letter to anyone who did not have a license: They were all very co-operative.

Registration was proceeding slowly but surely. The crowd was amazingly well behaved. Those "Star Trek" fans were great.

I was finally going to see Jeff Maynard's Light Show. Everyone had raved about it last year, and I was really looking forward to it. But it was not to be. I was dragged away on some emergency phone call, and by the time I got back, he was finished.

I went to get something to eat, since the last time had been at eight-thirty that morning. A loooong time ago.

Back at the booth, I looked at the 35mm projector that we need for *The Questor Tapes* and suddenly felt ill.

"Oh Wally, how big are those film cases?" These are the cases the reels are put in for projection.

"The usual two-thousand-foot-size."

"Um, Wally, I think the film is on larger reels."

"Nah, travel reels are always two thousand feet."

I climbed back out. (I was getting good, only took off three coats of paint, two layers of skin, and lost five years growth.) I went to check.

Uh-oh.

Mike and John and Jim Minter helped me drag them down, and we tried to fit them into the cases. No go. These were three-thousand-foot reels. Double uh-oh. I called Al from the booth and told him to make an announcement about the film, and why we could not show it as planned.

AL: "They don't have to know why."

JOAN: "Of course they have to know why!"

I raced downstairs and sadly told the fans the unhappy news. As the ohs and ahs filled the air, two gentlemen got up from the third row and made for the dais.

"We're from WXYZ-TV. If you'll send some people with us we'll put the film on two-thousand-foot reels."

They were film editors! There *are* guardian angels, and they wear rumpled Army jackets.

Not letting go of my angels for a moment, I rounded up some of my press room kids and sent the precious cargo off in two cabs with each helper's arm hugging a reel of *Questor*. Lauren, Diane, Ellen, Carol, and the rest waited patiently while the guys unwound the film from the three-thousand-foot reels and re-wound it on lovely, adorable two-thousand-foot reels.

Meanwhile, back at the Americana, the catastrophes were taking place right on schedule. Wally discovered that he had no negative *or* positive carbon arcs (whatever *they* are) for the 35mm projector. It seems that they are absolutely essential to 35mm projectors—I mean, like zilch and no *Questor Tapes* without them. And the Americana does not supply them. It seems you must order them from the hotel electrician prior to the convention. But since the hotel never mentioned this little fact and since we had never used 35mm machines before . . . Another reason why the urge to do damage hits every time I pass the southeast corner of Fifty-second Street and Seventh Avenue. Aaaarrgh!

We denuded the ballroom of helpers and scattered them into the cold night air with instructions to hit every movie theater in a ten-block area. They were to call us if they hit paydirt, and we would send $$ or $$$, if necessary. Cashiers were startled out of their collective wits in every theater on and off Broadway. Most of them didn't even know what carbon arcs were, let alone if the theater had an extra set—for sale—to a wild-eyed, desperate-to-see-*The Questor Tapes* kid. But at last, at the glorious, beautiful (we may erect a shrine) Guild on Fiftieth Street, there was an usher having a smoke who overheard our helper's frantic pleas. He checked and, sure enough, they had a couple of extra sets of whoosie-whatsises—for only $$! An hour late to be sure, but *The Questor Tapes* were shown to a wildly enthusiastic audience. It was a beautiful pilot, one of the best things Gene Roddenberry has ever done. Needless to say, NBC did not exercise the option. No comment. (No printable comment, anyway.)

SATURDAY, FEBRUARY 16, 1974

More of Friday—much more. The lines formed earlier and got longer earlier. Registration opened at 10:00 A.M., and the mob scene really began. By the time Dorothy Fontana opened the convention, the ballroom was filled and then some. This was BFM (before fire marshals). Oh yes, this was our introduction to some of New York City's finest. We had held two other conventions in New York, and had never had the opportunity to meet these gentlemen before. There is always a first time. It seems a parent took one look at the hordes of fans waiting (very patiently, I might add) and got hysterical.

"My son is here! He's being trampled! He can't breathe! Get the police! Get an ambulance!"

Her son was later discovered, in line, reading the latest *Monster Times* and eating a Mounds bar. Sigh.

Enter fire marshals. They were nice. Really. They only closed down the huckster room for about an hour to clear it out and establish a line of traffic. Other than that, they were most understanding. We didn't hassle them, and they didn't hassle us. They said everyone was amazingly well behaved and orderly, but we had to limit the registration each day to so many people and so many one-day people. Okay.

They were a little disturbed by the crowds in the ballroom, but since no one was smoking and we had set up exits and en-

trances, they didn't make much of a fuss. From then on, however, every few hours a troup of fire marshals would show up to:
"Clear the aisles!"
"Open the doors!"
"Shut the doors!"
At this point, I would like to extend our thanks and appreciation to the fire marshals of New York City. Thank you, fellas, for keeping us safe. See you in 1975.

At one point, Walter Koenig made the mistake of walking around the convention without any security guards. As he came out of the dealer's room, the programing came to a temporary close in the main ballroom just across the way. The space between the two is only about thirty feet wide.

The crowd saw Walter—Walter saw the crowd. Elyse saw Walter for about 2½ seconds before he was engulfed by masses of fans. By some strange alchemy, he was pushed to the forefront of the crowd. Elyse gave one of her famous shrieks—"STOP!!!"—at the top of her blue-eyed lungs. Elyse's voice, as we have described before, is very high and piercing, especially when she wants to be heard. This time the windows cracked for a radius of three city blocks. More important, the fans stopped dead in their tracks, luckily for Elyse. She is five-one and would have become a natural-blond smudge on the carpet if they hadn't stopped.

The noise filtered through to the Princess Ballroom, where the art show was being set up. Devra poked her head out to see what was the matter. Walter, seeing an avenue of escape, ducked inside. Elyse, suddenly realizing just how large a crowd she was holding at bay, followed at double-time. Once inside, the reality of what she had done hit her, and she suddenly sat down on the nearest chair. As though oblivious to his hairsbreadth escape (more than likely in a daze), Walter took the opportunity to inspect the artwork. And the art show group got a chance to inspect one of the stars. This was a rare occurrence, since they are pretty much confined to that area during the daily programing. Devra has said she sometimes expects to see beds brought in and a kitchen set up.

Since the membership had to be limited each day, a strange thing began to happen in the lobby of the Americana. Kids who had bought daily tickets in the morning were selling them in the late afternoon—for exorbitant amounts of money! Ticket scalpers at twelve!

The stars were rousingly received by the fans when they made their speeches. One of the most thunderous receptions was for DeForest Kelley. When De made his appearance, the roar of excitement was deafening. De said he could actually feel the love sweep across the stage.

"It was one of the most emotionally charged moments of my life. The warmth and love was an almost palpable wave." He was so touched he had to wipe his eyes several times during his speech.

All of our guests—George, Nichelle, Walter, Dorothy, and Fred Phillips—said the same thing. Makes you feel sorta good, doesn't it?

Hal Clement gave the fans a lesson in astronomy, "Star Trek" style. They loved it. Hal teaches in Massachusetts under his real name, Harry Stubbs. I think those students must be very lucky.

The Tribble Man himself was a star attraction. David's speech was as clever and amusing as he is. I'd like to mention right now that David was of immeasurable help to the convention and the Committee. He was always there when needed with a bright quip or a funny story. Get David to conduct your auctions; he does good work.

After the con had ended for the day and Michael was comfortably settled in the "Black Hole of Calcutta," I went up to my room to give my poor feet a rest. I had no sooner gotten my tired tootsies up on the bed when the phone rang. It was De. It seemed the Kaiser Television Network had asked him to do six fifty-five-second spots on the convention, to be broadcast the following week. He had done a rough of the first one and came to me for *help!* I had never done anything like that, but I figured, why not?

I called Jackie to come and help. The main thing to keep in mind was De's drawl. It is charming and delightful, but that means less words in the time allowed. We used De's first draft with a few minor changes. With that as an example, I wrote the spots, and Jackie corrected my grammar and stuff. Jackie said

James Doohan holding a Saurian brandy bottle belonging to Steve Rosenstein. Steve reclaimed it for posterity after the picture was taken. *(Jeff Maynard)*

Isaac Asimov in a playful mood with a phaser as Elyse Pines Rosenstein looks on. *(Jeff Maynard)*

Here's a glowing Nichelle Nichols in the dealers' room autographing her record album. Isn't that a glorious poster of Nichelle? *(Jeff Maynard)*

James Doohan and Shirley Maiewski (now chairperson of the "Star Trek" Welcommittee) illustrating the advantages of close co-operation between the stars and the STW. *(Jeff Maynard)*

Walter Koenig looking grand and enjoying a good laugh at the Committee dinner at the 1974 con. *(Benjamin M. Yalow)*

David Gerrold doing the M.C. "bit" and doing it well at the 1975 con. *(Benjamin M. Yalow)*

Nichelle Nichols singing "Beyond Antare at the 1974 con. *(Benjamin M. Yalow)*

Mariette Hartley during her surprise visit to the 1974 con. *(Benjamin M. Yalow)*

Isaac Asimov keeping the fans happy his speech on—Isaac Asimov! *(Jeff Mayn*

she was so tired from working in the dealers' room that she let a few errors slip through. Jackie helped me type the spots up (my handwriting has been known to give people fits of deep depression).

DEFOREST KELLEY'S REPORTS ON THE NEW YORK "STAR TREK" CONVENTION 1974[1]

MONDAY, FEBRUARY 18, 1974

Hi, this is DeForest Kelley, "Star Trek's" Dr. McCoy, with my special report from the "Star Trek" convention in New York. The convention is being held at the Americana Hotel in downtown Manhattan and is sponsored by a committee of fourteen people, each with a specified duty such as art show director or press and publicity. I attended a press party Thursday night, and I was flabbergasted to learn that they'll expect more than twelve thousand fans here by Saturday. The Americana is already receiving fans from California to Canada, and as far away as Hawaii and West Germany. They're here with cameras and tape recorders, artwork—you name it, they've got it—and they're all downstairs anxious and ready to register and get on with this show. This is DeForest Kelley, "Star Trek's" Dr. McCoy, and I'll have more news for you on "Star Trek" tomorrow night.

TUESDAY, FEBRUARY 19, 1974

Hi, this is DeForest Kelley, "Star Trek's" Dr. McCoy, with my special report from the "Star Trek" convention in New York. Hey, did you ever start up a conversation with Spock and find out he was a made-to-scale dummy? Carol Swoboda from North Carolina has made one so real you're sure he'll open his mouth and say, "Totally illogical, Dr. McCoy." The art show has contained some of the finest work by young and talented people I've ever seen, but would you like to buy a tribble or a picture of Captain Kirk? You can do it all—they've got this and more down in the dealers' room. Now, if it's related to "Star Trek" in any way, I'm sure it was somewhere in that room. Professional dealers and fourteen-year-old entrepreneurs

[1] Taped messages broadcast during "Star Trek" reruns on Channel 48, Philadelphia, printed through the courtesy and permission of Kaiser Broadcasting Company, WKBS-TV.

sit side by side just hawking their wares. It's a lot of fun. This is DeForest Kelley, "Star Trek's" Dr. McCoy, and I'll have more news on the "Star Trek" convention tomorrow night.

WEDNESDAY, FEBRUARY 20, 1974

Hi, this is DeForest Kelley, "Star Trek's" Dr. McCoy with my special report from the "Star Trek" convention in New York. The program started off this morning with Dorothy C. Fontana, story editor and scriptwriter of the live-action "Star Trek" and Associate Producer of the animated series. Soon to follow were George Takei, who now produces his own talk show over KNVC in California, and Nichelle Nichols, who has taken time from her nightclub appearances and recording dates to appear here this weekend. Walter Koenig, better known as "Chekov," whose well-received directing efforts may bring him to Broadway, is to appear later this afternoon. My own entrance onto the stage was greeted by the most thunderous and moving ovation it has been my astounded pleasure to receive. The waves of love flowing across the auditorium were almost visible. This is DeForest Kelley, "Star Trek's" Dr. McCoy. I'll have more news on the "Star Trek" convention for you tomorrow night.

THURSDAY, FEBRUARY 21, 1974

Hi, this is DeForest Kelley, "Star Trek's" Dr. McCoy, with my special report from the "Star Trek" convention in New York. Isaac Asimov is one of the foremost science-fiction writers in America today, and his speech at the convention ran ten minutes over his allotted hour, but no one noticed. The first five minutes were devoted to "Star Trek," and the remaining time was devoted to Issac; nobody minded that, either. A lecture on astronomy? Sure, when it's given by Hal Clement, with huge color slides and fascinating "Star Trek" asides. Hal is a real fan, and he attends every convention on the Eastern Seaboard. David Gerrold, who wrote *The Trouble with Tribbles* and became immortal in the minds of all "Star Trek" fans spoke today, too, and his speech was both funny and fascinating. This is DeForest Kelley, "Star Trek's" Dr. McCoy, and I'll have more news on the "Star Trek" convention for you tomorrow night.

FRIDAY, FEBRUARY 22, 1974

Hi, this is DeForest Kelley, "Star Trek's" Dr. McCoy, with my special report from the "Star Trek" convention in New York. The huge ballroom here at the Americana was crammed to capacity and then some every time the six uncut, full-color "Star Trek" episodes were shown, from *City on the Edge of Forever* to *The Ultimate Computer*. They were received with joy and rapt attention. The infamous blooper reel was shown several times a day. Each time, the hall reacted with the same hysterical glee. The idea of Spock walking into a nonfunctioning door, or Kirk being picked up and carried off the set kicking and yelling, or me flubbing a line and breaking up, seemed to crack the funnybone of every fan. I can't really describe it; you must see it for yourself. This is DeForest Kelley, "Star Trek's" Dr. McCoy, reporting to you from the "Star Trek" convention in New York.

SATURDAY, FEBRUARY 23, 1974

Hi, this is DeForest Kelley, "Star Trek's" Dr. McCoy, with my special report from the "Star Trek" convention in New York. The feeling in the convention is running high concerning the possibility of "Star Trek" returning to television. The more realistic fans, however, feel that a movie is likely. George Takei, Nichelle Nichols, and myself think that the publicity generated by this convention and—now, get this—the fourteen thousand fans that attended it—could possibly start those stubborn heads at Paramount thinking. Yes, fourteen thousand! Now, that doesn't count the thousands of fans that had to be turned away because there was no room. There was no room for a tribble, let alone a fifteen-year-old Trekkie from Brooklyn. I get the feeling that I was most fortunate to be invited to be here as a guest. This is DeForest Kelley, "Star Trek's" Dr. McCoy, reporting from the "Star Trek" convention in New York.

De recorded them over the phone to Cleveland the next day. They timed out perfectly. Pretty good for beginners, huh? I even got a job offer out of it. Wasn't that nice? I didn't take it, of course, but I was very flattered.

De is a very sweet man, and also a very private one. I am really proud that I can call him a friend. He is one of the kindest men I've ever known.

I came into his room one afternoon to take him downstairs for an appearance and found several helpers sprawled happily on the floor at his feet. They had delivered some orange juice to his room (why it had taken three of them to deliver one quart of orange juice . . . ?) and stayed to talk, at De's invitation.

"It gets so lonely, you know, Joan," he told me later. "You have to stay cooped up in your room, and leaving the hotel is such a hassle. I thought we'd have to get Fred to give me a false beard and nose so I could go and buy a pair of shoes this morning.

"Those kids were such a delight today. I loved talking to them, they're so bright and intelligent. They are very dear."

And so are you, De, and so are you.

The Committee dinner was scheduled for tonight. Well, we figured that was one way to guarantee that we would have one decent meal during the con. The press room was closed for the day, and the films were on schedule, I hoped.

I soaked in the tub for fifteen beautiful minutes and then called De's room. He said he didn't think he felt like coming to the dinner, since he was a bit tired. I told him how many of the Committee and guests were looking forward to meeting him; I also said he would not have to stay for the entire dinner—he could leave after the cocktails, soup, whenever he wished.

"All right, you've talked me into it."

"Great, I'll pick you up in about fifteen minutes."

After all, Isaac Asimov and Hal Clement are worth putting on your shoes for any time. Besides the shoes, I put on my new coral matte jersey sheath and matching jacket.

When I knocked on De's door, just down the hall from mine, he was on the phone with his wife, Carolyn. We had met in 1969 when she and De had come into New York to see some theater. Now, that was a wild story.

I was still working at CBS when I got a call from Philadelphia. It was De. He was in town to surprise Bill Shatner, who was appearing as cohost on "The Mike Douglas Show" that week. If you didn't catch the show, you really missed a goodie. Early in the program, Mike Douglas made believe he had hurt his hand. About halfway through the show, as he had Bill describing the other cast members, they started talking about De. Mike said he

could certainly use someone like Dr. McCoy and then asked if
there was a doctor in the house. And there, walking down the
aisle in his costume, was De. Bill was absolutely dumfounded.
What a surprise!

When De and Carolyn got to New York, they invited me to
lunch with them. We had a lovely time until they had to leave
for the theater. Carolyn is a very pretty woman and very
charming, too.

I walked them over to the theater and went home. De told me
later that people knew him the moment he walked in. He was
seated among a group of nuns, and fans from all over the theater
were passing down programs for him to sign. The hum got
louder and louder, and he was never so glad to see a curtain go
up in his life. They were seeing *Cabaret* and had planned to go
backstage to see Joel Grey. No way. The theater had called the
police because they were afraid of a riot, and De and Carolyn
were hustled out as the lights came up after the last act. This
was the first time something like this had happened, and they
were really shook. He commented later that California fans
seemed more blasé.

Back to the here and now. De told Carolyn I had just come in
to take him to dinner. Carolyn and I spoke for a moment, and
she said to take good care of De. I said it would be my pleasure.

Everyone was in the bar of the Club Suite. As we entered, De
caught sight of Joyce. Before this he had only seen her in loose-
fitting shirts and slacks, which did not do justice to her great
bod. This evening she was wearing a silver knit top that fit like
crazy and a long, slinky black satin skirt.

De beamed at her and said, "Good grief, girl, you've got a
great build. Why have you been hiding it?"

Joyce just beamed back. As a matter of fact, if New York had
been hit with a blackout at that moment, I think she could have
lit mid-Manhattan all by herself.

Hey, I just realized—Joyce hasn't worn any of those loose-
fitting things since, and the world is better for it. You know why
if you saw her at the 1975 convention, where she wore a copy of
Bill Theiss' famous "Look, Ma, no hardly anything" dress from
Who Mourns for Adonais? You can't wear that without being
built with a capital *B.*

I introduced De to the other guests and the few Committee

members who had not had the time to meet him before. Yes, it
does get *that* busy, and if you're buried in the Art Show or stuck
in the worry room, King Kong could make an appearance and
you wouldn't know it until you slipped on a banana peel.

De seemed to be enjoying himself, and I breathed a sigh of relief. We went into dinner, and each guest sat at a different table
—spreading the wealth, so to say. Debbie Langsam was at our
table, and before long she and De were in deep conversation.
The soup had just been served, and it was not very good. And I
am being kind. The roast beef later was fantastic, but the soup
was ugh. Everyone was taking guesses as to the various ingre-
dients—old railroad ties and unwashed socks were high on the
list. Then a helper came in with a message from Al. He was
downstairs keeping an eye out for the ever-vigilant fire marshals, and he wanted Debbie with him. That's what happens
when you are assistant chairman of a convention. She sighed,
finished her soup, and left.

Fred Phillips came over to our table after dinner and said he
felt like seeing a little nightlife.

"I know just what you mean," De said. "I feel as if I've been
cooped up for weeks."

That's what happens when you're a star. It was a traumatic experience every time we would try to get De or any of the guests
out of or into the hotel. We would corral some security guards
and large helpers and form a phalanx with De in the middle.
We'd take an elevator to one of the lower levels, see him to the
street, and wave bye-bye.

Sometimes fans would get into the same elevator and, not
spotting De behind the six-four guards, would discuss various
topics, including De. Sometimes I'd get a glimpse of a reddening
ear or a twinkling blue eye (and are they ever blue!).

Of course, the main thing to remember in a situation like that
is to keep walking and step over the fainting bodies; it's the only
way. We had to literally do that with Bill Shatner—but that's another convention.

The whole crowd was now on their way to the Princess
Ballroom, where the Art Show was being held. We were opening
up the room so that the guests could see the art and those who
were judges could make their selections.

It was a beautiful Art Show, and I got the following rundown of some of the highlights from Devra: "The Art Show included a 'Birth of Spock' triptych by Molnar that was very clever; Spock as the *Time* 'Man of the Year'; an excellent Nomad model; a miniature Klingon ship contest, and a full-size dummy of Spock. People were constantly coming up to the chair where we set it and saying, 'You can't sit there! Where's your name badge?' The artist, Carol Swoboda, brought it to New York on a bus, wrapped in a huge trash bag. Somewhere along the way, the head fell off and rolled down the aisle. Ax murder! Crazy lady carried body in bus! Ah, the things we do for art."

After a little while, De turned to me and said, "You know, a friend of mine is playing at a place called Jimmy's. Is that near here?"

"As a matter of fact, it's just down the block from here."

"Great. Let's get Fred."

Going up in the elevator, I turned to De and asked who his friend was.

"A great singer. We used to be shopping-cart buddies. We went to the same supermarket for a while. His name is Lou Rawls."

Oh boy. I got my coat, and we all met in De's room. As we were leaving, I looked at my watch.

"Wait a second. Let's turn on the news and take a look at CBS. They were here this afternoon, and they should have something on the convention."

"Okay," De said, "but I bet they don't even mention my name."

"How can you say that?"

"Well, nobody interviewed me, and I don't even think they know I'm here."

"That's silly. I told everyone you were here. I bet you a drink you're wrong."

I lost.

They mentioned the crowds, large but well-behaved, the dealers' room, crowded and bustling, and they mentioned Bill and Leonard and Gene—none of whom were there! Not one word of the people who were there—like De, Nichelle, Walter, Fred, David, Isaac, Hal . . . I began to wonder if the person who had written the report had even been at the convention. I could have died. The news team had come during one of my frequent treks to the projection booth, and I had missed them.

We walked into Jimmy's, and the place was jammed. We could hear the *maître d'* saying that there was no more room upstairs. Our eyes flashed to the sign with Lou Rawls' picture and, sure enough, he was playing upstairs. De walked over to the harassed *maître d'* and asked if it were possible to send a note backstage, since Mr. Rawls was a friend. The man's eyes widened, then narrowed, and I saw his lips form the world "Bones." Suddenly we were whisked into an elevator and taken "upstairs." You never know when or where you will find a "Star Trek" fan!

The next thing we knew, this vibrant, handsome young man was shaking De's hand and getting us seated at a table.

After his first song, he introduced De from the audience and gave the con a plug, too. Oh boy, that's all we need, more people. Just as Lou was taking his last bow, a man came over to the table and escorted us to Mr. Rawls' dressing room. Lou Rawls came bounding in—still full of that unbelievable energy. He wanted to hear all about the con.

"Could I come over and visit? Get a look at what's going on?"

Boy, could he! He promised to come over the next day to say hello.

While we were talking I got up to get some ice for my drink, and my back suddenly gave a twinge. It was a very deep chair, and I had to really haul myself out of it. Mr. Rawls asked what was wrong, and I said I had been having a little trouble with my back. Before I knew it, one of his friends took me by the shoulders and shook me like a puppy. I could feel and *hear* all sorts of little and not so little creaks and cracks. He set me down, and I almost fell on my face. But my back felt just fine!

Sunday was a very busy day, since we had set press interviews for Nichelle and Isaac. Every once in a while, the phone would ring. I would see one of the helpers answer, and her face would go kind of blank, and I knew that De was calling. I would take the phone out of her limp hand and say, "No, he hasn't shown up yet, De. I'll tell you when he does, don't worry."

I had told the Committee about Lou's appearance, and we had thought of introducing him from the stage as a "typical fan." However, Mr. Rawls didn't show up until after the day's program was over.

We were just leaving the press room, and there he was, coming off the elevator. He had had an interview, and it had taken much longer than expected. Well, the fans didn't get to meet him, but all my people in the press room did, and they loved it.

Lou suddenly turned to me and said, "You know, there is one thing I have heard about and never seen. Do you think I could see the blooper reel?"

So there we sat—about seventeen of us in my room, with Lou Rawls howling and applauding the bloopers. After sitting through it twice, I got Lou a program from the convention to take home to his little boy who, he said, is almost as big a fan as he is.

Jackie met Lou Rawls on Monday, when she went to De's room to say good-bye. Lou answered the door and almost bowled her over with his charm. The thing that really got her was when they said good-bye. He kissed her hand. She told me later that was the first time that had ever happened to her, and she thought more men should do it. It makes you feel just grand, she said.

We also had our share of rumors—as a matter of fact, they were rife; and rampant, too. The most mentioned was Leonard Nimoy—when was he going to appear, if he was going to appear. Leonard had mentioned that *if* he were in town during the convention, and *if* he could make it, he would attend. We have never advertised anything we didn't think we could supply, so we hadn't mentioned anything. *If* he couldn't make it, we were not going to get killed for saying he *was* going to appear.

The previous year he had appeared on Sunday, and in 1973 that's when the rumors were most rife. But in 1974 he fooled everybody and didn't show up till Monday.

Jackie, who had kept the "secret" so well in 1973, was besieged with "When is he coming this year?" Well, "this year" she didn't know. She was so good at "not knowing" in 1973 that when she really didn't know in 1974, nobody believed her!

SUNDAY, FEBRUARY 17, 1974

The first Art Show auction went quite well, and some fortunate people picked up things that anyone would be proud to have in his home. David was the auctioneer and did his usual great job with charm and humor.

At 11:00 A.M. (well, actually closer to 11:30 A.M.) Nichelle made her speech. She knocked them all for a loop and a half. She was candid and open and funny and beautiful. And she sang *a cappella*. It was one huge love-in. She could have sat there for the next two days and no one would have left the room. If it weren't for the security guards, they would have carried her from the ballroom on their shoulders and sipped champagne—no, Pepsi—from her slipper, only she was wearing boots.

George. Now, you know we love George. But George has a lot of friends in New York, and George loves to visit these friends—so much so that he sometimes forgets what brought him to New York in the first place. So George was a bit late—about twenty minutes—for his first stage appearance. Thom had been his escort (when he finally found him) and took him to the ballroom door and pointed him toward the stage and Elyse, who was awaiting his entrance. Somehow George got lost—between the door and the stage. Elyse saw Thom and frantically relayed her distress. A large crowd had formed, and in the middle was George, happily signing autographs. Elyse discovered extra gray hairs that day.

All was forgiven once George flashed that beautiful smile and apologized. He walked onstage to a standing ovation.

In 1973, Jackie, Sondra, and I shared a room, and I had everyone in afterward for the Dead Dog Party.

Sondra and Jackie sat on one bed with George and half a dozen other people, and in the screaming bedlam (at least equivalent to a SST landing) they interviewed George for *Star Trek Lives!* Jackie had to transcribe from that tape. The noise *was* incredible, but she could isolate George's marvelous voice without trouble.

His voice is an electronics man's dream.

Isaac was on at 2:00 P.M. Need I say more? Isaac's speeches are mostly about Isaac, and the fans couldn't be happier. A more erudite and charming man would be hard to find.

At 3:00 P.M. Fred Phillips did a make-up demonstration on Chairman Al. Poor Al lost his real mustache for a fake Klingon one. I don't think Al knew Fred was going to denude his upper lip till Fred whipped out his trusty razor and did the deed:

AL: Hey.
FRED: ?????
AL: Fred?
FRED: I've got to do it.
AL: Oh.

I must say Al made a fabulous Klingon. However, it almost scared his little daughter out of her wits, so he washed it off a while later. Too bad.

Since the costume judging began at 7:15 P.M., Dana started marshaling her forces at 5:00 P.M. Dana always has some sort of theme for the costumes she and her helpers wear. This year she was going as Bruce Lee, and Dave, her assistant, was to be Caine from *Kung-fu*. Fred Phillips was a doll and did the makeup job: It was fabulous!

Some of the Committee decided they had better grab a bite while they had a chance. Joyce, Devra, Barbara, Wendy, Louise, and Jay, the security guard, decided on Chinese food. What else is new? Joyce and Wendy took a cab and went to the Chinese take-out around the corner from my apartment. There must be dozens of Chinese restaurants within a couple of blocks of the hotel, but Joyce remembered with great fondness the delicious egg rolls and even more delicious prices this little place offered. They carried back shopping bags full of quarts and quarts of wonton soup, chow mein, egg rolls, and other assorted goodies. The crew settled down in the room. Joyce, Devra, and Barbara shared and dug-in with Gusto (he wandered in from across the hall).

In the middle of the oriental orgy in walked Nichelle. Seeing her hungry look, they loaded up a plate and she went happily on her way. Five minutes later the phone rang. "This is Lieutenant Uhura. Where the hell's the soy sauce?"

Dana and her crew were not to eat till later—much later—in the evening. That's what comes of being so conscientious.

There's a book out, one of those big jobbies they put out for Christmas—you know, they call them coffee table books. It's called *When Two or More Are Gathered Together,* by Neal Slaven, and published by Farrar, Straus & Giroux in 1976. Well, that rather odd-looking group of people in the photo section are the Costume Ball winners of the 1974 "Star Trek" convention.

Two nice young men approached me at the con and asked if they could take pictures of the winners for their book. They explained that the book was about all the different and strange things people do when they get together in groups. The book contains such diversified groups as the Mormon Tabernacle Choir and Ringling Brothers Circus. Hmmm, maybe we did belong after all. Anyway, I told them they had to check with Dana, since she was in charge of the Costume Ball, and the members of the Committee tried not to intrude into someone else's area. She said it was fine with her, and we all agreed it would be a gas.

I got my helpers (yes, they *do* work hard—and often), and we piled all the chairs on the side of the room so the cameras and lights could be set up. We even cleaned the carpet. Well, we got down on our hands and knees and picked up lint and gook till you could see what color the rug was, that's what we did.

Leaving the boys to watch the ball from the balcony window overlooking the ballroom, we scattered to our rooms to get dressed for the festivities. I had a replica of one of Kirk's shirts (the one that wraps around) and added tights, boots, and hot pants to make my costume. Of course, no one from the Committee can enter the Costume Ball, but some of us liked to get dressed up anyway.

I got downstairs just in time to see the end of one of the skits that was dedicated to David—to teasing David, that is. They were very good, but David is gooder. You don't take on that lad unless you are very fast with your lip. The fans ate it up; and frankly, so did David.

Everyone was asking me if my shirt was real, and I had to admit it wasn't. The color was a bit off, but the braid was almost exact, and we had gotten the insignia from Lincoln Enterprises, so it really looked good. A lot of people took pictures, and it turned out to be an ego-boo[2] evening—for me, anyway.

The ball ran smoothly, as ususual, even though it was incredibly crowded. Everyone sat on the floor instead of chairs, but

[2] Ego-boo or ego-boost. To be made much of and feel really good.

they were very good about keeping aisles and keeping them clear (fire marshals, you know).

Dana has a fiery temper and it has often been said that compaired to her Krakatoa is a sputtering match. Well, Al got a load of lava—close up. It seems he had been contacted by a man who had just opened up a new restaurant downtown and thought it would be good publicity if he offered free dinners to the winners and the Committee. Nice idea. One or two problems. Al hadn't thought to tell anyone—like Dana or the Committee. Also, he seemed to have forgotten the picture session after the ball. He then compounded that boo-boo by making the announcement in the middle of the judging—without asking Dana first. Krakatoa, kids.

Even so, the Costume Ball was a great success, as usual. Dana puts a great deal of forethought and effort into it, and it shows. The costumes were both gorgeous and imaginative that year. The judges besides David were: Jeff Maynard, Fred Phillips, Nichelle, George, Walter, and Hal Clement. It was a hectic but happy time for all the winners.

Most of my helpers were there, helping, as usual. Ellen, Carol, Germaine, Allyson, Michael, and Ruth shanghaied me and took me to dinner. Guess what we had? That's right. Chinese food!

MONDAY, FEBRUARY 18, 1974

Monday was a daze, not a day, for me. I was pooped, and the con did not end till 5:00 P.M. I had had another gall bladder attack the previous evening and had not been able to sleep, even with the medication. I couldn't wait for the operation. To be able to eat like a human being again. The no-fat diet I was on made me look as if I had spent the last year as a guest in Dachau. I had lost about fifteen pounds and all my clothes were hanging on me—or off me, take your pick. All I know is that I was having fantastic dreams about mayonnaise and corned beef and mayonnaise and lamb chops and mayonnaise . . . Yeah, I'm a mayo freak. (When I was a kid I used to make mayonnaise sandwiches. Don't laugh—my brother, Stuart, used to make mustard ones. It wasn't that we didn't have anything else to put on sandwiches, we just liked mayo and mustard.)

I'm sitting here saying to myself, "Okay, Joan, what were you doing on Monday? What were you doing besides running around and yelling?" Yes, dear friends, Joan was quite snappish that Monday. I think it was a combination of the attack I had had the previous evening (can you have too much Chinese food?), the impending operation (this was the sixth operation in five years, and I was beginning to feel as if I could give Job a run for his money), plus the schism in the Committee. However, for the benefit of those people (and I don't think there were *that* many) who felt the Winston Wrath, it was nothing like the real thing. I don't explode very often, and it takes a great deal to get me started, but when it erupts, everybody had better head for the hills, another country, or a convenient closet. Elyse and Steve insist that lightning flashes from my eyeballs and flames shoot from my nostrils. I don't know about that, but they do say that having seen it once they do not wish to witness it a second time.

But not only my nerves and my temper were frayed; the whole Committee situation was coming to a head. It was obvious that Al wanted different things from the convention than most of the rest of us. Al had approached me about joining him in his new ventures, but I had not as yet given him a definite answer. I don't think he realized how close I was to the rest of the Committee. I felt Al wanted to make the conventions into commercial ventures, while we wanted to remain fan-oriented. We tried to keep all this from the guests and the fans, and I think we succeeded. Everyone seemed so surprised when the parting came.

I didn't make the art auction that morning, but I understand it was very successful. I was a bit busy since we had finally gotten the word that Leonard was coming that day. I begged that, this time, he have his press interview first and then go down to the ballroom—and also to tell the fans beforehand so they would not go into hysterics and mob the stage. And that's what we did. Of course, the security guards with the whips and chains didn't hurt at all.

The announcement was made during the art auction. While David was preparing the delirious fans for Leonard Nimoy's appearance, I was not twiddling the old thumbs, no siree. I had spent a good hour on the phone, calling all the major and local media in the city (ABC first, of course). One desk man was very bored and asked, "Who's he?" I suggested he ask his secretary, since she had almost crawled through the phone when I mentioned Mr. Nimoy's appearance. "Okay," he said, "I will." He must have, because they sent over a camera crew. And so did ABC.

HOW TO GIVE A COMMITTEE MEMBER
A HEART ATTACK

Dave Simons, our helper herder, was delegated to wait outside the secret (we hoped) entrance to the hotel for Leonard Nimoy. Dave got there about twenty minutes early and got worrieder and worrieder. He was expecting Leonard to arrive in a cab. But as he looked down the street for the fourteenth time, he was tapped on the shoulder, and a deep, famous voice said, "Are you waiting for me?" There stood Leonard Nimoy. At eighteen you can't really afford to lose ten years' growth. Just what we needed: an eight-year-old Committee member!

The Americana had one convenience—a lot of interconnected hidden stairways. And were we thankful that day. Dave brought Leonard into the press room without the fans even suspecting his presence in the hotel.

My guys from ABC came and set up in back of the press room. Leonard came in, looking fantastic in a patched dungaree outfit. He gave me a warm handshake and a quick kiss (I admit it—I put my cheek in the right place for it) and said he was very glad to see me. I think he was also glad to see the great press turnout. At one point during the interview, he talked about television and how programs got started (and stopped), and he mentioned CBS. I patted his hand, and as he turned to me I said, "ABC, Leonard, ABC." He looked startled for just a moment, and then with a huge, gorgeous grin, said, "Of course, ABC." My guys in the back of the room almost cheered.

He spoke at length of the love and affection he and everyone connected with the show had for "Star Trek," as well as his great respect for Gene and all the crew and actors who had worked with him. He was most sincere, and he greatly impressed the people from the media.

Meanwhile, in the ballroom, small children from about eight

or nine and under were being seated on the floor in front of the stage. This was David's brainstorm. He figured no one would rush the stage and take the chance of trampling all those little kids (he hoped). As a matter of fact, David had stated that if one hair on any of their heads was even bent, the perpetrator would be permanently bent, like a pretzel.

George, Nichelle, De, and Walter were holding a panel, answering questions from the fans, with David as moderator. We managed to get Leonard down without anyone the wiser and signaled to David. He made the announcement and—*Pandemonium*, but controlled. No one rushed the stage or pushed forward. Everyone kept their seats and shrieked their joy to the heavens—for about five minutes.

During Leonard's speech a helper sent a little boy of about four or five down the aisle, telling him to sit down front so he could see Mr. Spock. The boy got two thirds of the way down the aisle and saw Leonard Nimoy in his gorgeous denim outfit, long hair, and nonpointed ears. The boy stopped dead and cried, "That's not Mr. Spock," did an about-face, and walked back to his seat. The audience howled, and so did Leonard.

Leonard spoke for about thirty-five minutes on a multitude of topics, with the fans hanging on every word. When he finished, they cheered again. What a time.

I wish I could give far more of a rundown on his speech, but we were all so excited by his appearance we forgot to tape it. (Sorry about that, folks.)

We got Leonard out of the ballroom, into a freight elevator, and onto the street in thirty seconds. He was almost dazed. He stood and talked to De for a few minutes while we got Leonard a cab. We were delighted he came, but sad he could not stay longer.

Dick Hoagland from the Hayden Planetarium was on after Leonard, and although Dick started with a half-empty room (many of the fans had to leave to recharge their batteries), the room was full when he finished. He used both film (from NASA) and slides to illustrate the heavens and how we would eventually reach them. The many "Star Trek" asides made his talk that much more interesting. Let's have him again, gang.

Last, but most certainly not least, we finished the convention with a panel of Dorothy Fontana, David Gerrold, and Fred Phillips. They also answered the fans' questions and told stories of amusing happenings on the set and, as the con ended, I think the fans went away happy.

But that was not the end for us. All had to make sure their area was cleared and cleaned and any equipment, rented or otherwise, was packed up and returned or stored in a safe place. The biggest worry was the projectors. They were worth a fortune and, although we had insurance, we didn't want anyone taking one home as a souvenir. Correction: *The big worry* was the films. They had to be mailed back to the various studios as soon as possible. We wanted to keep our reputation untarnished so we could borrow from them again the following year.

We wandered around making sure nothing was left lying around. I came upon one of the helpers crying her eyes out. She had been giving us a hand in the press room and had lost her purse—with almost her entire "Star Trek" collection of pictures and film clips.

"Abby, why did you bring all that with you?"

"I . . . I . . . wanted to show it to my friends," she wailed. "And I got everyone to autograph my *Making of 'Star Trek,'* and that's in the bag, too." Just the sound of her voice made me feel like crying, too.

I sent helpers and friends all over the hotel and took Abby up to my room. I talked with her quietly and promised that if her bag wasn't found I would give her some pictures and stuff from my own collection to help her replace her loss. The rest of the Committee said they would do that, too. At this point Walter Koenig walked into the room. He had heard what happened and, very sweetly, took the time to talk with her and try to calm her down. Just as she was starting to smile back at him, Ellen ran in to say the bag had been found. It had been hanging on the press room coat rack when the hotel man took the rack away. He had noticed it later and turned it in to the lost and found.

Talk about happy!

After a while, the Committee began to wander into the con suite and collapse onto various surfaces in various positions of tired. The assistants and helpers who could still stand and articulate drifted in and plopped down. We kind of mumbled and sighed at each other for a while.

Some of the guests were staying over for a few days. De had some business to transact, and Nichelle had some people to see, that sort of thing.

After a while I went back to the room to lie down, and my press room kids and some of the fans came to say good-bye.

Then I got a call from Elyse. The Committee was going out to dinner. George, De, and David were coming with us. We went to a smorgasbord restaurant and stuffed ourselves. It was a good way to end the weekend, talking and dining with friends.

"STAR TREK" TRIVIA CONTEST QUESTIONNAIRE
INTERNATIONAL "STAR TREK" CONVENTION, 1974

1. Melenex causes
    A. Temporary skin discoloration and disorientation   B. rash
    C. Brief unconsciousness and temporary skin discoloration
2. Spock as Selik named some relations. They were
    A. Sitar and T'Pau   B. Shariel and T'Pel   C. T'Pel and Sasek
3. Mudd's love potion came from
    A. Sirius 9   B. Venus   C. Rigel 12
4. The Antares was a
    A. Small Class J cargo ship   B. Science probe vessel
    C. Shuttlecraft
5. Code Factor 1 is
    A. Invasion status   B. Code broken by the Romulans
    C. Code name for destruct sequence
6. Whose father helped Kirk get into the Academy?
    A. Mallory   B. Garrovick   C. Hansen
7. A city on Vulcan is
    A. l-Langon   B. I-Chaya   C. ShiKahr
8. In one of the animated episodes our beloved captain blew the Star Date. He said:
    A. 50.6   B. 52.2   C. 56.7
9. What time did the red hour begin?
    A. 6 P.M.   B. 6 A.M.   C. Noon
10. In *More Tribbles, More Troubles* the Klingons' new weapon was
    A. A more powerful phaser   B. A safe tribble   C. A stasis field

11. The *Shore Leave* planet is located near
    A. Omicron Delta   B. Beta Lyrae   C. The Neutral Zone
12. Harry Mudd has been known to use the alias
    A. Harcourt Fenton   B. Leo Francis Walsh   C. Cyrano Jones
13. Who called Spock, "Mr. Ears"?
    A. Kevin Riley   B. Tommy Starnes   C. Charlie Evans
14. Star Fleet uniforms are made from algae-based
    A. Nylon   B. Xenylon   C. Syntho-cotton
15. A tribble predator is called a
    A. Glommer   B. Kzin   C. Quadro-pod
16. In *Return of the Archons* the other two members of Riger's underground triad were
    A. Marplon and Tula   B. Tamar and Marplon   C. Hacomb and Marplon
17. How many science labs are there on the *Enterprise*?
    A. 2   B. 8   C. 14
18. Besides *"Corbomite Maneuver,"* Captain Kirk used the same bluff in
    A. Enterprise *Incident*   B. *Balance of Terror*   C. *The Deadly Years*
19. Who said, "Loneliness is a flower dying in the desert"?
    A. Miramanee   B. Rayna   C. Mira Romaine
20. Tribbles are born
    A. Pregnant   B. Fat   C. Hungry
21. The Horta is a life form based on
    A. Carbon   B. Silicon   C. Fluorine
22. Marc Daniels and Joseph Pevney each directed the same number of episodes. How many did they each direct?
    A. 12   B. 14   C. 16
23. Who called Kirk a "swaggering, overbearing, tin-plated dictator with delusions of godhood"?
    A. Koloth   B. Kor   C. Korax
24. How many years did Spock say it would take Cyrano Jones to clear Space Station K-7 of tribbles?
    A. 19.3   B. 16.5   C. 17.9
25. How many settings did the slaver weapon have?
    A. 7   B. 8   C. 9
26. How old (in years) was the pod ship from *Beyond the Farthest Star?*
    A. 200 million   B. 300 million   C. 400 million
27. How many drops of cordrazine can save a man's life?
    A. 2   B. 4   C. 5

28. Tal-shaya is
    A. An ancient form of Vulcan execution　B. the name of
    Spock's pet sehlat　C. A Vulcan city
29. Blue-skinned aliens with antennae are known as
    A. Tellarites　B. Andorians　C. Orions
30. Coradin was
    A. A planetary system　B. A drug　C. An alien ambassador
31. What was the name of the officer who interrogated Kirk in
    Tomorrow Is Yesterday?
    A. Webb　B. MacPhearson　C. Fellini
32. In Miri, the Onlies aged one month for every —— of real
    time.
    A. One year　B. Ten years　C. One hundred years
33. What does the Mediscanner K-3 indicator measure?
    A. Pain level　B. Blood pressure　C. Respiration
34. At what light intensity did the Denevan creatures die?
    A. 1,000 candles/sq. in.　B. 1 million candles/sq. in.
    C. 10 million candles/sq. in.
35. What was Sam Kirk's occupation?
    A. Lab technician　B. Research biologist　C. Physicist
36. Who did Kirk call a "chairbound paper pusher"?
    A. Stocker　B. Pike　C. Kommack
37. What was Kirk's brother's first name?
    A. Sam　B. Peter　C. George
38. Dr. McCoy used —— to bandage the Horta.
    A. Plaster　B. Thermal concrete　C. Bandages and tape
39. The life cycle of the Horta is —— years long
    A. 500　B. 5,000　C. 50,000
40. Lieutenant Commander Scott's prize bottle of scotch is
    —— years old.
    A. 25　B. 50　C. 100
41. Tribbles are frightened by
    A. Klingons　B. Romulans　C. Vulcans
42. Landru was a
    A. computer　B. President of the Archons　C. Robot
43. Theragin is
    A. A Federation planet　B. A Klingon nerve gas　C. The
    ambassador from Organia
44. The name of the other shuttlecraft mentioned in Galileo
    Seven was
    A. Columbus　B. Magellan　C. Copernicus

45. The *Valiant* is mentioned in two episodes. In which episode is it not mentioned?
A. *The Doomsday Machine* B. *A Taste of Armageddon* C. *Where No Man Has Gone Before*

46. The only episode in which Scotty uses Kirk's first name is
A. *Wolf in the Fold* B. *Return to Tomorrow* C. *Mirror, Mirror*

47. The only episode in which the U.S.S. *Enterprise* is shown orbiting from right to left is
A. *Mirror, Mirror* B. *Shore Leave* C. *Alternative Factor*

48. A planet adaptable for human life with the use of pressure domes and life-support systems is identified as ———.
A. Class K B. Class M C. Class J

49. How long had the creatures been on Deneva when the *Enterprise* arrived?
A. 6 months B. 8 months C. 10 months

50. Balok offered Captain Kirk ——— to drink.
A. Tranya B. Trova C. Saurian brandy

51. The murder weapon used in *Wolf in the Fold* was made on ———.
A. Rigel 4 B. Rigel 2 C. Rigel 7

52. Tritanium is ——— times as hard as diamond.
A. 27.4 B. 24.1 C. 21.4

53. The Vulcan mindmeld was first used in what episode?
A. *Devil in the Dark* B. *Dagger of the Mind* C. *Changeling*

54. The *second* episode (in air-date order) in which the Klingons appeared was ———.
A. *The Trouble with Tribbles* B. *The Deadly Years* C. *Private Little War*

55. Which Star Fleet order means "Do not approach this planet for any reason"?
A. Code 1017 B. Code 701 C. Code 710

56. Kaferian apples were mentioned in what episode?
A. *The Way to Eden* B. *The Apple* C. *Where No Man Has Gone Before*

57. In which episode did Uhura *not* sing?
A. *The Corbomite Maneuver* B. *Charlie X* C. *Conscience of the King*

58. The name of the other probe in the *Changeling* is ———.
A. Tongo Rad B. Tan Ru C. Nomad

59. What is the serial number of the U.S.S. *Republic?*
    A. NCC-1371   B. NCC-1071   C. NCC-1031

60. Who portrayed Balok in *The Corbomite Maneuver?*
    A. Howard Clinton   B. Michael Dunn   C. Clint Howard

61. Who said to Kirk, "We think much alike, Captain, you and I"?
    A. *Flint*   B. *Balok*   C. *Alexander*

62. Who was the court buffoon in *Plato's Stepchildren?*
    A. Alexander   B. Parmen   C. Dr. McCoy

63. What was Leila Kalomi's job?
    A. physician   B. biologist   C. botanist

64. Where did the Horta hide the PXK reactor part?
    A. The Chamber of the Ages   B. The Vault of Tomorrow   C. The Altar of the Mourned

65. Who said, "Only a fool fights in a burning house"?
    A. Garth   B. Kang   C. Khan

66. Who is the inventor of the M-5?
    A. Daystrom   B. Cochrane   C. Flint

67. Which of the following was *not* an ally of Colonel Greene?
    A. Kahless, the Unforgettable   B. Genghis Khan   C. Zor-Kahn

68. Who was the head of the colony on Omicron Ceti III?
    A. Elias Sandoval   B. Commander Hansen   C. Ben Childress

69. Who ran the Twenty-first Street Mission?
    A. Roberta Lincoln   B. Edith Keeler   C. Janice Lester

70. Who was the Dolman of Elaas?
    A. Elaan   B. Losira   C. Natira

71. The Medusan ambassador was accompanied by ———.
    A. Mira Romaine   B. Janice Lester   C. Miranda

72. Who was left by "the old ones"?
    A. Andrea   B. Ruk   C. Miramanee

73. Who commanded the attack force against the *Enterprise* while it was controlled by M-5?
    A. Commodore Wesley   B. Commodore Decker   C. Commodore Mendez

74. Who did Kirk fight on the *Shore Leave* planet?
    A. Riley   B. Finnegan   C. Cogley

75. What is the serial number of the *Enterprise?*
    A. NCC-1071   B. NCC-1017   C. NCC-1701

76. Which of the following is *not* a Klingon?
    A. Kodos   B. Korax   C. Kor

77. Garth was from ———.
    A. Axanar   B. Izar   C. Tau Ceti

78. Who said, "A shame, Captain; it would have been glorious"?
    A. Kor   B. Kang   C. Koloth
79. Who was Flavius Maximus?
    A. A dictator   B. A senator   C. A gladiator
80. Khan Noonian Singh made reference to which of the following?
    A. Reginald Pollack   B. Shakespeare   C. Milton
81. How did Kirk defeat the Gorn captain?
    A. By pushing a boulder off the ledge   B. By using gun-powder made from native sources   C. By inducing a rockslide with his communicator
82. What reversed the aging process in *The Deadly Years*?
    A. Adrenalin   B. Hyronalin   C. The transporter
83. In which of the following did Spock say, "He knows, Doctor; he knows"?
    A. *Arena*   B. *City on the Edge of Forever*   C. *Mark of Gideon*
84. What is the antidote to Rigelian fever?
    A. Ryetalyn   B. Adrenalin   C. Theragin derivative
85. McCoy never had which of the following?
    A. Tonsillitis   B. Xenopolycythemia   C. Synthococcus novae
86. What was the Land of Murdering Oppressors?
    A. Talos 4   B. Ariannus   C. Cheron
87. What was "invented by a little old lady in Leningrad"?
    A. Scotch   B. Vodka   C. Gin
88. Which name was destined to go down in galactic history?
    A. Leonard James Akaar   B. Kor   C. Garth
89. Who needed no urging to hate humans?
    A. Kor   B. Kang   C. Kahless
90. Who has no brother?
    A. Kyle   B. Kirk   C. Chekov
91. The Vulcan mindmeld was not used in ——.
    A. *Dagger of the Mind*   B. *Devil in the Dark*   C. *This Side of Paradise*
92. What place is even better than Leningrad?
    A. Space Station K-7   B. Mudd's planet   C. Wrigley's pleasure planet
93. Of the following, who was *not* in the landing party in *I, Mudd*?
    A. Scotty   B. Uhura   C. McCoy
94. "Let's get the hell out of here" ended which episode?
    A. *Catspaw*   B. *City on the Edge of Forever*   C. *The Cage*

95. "The Preservers" were mentioned in what episode?
    A. *For the World is Hollow and I Have Touched the Sky*   B. *The Squire of Gothos*   C. *The Paradise Syndrome*
96. Who didn't know about quadrotriticale?
    A. Kirk   B. Chekov   C. Spock
97. Who, at the age of twenty-four, made the discovery that won him the Nobel and Z-Magnees prizes?
    A. Dr. Richard Daystrom   B. Zefram Cochrane   C. Jackson Roykirk
98. On whose humanity did Captain Kirk gamble his life?
    A. Commodore Wesley   B. Spock   C. Melakon
99. What was Gary Seven's computer?
    A. Beta 4   B. Beta 5   C. Memory Alpha
100. How many planets are there in the Fabrini system?
    A. 3   B. 6   C. 8

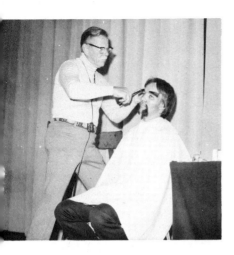

The famous "Star Trek" make-up man, Fred Phillips, changing our chairman, Al Schuster, into a Klingon at the 1974 con. Find out what Fred did to Al's *real* mustache! *(Jeff Maynard)*

Still in make-up, Al Schuster congratulates the New York City fire marshals on their good work at the 1974 con. *(Jeff Maynard)*

Nichelle Nichols congratulating Michael Breen, who won first prize as young Spock in the twelve-year-old-and-younger competition at the 1974 Masquerade contest. *(Jeff Maynard)*

Here at the 1975 Chicago convention, Walter Koenig, George Takei, William Shatner, and James Doohan applaud the entrance of Nichelle Nichols onto the stage (unfortunately, the camera wasn't able to get her in the picture, too). *(Jeff Maynard)*

Behind her table in the dealer's room at the 1975 Equicon, Nichelle Nichols meets and greets her fans. *(Richard Arnold)*

William Shatner during his first "rap session" at the 1975 con. (*Jeff Maynard*)

William Shatner describing the complex make-up he had to wear in one of his films, *The Devil's Rain*, during this same session. (*Jeff Maynard*)

CHAPTER V

ON SELLING A BOOK;
OR,
HOW I LEARNED TO LOVE MY PADDED CELL

It's hell to write a book, but it's worse to try to get it published. Talk about rejection. We could give a course. Sondra and Jackie have more experience than I do. They submitted their version of *Star Trek Lives!* to Ballantine, and after sixteen weeks got a nice letter, and that was all. The real veteran is Jackie. She has been marketing stories since 1967. Her fantastic (no, I *won't* delete that, Jackie) *House of Zeor* took two years and piles of rejection slips to sell. (The hardcover version was published by Doubleday in 1975, and Pocket Books is bringing out the paperback edition in June of 1978.

Then Sondra pulled me into it. It had been suggested that they should make it reflect "Star Trek" fandom more truly by putting some funny stuff into it. Well, Sondra decided I was going to write the funny stuff.

I had not really written much up to that point. I had taken creative writing in school and had had an article of the "Star Trek" set published in *The Monster Times.* Oh, and I had written an outline for a "Star Trek" episode.

Jackie told me later that when Sondra told her about me she was amazed. We had met only briefly at cons, and she knew me mostly as a talker. Well, everybody knew that. But a writer . . . "Joanie doesn't write. She talks!" Sondra thought she knew better and kicking and screaming every foot of the way, I was made part of the "daring duo," which then became the "terrific trio"! (Later Sondra was to be the prime force in getting my name on the cover of the book with hers and Jackie's. She also got me a percentage of the royalties.

We made up a query package to send out to the publishers. That's about three chapters and an outline of the whole book. Sondra and Jackie had done the outline, and the first two chapters. Sondra used my chapter on the 1972 "Star Trek" convention as the third for the query package.

While I was writing my chapter on what it was like being on the "Star Trek" set, I called up various acquaintances at agencies all over town and asked if they would be interested in handling our book. Lo and behold, one was. We had an agent!

Of course, I had to explain to the very nice young lady assigned to us (1) what "Star Trek" was; she didn't know (sigh); (2) what publishers Jackie knew would be interested; and (3) what to say to the editors (second sigh).

The agency sent it to Fred Pohl at Bantam and we waited, not too patiently, I might add. After ten weeks and a few phone calls we got a letter. The upshot of the calls and letter was that he liked the book very much, and would have liked to publish it—but said that his "Star Trek" schedule was already fully committed to the Blish books. However, because he liked it he was recommending us to an editor friend at Pyramid.

The book went the rounds and she would get these letters saying they liked it very much but did not know what to do with it, so they were sending it on to the so-and-so editor at Whoozywhatsis Publishers. This went of for about eight months, and we finally got a call from our agent. She felt that she had not really done anything for us (she was right; she hadn't), so she was releasing us and we were once again on our own.

All during this time the manuscript would get lost or dog-eared, and poor Jackie would type it all over again.

The various editors would write and tell us that everyone in the office loved the book but they did not publish that kind of "stuff." However, a free-lance editor, Roger Elwood, was very interested and might be able to find us a home. Could we be a little patient and see what he could do? We certainly could!

However, we still sent the book to other publishers as Sondra and Jackie worked on the other chapters of the book. I worked on the 1975 convention . . . and my very demanding job at ABC.

After almost a year, Roger told Jackie that he was having a more difficult time than expected and he was releasing us from our promise. Free again, drat it!

At that time, Joyce Yasner of the Committee landed a job as an assistant editor at Ace Books. She suggested we submit the book to Ace, since they published all kinds of "stuff." I talked with Jackie and Sondra, and they said okay. I made an appointment with Pat LoBrutto, the SF editor at Ace, for lunch and promptly fouled up. I thought it was for Wednesday; he thought it was for Tuesday. You can imagine my horror when Joyce called my office at 2:00 P.M. Tuesday, gently yelling, "Where the hell were you?"

"I was at lunch, and why are you yelling at me?"

"I am yelling," Joyce yelled, "because Pat and I waited over an hour, and you never showed your face."

". . . But but but, " I butted, "the date is for tomorrow!"

"No, it was for today!"

Oh boy. I called Pat to apologize, and he was very nice about it. I asked if he could see me the next day at his office at Ace. We made a date, and this time I kept it.

I swept in the next day and, he said later, overwhelmed him. All I did was act out part of the set chapter. Anyway, he said he'd love to read it, and I left our precious package with him.

Five weeks later, Fred Pohl from Bantam called Jackie. Let's go back in time for a minute to 1973 and the world SF con in Toronto (Torcon) where, by the bye, the first ST animated episode was shown in a première performance.

I met Fred Pohl in the lobby of the Royal York Hotel and really let him have it.

"I think you made a mistake in not buying our book."

"Well, we're all entitled to make a few now and then."

"Well, I think you'll come to realize this was a doozie. What didn't you like about it?"

"Oh, I liked it. But I felt the Blish books were enough. I especially liked your chapter. You have a nice, light stream-of-consciousness style."

Why is it we never have a witness or tape recorder at these moments? I had a style; Fred Pohl said so.

That was in 1973.

At the 1974 world SF con in Washington, D.C., it was Jackie's turn to "get" Fred. They met at the meet the authors party (her House of Zeor had just been published in hardcover by Doubleday, and she had also been nominated for a Hugo Award that year for Best Fan Writer; she came in second).

Their conversation was quite short.

JL: "Remember the ST book? It's still available if you're interested."

FP: [Various polite but noncommittal sounds.]

Okay; the scene was set. The book is at Ace. We are on tenterhooks.

Jackie's phone rings, and it's Fred Pohl.

"Do you still have that ST book?"

She explained that Ace had it.

"Have they made you an offer?"

"No."

"Well, I'll send you a letter of intent, with copies for Sondra and Joan."

It seemed that James Blish was quite ill, and Bantam had a hole in their spring list—a "Star Trek" hole. Fred remembered our book and figured we *must* have finished it by then.

Jackie immediately called Sondra and me, I screamed, and then after hasty long distance conferences I called Pat at Ace. I explained we wanted the book back because we had an offer, and told him from whom. He asked if he could please have it till Friday (this was Wednesday) and get back to us. I said okay.

On Friday we all received the letter of intent from Fred. This stated in terse terms the amount of the advance and the percentage of the cover price Bantam was willing to pay. That day a VP (not Pat) called from Ace. I told him of the letter, and he said he had to check with the president, who had already left for the weekend, before he made his offer. But he did not intend to make it a bidding match.

Sondra, Jackie, and I conferred several times that weekend. (Ma Bell fell in love with us.) The Ace VP called Sunday afternoon with their offer. It was about the same as Bantam's, but Bantam had better distribution (No. 1 is what they were), so we decided to go with them.

Happy ending, right? Wrong! The negotiations for the contract began at that time. You may think you just tell them what you want and they hand you a contract. Well, it doesn't work *quite* that way. There are lots of phone calls first.

This went on for several months. Since we did not have an agent, I had to act as agent on Jackie and Sondra's instructions. Our phone bill began to assume the dimensions of the national debt.

Prior to this, Fred had asked me for an additional chapter for the book. Sondra thought I could do it—so I gamely gave it a try. This became "What Are They Doing Now?"

During this time, Sondra decided several of the chapters had to be rewritten and Jackie agreed. With Myrna Culbreath's help, Sondra set to work. Jackie drafted new material—including a sixty-eight-page chapter on the Kraith Series which never saw print—and rewrote Sondra's rewrites all through the book. Jackie also was doing the Acknowledgments page for the front of the book; that's where we gave the sources of all the fan fiction stories we quoted from in the chapter called "Do-it-yourself 'Star Trek'—The Fan Fiction."

One evening Sondra called and said she had some suggestions for the "What Are They Doing Now?" chapter. She wanted to add an introduction and ending to kind of tie it all together. She read it to me over the phone, and it sounded just fine. She also had some suggestions for my other chapters, but I said if she didn't mind I would like these left alone. Sondra can write better than I can, but not in my style. This she readily admitted. Also, she and Jackie had helped me with them in the first place, and we finally decided that the spontaneity might be lost if they were polished further.

Finally, after three months Bantam called and said okay, everything is set—where are the releases?

"Uh, releases?"

"Yes. The releases from all those people you quoted in the book," said the Bantam Legal Department. "We must have them within two weeks!"

"Two weeks!!!"

Sondra was busy with the book, so I frantically (there's that word again) called Jackie. We independently galloped through the manuscript and sifted out the names of all the people quoted therein (oops, that's my job rubbing off wordwise) to make sure we hadn't missed anyone.

Jackie had been in contact with most of these people all the time the book was being written. Every seven or eight months Jackie would contact anyone we might quote to make sure they had not changed their addresses or their minds. Every time the book was redone (this happened eight times), people would be dropped and others added. At one time or another, she had received letters from them giving us "permission to quote." But Bantam wanted them to sign a more formal release.

I went to a friend in the Legal Department at ABC and she gave me the wording. Then Jackie and I wrote a cover letter to go with the release. We enclosed stamped, self-addressed envelopes, attached copies of the galley showing exactly how they were quoted, and sent them out.

At this point we only had ten days left. Then Ma Bell must have thought I'd won a million-dollar lottery, because I called everyone on our list—about thirty-five people all over the country. Only one person had changed their mind. Whew! Everyone was marvelous and sent the releases back by return mail. There were a few problems. Some names were misspelled, and I had to hand in a correction sheet.

Finally, with an effort which seemed to us to rival the labors of Hercules, the manuscript was completed with about four new chapters, checked back and forth with Jackie, and turned in to Fred Pohl to meet the one-month deadline.

Fred now had the book, but Sondra had just sent me a whole pile of additional changes including the long phone interview she had just done with William Shatner. I was in his office inserting the proper pages when he received an interoffice envelope. It contained the cover copy for our book. He handed it to me, and I screamed.

After he climbed down from the filing cabinet and assured the office staff I had not been stabbed or anything, I explained my reaction. The copy read as follows:

Star Trek Lives!
By Joan Winston

That's all. No Jacqueline Lichtenberg or Sondra Marshak. Fred had just handed it to me before checking it, or he might have

been the one who yelled and me doing the explaining. They
fixed it. You betcha.

After I had inserted the last corrected page, Fred and I
walked down to the Production Department and handed in the
manuscript. It was a great thrill.

I got another thrill a week or so later when a young woman
called to say that she was copy editing our book. She said she
had to call to let us all know how much she was enjoying her
work. You never know when you will find a "Star Trek" fan. I
told Fred about the call; he said he'd never heard of anything
like that happening before. How about that?

I had no sooner hung up with Fred when my other phone line
lit up. Chris, my secretary, walked in and reported it was someone about you-know-what. You-know-what was what she called
"Star Trek." I picked up the phone and it was Elyse. She had
gotten a letter from Bill Shatner's agent; if things could be
worked out, Bill would come to the 1975 convention! We'd work
it out, we'd work it out!

CHAPTER VI

WHAT LITTLE BREAKDOWNS ARE MADE OF;
OR,
THE CAPTAIN'S COMING, DOUBLE THE GUARD
(The 1975 "Star Trek" Convention, February 14–17, 1975, the Commodore Hotel, New York, New York)

THE 1975 "STAR TREK" CONVENTION—HOTEL COMMODORE

Friday, February 14, 1975

11:00 A.M.	Films
2:00 P.M.	Special effects: Mike McMasters
3:30	Fan panel
5:00	Dinner break
7:30	"Andromeda Light Show": Jeff Maynard
8:30	Films

Saturday, February 15, 1975

10:00 A.M.	Panel: "From Script to Seam" William Theiss, David Gerrold
11:00	Hal Clement: "The Peeling of the Apple"
12:00 NOON	Gene Roddenberry
1:00 P.M.	William Shatner: rap session
1:30	Lunch break
2:30	Richard C. Hoagland: "From Stonehenge to 'Star Trek' and Beyond"
4:00	Panel: "Aboard the Good Ship *Enterprise* . . ." William Shatner, Gene Roddenberry, George Takei
5:00	Majel Barrett Roddenberry
6:00	Dinner break

7:30   "Andromeda Light Show": Jeff Maynard
8:30   Films

Sunday, February 16, 1975
10:00 A.M.   Art Auction No. 1
12:00 NOON   Isaac Asimov
1:00 P.M.   Lunch break
2:00   William Shatner
3:00   Writers' panel:
           Isaac Asimov, Gene Roddenberry,
           Hal Clement, David Gerrold
4:00   William Ware Theiss: costume demonstration
6:00   Dinner break
7:30   Masquerade prejudging (East Ballroom)
9:00   Federation masquerade

Monday, February 17, 1975
11:00 A.M.   Art Auction No. 2
1:00 P.M.   Lunch break
2:00   David Gerrold
3:00   George Takei
4:00   Convention ends

All items listed in the program will be held in the Grand Ballroom unless otherwise noted.

FILMS
Films will be shown in the East Ballroom at the following times:
Friday: 2:00 P.M.–3:00 A.M.
Saturday: 10:00 A.M.–3:00 A.M.
Sunday: 10:00 A.M.–6:00 P.M.
            10:00 P.M.–3:00 A.M.
Monday: 11:00 A.M.–4:00 P.M.

ART SHOW
The Art and Handicraft Show is located in the West Ballroom and will be open as follows:
Friday: 4:00 P.M.–6:00 P.M.
Saturday: 10:00 A.M.–6:00 P.M.
Sunday: 9:00 A.M.–6:00 P.M.
Monday: 10:00 A.M.–4:00 P.M.

DEALERS' ROOM

The Dealers' Room is located in the Windsor Complex, on the Lobby
floor, near the main stairs to the East Forty-second Street entrance
of the hotel. The hours are:

Friday:	9:30 A.M.–8:00 P.M.
Saturday:	9:30 A.M.–8:00 P.M.
Sunday:	9:30 A.M.–8:00 P.M.
Monday:	9:30 A.M.–4:00 P.M.

PLEASE NOTE

The taking of *flash* photographs during the program items is prohibited. Smoking is prohibited in the main function rooms by law.
You may take available-light photos and tape the proceedings from
your seat: *no microphones will be allowed on the stage or podium.*

All proceedings (tapes, transcripts, photographs, motion pictures,
etc.) are the property of the "Star Trek" convention. You may tape
and photograph for your own use. However, COPIES MAY NOT
BE SOLD, PUBLISHED, OR IN ANY OTHER WAY DISTRIB-
UTED WITHOUT OUR EXPRESS WRITTEN PERMISSION.

GRAND BALLROOM:	Main program
EAST BALLROOM:	Film program
	Masquerade prejudging
WEST BALLROOM:	Art and Handicraft Show
GRAND BALLROOM FOYER:	Registration
	Information desk
PARLOR "A":	Convention headquarters
	Lost and found
	Helpers' headquarters
PARLOR "B":	Press room
WINDSOR COMPLEX (LOBBY FLOOR):	Dealers' room
FIRST FLOOR:	Group meeting rooms (times and room numbers to be posted)

The day after the 1974 con we got together to discuss our
plans for the 1975 convention. Devra was elected chairperson,
and I became vice chairperson.

We had not been too happy with the Americana, so we returned to our old faithful, the Commodore. We reserved Wash-

ington's birthday weekend and sent out letters to all the guests who had previously appeared at our cons and to those who hadn't. Included, quite naturally but not too hopefully, was Bill Shatner. All the letters went out sometime in May. Elyse was quite a busy little girl.

The answers started to trickle in, with all saying they would love to attend, schedules permitting. Then Elyse phoned excitedly that fateful day. Bill Shatner's agent had written to say that perhaps Captain Kirk might be able to come to our convention, under certain terms and conditions, and asked us to contact him.

Elyse usually took care of this, since she was in charge of programing, but she and the rest of the Committee felt that since I knew Bill and his then agent, Ted Witzer, I should do the talking. And that's why Ted Witzer was on my phone that day. We talked agent talk, and I told him I'd get back to him and called each of the Committee. I could not make that large a commitment without their okay. We took a vote, and I got in touch with Ted to say we had a deal and a contract would soon be on its way.

Yahoo! This was to be the first convention that Bill had ever appeared at. Of course, there was an escape clause, but that was perfectly normal business procedure. Bill had thirty days prior to the con to inform us that a pilot, series, or movie commitment would prevent his attending. That was the way we worded all our advertising, too.

We had also gotten a very nice letter from Leonard Nimoy, but he seemed to be more interested in why we had split with Al and made no mention of appearing at the con.

We had set our other guests, and it was quite a list.

Isaac informed us that it had become a tradition to attend, and he was not about to go against tradition. Hal Clement, as always, said he would be delighted to come. David Gerrold pleased us immeasurably by his acceptance. He, too, had become a tradition. Jeff Maynard returned with his fantastic Light Show. George—now, there was someone we could always count on.

Fred Phillips regretably was unable to make it back. He had an assignment that would not permit his attendance. But we were able to get an old friend of mine, and now of the whole Committee, Bill (excuse me—William) Ware Theiss (tease,

tease), the gravity-defying costume designer for "Star Trek."
And—Tra-rah-ta-ta-ta—the one and only Roddenberrys, Gene
and Majel. Now, that's a guest list!

Also our usual surprises. What surprises, you ask? Read on
McFan, read on. (Jackie, is that what you mean by precogni-
tion?)

When we split with Al, it was intimated by many people that
since we were a group of amateurs, any convention we tossed
would be an odds-on bet to floppola. Well, we were bound and
determined that this con was going to be one of the best anybody ever saw—that is, if hard work, determination, blood,
sweat, and tears made a good con.

Since we had no money from the 1974 con, Ben and Devra
dug down and kept our heads above water by coming up with
the needed funds. Ben gave us the money for printing, paper,
postage, etc. Devra dug into her savings account and put down
the hotel deposit.

"If we don't succeed with the con," Devra said, "I'll have the
biggest birthday party you ever saw." The Commodore ballroom
holds over two thousand people.

The first flier went out sometime in March, I believe. We
listed the graduated registration rates and other information. We
reserved tables at various cons in the area so we could sell memberships, give out fliers, and sell assorted "Star Trek" stuff.
Devra made and sold delicious candy, and I remember that at
one con we made more from the candy than from the memberships.

The regular round of meetings had started. They were at the
hotel, or Devra's or Elyse's. Joyce, as secretary, took voluminous
notes and sent out minutes to one and all to remind us of the
topics discussed, or enable us to catch up if we were unable to
attend. I admit I missed quite a few meetings in Brooklyn.

Because of the rising costs, we paid for the paper for the progress reports and program book in advance. As well as the plastic
for the shopping bags.

That's another thing. We decided, and it was taken for
granted, that we would continue to give the fans that extra
something that they had come to expect from us. Like the big,

multipaged program book chock full of pictures, and the big plastic shipping bag to carry all their goodies in.

It's so easy to say, "The fliers went out." First the fliers had to be written, then printed, then all the address labels made up, then pasted on, Zip-coded, and taken to the post office. This was usually done at either Elyse's or Devra's home. We would call up a faithful corps of helpers—Ellen and Carol Schlakman, Ruth Schoenberger, Alina Chu, Linda Deneroff, Diane Duane, Lise Eisenberg, Karina Girsdanski, Cheryl McDaniels, Pat O'Neill, Jeremy Paulson, and many, many more. If these names sound familiar, they should. They have been working with the Committee for years. (Just gluttons for punishment, I guess.)

At first we would have meetings once a month, then twice a month as the time grew nearer. I could not make all of them, since my job kept me hopping. But the Committee was very understanding. If I couldn't be there in person, I was there in spirit. Unfortunately, a spirit can't staple, paste, or answer mail (not mine, anyway).

Money started to come in, and that eased the financial situation quite a bit. Dealers were buying tables, but Stu Grossman (a dear, but a worrywart) thought it was not fast enough. Dana was not working at the time, and she processed almost all of the memberships herself up to the very last days. One heck of a job. Ask Joyce, who did it for the 1976 con. Then again, *don't* ask them, or you will never get anyone to do registration again. Ever. All the preparation is scutwork, but this is the worst. Hats off to Dana and Joyce.

Elyse and Steve were gathering all the info for the progress report. We were determined that it was going to go out on time this year. We always said that, but it had never happened. This year, lo and behold, the progress reports were all in the mail before Halloween.

This made Thom, Dana, and me very happy, since we could go to Lin Carter's famous annual Halloween bash without having to feel guilty about not having to work that weekend.[1] I'm glad I went, since I won first prize in the Costume Contest. The

[1] Lin Carter writes sword and sorcery books, does lots of anthologies, and is a good friend.

Carters always had a theme for their parties, and in 1974 it was the 1930s. I came as a Busby Berkeley girl. I wore black net stockings, black satin shorts, a silver lace blouse with big bows to match, in a high pompadour. And real tap shoes with huge satin bows. I even sang a song and did a tap dance. I think they gave me first prize because they were so stunned at (1) my complete lack of talent and (2) my nerve at displaying same in public.

(Back to the con, Joan, and leave the dancing to Ginger and Eleanor.)

At one of the meetings I did attend we discussed our television ad. The 1974 convention was the first for which we had a TV ad. Elyse was the one who contacted WPIX and made all the arrangements. That ad was on the air near the end of January 1974. For the 1975 convention we decided that we would have it earlier in the year, since some of the fans might be a little confused by our change of name. The old name, International "Star Trek" Convention, had bad memories for some of the Committee, so we decided to go back to the original name, The "Star Trek" Convention. That's what we called it back in 1972. That con had been a hectic but very happy one for all concerned, and we hoped that the name would be a good-luck charm. Lord knows, we felt we needed all the luck we could get.

Because of the change of name, we wanted to have two ads for the 1975 con. The first was to take place in May 1974, and the second, as before, in January, just prior to the con. Elyse wrote the copy, and an announcer from WPIX was to read over the graphics (slides of pictures and copy), which the station was to make up for us. And there was the rub. In writing the script, Elyse had numbered the slides ST No. 1, ST No. 2, and ST No. 3. When the station people received the slides, they called them ST No. 2, ST No. 3, and ST No. 4. The station had a "Star Trek" logo (identification), which they used between station breaks. It was a picture of Kirk, Spock, and McCoy, and this was identified in their files as ST No. 1. Aha, you see the light beginning to break. It took a bit longer for some people at the station.

What happened was this: The ad went on the air sometime in May, but instead of our slide appearing (a picture of the crowds at one of the cons), you got Kirk, Spock, and McCoy. Then came slide No. 2, actually our slide No. 1 (the crowd scene), and then slide No. 3, actually our slide No. 2, a slide from the series. Our slide No. 3 never got on the air, and that was the one with all the information on it—little things like the dates of the con, the hotel, and the membership fees. Sure, the announcer was saying them, but if you didn't have them in front of your little eyeballs, it was very hard to remember.

As a result, we got something like five thirty-second commercial spots for the price of one. The ad would usually be on the Saturday "Star Trek" episode, and Elyse would call the station on each Monday morning to tell them they had goofed—again. *Quel* bargain.

However, some of the fans must have been able to make sense of the ad, because the convention phone at Elyse's house began to ring and ring and ring. She and Steve got a telephone answerer with a special tape to handle the calls when they were not at home. We had fans tell us they waited for hours to reach the number, and Steve discovered later that the tape would wear out every few days. That's a lot of phone calls. When Steve and Elyse were at home, the phone rang about every two or three minutes. It was a ring-a-ding time for the Rosensteins.

During this period, the tape wore out—which fact was not discovered for several days. However, the telephone exchange, not being able to connect with *our* number, slipped over one digit, and a very nice but rapidly confused lady began to receive calls at all hours of the day and night with fans asking plaintive questions about hotel rates and guest stars and movie schedules. The calls came at the rate of one every ten minutes. She called the phone company, and Ma Bell told the Commodore not to give out *our* number. *Mucho* confusion. At this time the hotel gave out Devra's number as a substitute. It was then we discovered the worn-out tape. Whew!

Quite a while later, after Devra had switched to a new branch of the library she overheard a co-worker telling a friend about these "weird" calls she'd gotten concerning a "Star Trek" convention. Being a brave soul, Devra "fessed up," apologized to the woman for all the trouble, and, to make amends, offered her a free membership. The woman accepted, and all was forgiven.

It was at about this time that we got the news that Bill

Shatner was to appear at Al's convention in January. Well, so be it. We could not have gotten an exclusivity clause, anyway. But if Al's was going to be his *first* con, ours was going to be his *finest*. And it must have been, because the several times I saw Bill during 1975 after our con he would always remark, "I had a real ball at your con." Glad to hear it, Bill, glad to hear it. As a matter of fact, at the January 1976 convention at the New York Hilton (you remember—the one where they had to call out the riot squad, the fire department, and such), Bill was asked a question that went something like, "What is your favorite kind of convention?" His answer was this (I'm quoting some fans; I did not attend): "If you want to see the stars, I guess this kind of con is your best bet. But if you want to see what 'Star Trek' is all about, meet the fans, and have a ball, go to the one in February." Now, that's a plug!

It was just prior to Al's con that we heard that Bill had signed for a picture called *The Devil's Rain,* to be shot in Mexico during the time of *our* convention.

Oy! I immediately called Teddy, Bill's agent and asked what the situation was. He said Bill was trying to arrange the production schedule with the producer so he could get off to come to our con. Bill was really looking forward to it.

The Friday of Al's con, Bill was set to do a then "$10,000 Pyramid" segment, and I went to the theater to see him. I found him in the make-up room, and he gave me a very warm greeting. He said quite frankly that he was terrified of the crowds, especially since he found on arrival that Al had no professional security guards for the guests. We had informed Teddy that we were spending a rather large amount of money on security. (I understand that Al did have professional security at the con, so there must have been a misunderstanding or cross-up in communication.)

Bill's fear of the crowds was quite understandable. As he walked out on the stage for his first appearance at Al's convention, the crowd rose to its feet and let out a roar of welcome. Bill paled and slowed almost to a stop, then squared his shoulders and continued to the center of the stage. He smiled, said hello, and the crowd was his. The captain had arrived!

It was very different the next day of Al's con. Bill was quite relaxed, and he joked and answered questions with good humor. During his talk, Al came onstage to announce that a little boy was lost, and was his father in the audience? Bill asked that the little boy (of about four) be brought up on the stage. He got down on his knees and, talking calmly and quietly, got him to stop crying, removed his hat and coat, and asked the child to do him the "favor" of keeping him company onstage until his father found him. And that's what the little boy did. Well, Bill should know how to handle kids, having three of his own.

When his hour was up, Bill said a sad farewell, and with kids crying "Don't go, please don't go" and other kids sobbing, he left the stage. I understand he was quite upset by this tearful farewell.

Meanwhile, I pulled a small coup. I arrived a short time before Bill was due to appear and walked into the ballroom. Mary Ellen Flynn of the 'Star Trek' Welcommittee had saved a seat for me. The people who wanted to ask Bill questions were already getting in line. I asked a young friend of mine if he would get in line and ask if Bill was going to the con (our con) in February. I figured if the kids had enjoyed this one, then they would enjoy ours also.

My friend asked his question just as Ben Yalow, Stu Hellinger, and Dave Simons walked into the ballroom wondering how they could get Bill to announce his appearance at the February con. They told me later they turned to each other and said, "Joan's here!"

As Bill stated, "Yes, I will be at the February Convention," and discussed how many miles he would have to fly to make it that weekend, you could hear the ballroom buzzing with "Gee, where is it, and when?"

Ben, Stu, and Dave gave out about fifteen hundred fliers in the half hour after Bill's speech. This did no harm to Al's con, as all these fans had already paid their membership fees for it. But it's an example of what one has to do to reach the people you feel would like to know about your con. It shows that all opportunities must be grabbed if you want to run a successful con. An important part is getting the news to the people who would like to attend.

Here are a few "helpful hints" developed after much trial and travail:

1. *Please:* Spend enough time planning the con. It is not something one can just put together in a few weeks. You really need six months to a year.

2. It must be publicized properly, using the local TV stations and papers and fanzines. And don't forget the local fan organizations. Their help is invaluable.

3. Go to as many cons as you can to see what they do right and what they do wrong. Learn from *their* mistakes.

4. Your committee should have at least eight to ten members, so that no one person is stuck with all the work. One person, however, must be in charge, to co-ordinate all events. But no ego trips, *please!* All decisions should be made by a majority vote. Let everyone have their say *once*, and then vote.

5. You should have a mature, responsible person as hotel liaison. Get everything in writing—*everything!* Don't take, "Oh, we'll have that for you. Don't worry." (famous last words). Put down every foot of space, every mike, every chair, all the opening and closing times. Don't let them rent the main ballroom out for a luncheon the Saturday afternoon of the con. It has happened.

6. Helpers: Put someone in charge. Make sure the helpers know who the committee is. Be sure to stress politeness: "Please" and "Thank you" should be branded on their foreheads. Try to allow for free memberships for them in your budget.

7. Have a worry room (lost and found, complaint department, first aid, etc.) and stick the chairperson or assistant chairperson there. Their locations must be known at all times. However, the other committee members should have authority to act in their areas.

8. Keep your sense of humor. You're going to need it.

There are many other things that I will probably remember after this book goes to press. However, as a safeguard, I am letting the Committee read this as I write it. I am sure they will come up with a load of other stuff.

Additional Committee Comments on Convention Rules:
    DEVRA: Go see a psychiatrist. It's easier and cheaper.

DEVRA: No. 4—4th and 5th lines. We could never learn this point, and spent hours arguing sometimes about the *weirdest* things, like the color of the badge cards. (That's funny, isn't it?)

STU H.: No, it's pathetic!

The fliers we gave out at Al's con must have reached the right people, since we received over twelve hundred memberships the last week prior to the deadline for advance tickets. We had set a limit of about eight thousand for the con and had fifty-seven hundred in pre-registrations by the deadline of January 15, 1975. This deadline, of course, was based upon the postmark, not the day received.

This gave us about a week to process all the cards and send them out so people would receive them prior to the con. We had decided to have huge boxes of plastic badge holders near the registration booths to speed up the actual registration. If the lines were too long, a pre-registered fan could just slip his previously received card into a holder and walk into the con. Later, when the lines had shortened, he could pick up his program book, shopping bag, etc.

This was a great idea, except for some bright, unscrupulous kids who found an equally unscrupulous color Xerox and went into business for themselves. That was the reason Devra came to me on Saturday and said that even though we had only registered sixty-eight hundred fans, the facilities were getting much too crowded. Devra, as chairperson, was canvassing the rest of the Committee as to a decision to close registration. We decided yes. Better to lose money than to be too crowded.

The counterfeits were discovered when a security guard found a ticket on the floor and brought it to the worry room. Devra noticed it was blank on the back. It did not have our disclaimer ("We are not responsible for . . . ," etc.). And that, dear friends, is why your badges were being so closely scrutinized every time you entered the Art Show, film, program, or dealers' rooms. Also why in 1976 you all got those lovely, specially designed badge holders that cost the Committee $$$$! Now, I am all in favor of free enterprise (oops), but there are limits, fellas, and if any of us, especially Stu Hellinger, finds out who you were, Alpha Centauri will not be far enough.

Meanwhile, January was a very busy month. Besides doing the thousand of membership cards, all the shopping bags had to be stuffed. No, little green men do not do it for us. The helpers, assistants, and Committee do it, that's who!

The Commodore gave us a large meeting room across from our storage room, and we set up an assembly line. Sort the trivia contest, staple, and pile. Place with masquerade rules. Then someone took them and inserted them into the program book, and then someone else slipped the whole *magilla* into a shopping bag—nine thousand times.

We had about thirty people doing the above, hearing, "We need more program books"; "I just ran out of staples"; "May I have a Pepsi?; "Can I call my mother?" "Where's the john?" "Isn't the program book gorgeous?" (you betcha!). All being yelled at once, of course.

We did over six thousand that Saturday and finished on Sunday. Those kids really worked, and so did the Committee. At some of the other work sessions we had real meals, not just sodas and snacks. Devra cooked us several of her fabulous gourmet dinners (with three desserts, no less). Elyse, having just moved into her new apartment the week before, cooked a spaghetti dinner for thirty of us. No, she is not a masochist, she's just a great cook who loves to share with people.

The week of the con finally arrived. Steve, Thom, and Dave rented a truck and started to cart everyone's paraphernalia to the hotel. The night before, the sky had opened up and dropped about eighteen inches of snow on little old New York. I was lending the con my projector and my reel-to-reel tape recorder. I was going to tape all the interviews in the press room. Later we were glad I did, since the tape recorder in the main ballroom had its mike stolen the first day.

There were several different groups doing film and tape specials of the con, and the guests got quite used to mikes and cameras being shoved at them from all angles. Please don't ask us what happened to those specials; we have no idea.

On Thursday, Steve's sister Amy commandeered the family car, and Ben and Elyse joined her to pick up the guests at the airport. No, we didn't use limousines. We couldn't afford them. Besides, the stars never complained; after all, it *was* a Chrysler.

This trip was for the Ta-rah-ta-ta-rah Roddenberrys. They arrived looking grand with about eight to ten pieces of luggage, plus a wheelchair for G.R. He had fallen on an icy street in Minneapolis while carrying a can of film for one of his lectures, and had hurt his hip.

When Ben had stuffed the car with all it could hold, and more, still on the sidewalk were two suitcases, the wheelchair, and Ben. It was at this time that Ben realized a twenty-three-year-old dream (he was twenty-three at the time). He leaped, he said, into a cab (how you leap into a cab with two suitcases and a wheelchair is something I would pay to see), slammed the door, and, pointing to the slowly moving Chrysler ahead of them, shouted,

"FOLLOW THAT CAR!"

The wheelchair was to be both a blessing and an albatross before the con was over. The blessing part was easy, since it made it possible for Gene to get around until his hip felt better. It also provided Claire Eddy and Pat O'Neill with a vehicle for their infamous "drag races."

I guess now is as good a time as any to relate the story behind "Claire's cable caper." Claire was assistant to Barbara Wenk, who was in charge of the helpers—no small task, with over 250 to assign, dispatch, and all-around handle. It was Friday, the first day of the con, and the helper headquarters had been set up on the left side of the worry room in Parlor "A" on the ballroom floor. The front of the room had tables for the worriers, like Chairperson Devra Langsam; Assistant Chairperson Thom Anderson; their assistants, Alina Chu and Michael Spence; and our lawyers, Sondra and Robert Harris. The "cable" was not TV but the telephone type. Several extra phones had been set up, and the wires were all over the place. Claire kept saying, "Somebody's going to trip over those and hurt themselves." Yup.

It started innocently enough on Sunday morning. Claire got a call from her roommate, Linda Deneroff, who said that her key would not open the room door. What was worse, she could swear that she heard strange noises in the room. Since both girls had all their valuables in the room, Linda had a right to be disturbed.

Claire's key was in her purse. Claire's purse was on the table near all those wires. Claire ran for her purse. Claire tripped over

wires. Claire made one-point landing on her ankle. Ankle immediately began to assume elephantine proportions. Claire went to
hospital. And that is how Claire got her very own wheelchair for
the whole weekend!

(Oh, I forgot to tell you, when they finally got into the room,
there was nobody there. Linda got some strange looks from the
hotel man who let her in. To this day she swears she heard
noises. And she still gets strange looks.)

Then Gene left his own wheelchair in the con suite one afternoon. Jeremy Paulson sat in it because it was the only empty seat
in the den. Claire was just leaving the living room via *her* wheelchair when the next thing she knew Jeremy was beside her in
his. Gazing down the long, elegant, now empty hallway, he said
out of the corner of his mouth, "Wanna drag?"

So we ended up with our very own Indianapolis 500—only
ours was the "Star Trek" 50 (feet, that is).

The press party was set for Friday night and was a killer-
diller. Everyone was there except Bill Shatner, who was flying in
from *The Devil's Rain* location in Durango, Mexico. Elyse, Ben,
and Amy (Steve Rosenstein's sister) were to pick him up at Kennedy Airport at 11:05 P.M.

The party started at approximately 6:00 P.M. and was in full
swing by 6:07 P.M. K.C., one of the helpers who was serving as
bartender, had bought me a present: a beautiful bottle of champagne. (I don't know why he bought me a present, he just did.)
I shared this with Majel, who loves the stuff, too.

One of the helpers came to tell me that four blind kids were at
the door of the con suite asking to speak to me. They were Lisa
Hess, David DiCarlo, Janice Harvey, and Andy Jadelskyj. Andy
had a lovely pale beige Labrador as his seeing-eye dog. I invited
them in and walked up to Gene and said, "Here are some fans of
yours who have never seen 'Star Trek,' but who love it just the
same." Gene, Majel, and Bob Lansing turned around and
stopped, stunned. The kids, sweetly and articulately, told them
how much they enjoyed listening to the program. As they talked,
the four of us stood there with tears streaming down our cheeks
and trying very hard not to let on. It was a beautiful moment
and one none of us will forget.

Bob Lansing had played Gary Seven in *Assignment: Earth*, an ST episode that was also considered a pilot for a possible new series. Gene had mentioned that Bob was a friend and gave me his phone number so I could invite him to the press party. Well, he came to the party and ended up staying for the whole convention. Stu got him a room and he appeared on panels, gave autographs, and was a judge at the Costume Ball. Everytime he would get set to go home something would come up, and he would decide to stay all over again. We ended up getting him several sets of fresh underwear and socks because we were afraid if he ever did get home he might not come back. He didn't leave until the end of the Dead Dog Party and said he could not believe the fantastic time he had had. It was a pleasure, sir.

Just before 10:00 P.M., Elyse, Ben, and Amy left the hotel to pick up Bill at the airport. We had gotten a call Thursday from Teddy saying that Bill had decided to stay with some friends in Brooklyn instead of at the hotel. But since we had said in our contract that we would pick him up at the airport, we would pick him up at the airport.

It was a couple of traffic snarls that made the Committee five minutes late. It was tailwinds that made Bill's plane fifteen minutes early. By the time our group got to the terminal, Bill had left. However, they were not certain, so they spent an hour wandering around, afraid to page him because they might start a riot. They were miffed. I was upset. Bill was due onstage at 1:00 P.M. for his first rap session, and I didn't know if he had his schedule with him. I called Bill's agent, Ted Witzer, waking him up, and he said he would get in touch with Bill and have him call.

Just then a fan, slightly dazed, said that someone who said he was William Shatner (a bit of a tremolo in her voice at this point) had called and that he would call me at 11:30 A.M.

And he did. As soon as I realized it was really him, I called out, "Okay, Elyse, you can tell the police to stop dragging the river, *It's* alive!"

"Uh, you're mad at me, aren't you, Joanie?"

"Bill, why should I be mad at you? The Committee loved wandering around Kennedy Airport for an hour last night!"

"Oh boy, is she mad at me." Bill then explained how the plane had been early and a crowd had started to collect and that he had jumped into a cab; besides, he did not feel we should have had to drive all the way out to his friend's home in Brooklyn at that time of night. It was not until then we discovered that a mix-up in communications had happened and Bill had thought we'd been notified not to pick him up.

Suddenly I was unmad. I told him when he was due onstage, and he promised to be at the "secret entrance" a quarter of an hour before time. Since the Commodore is supposed to be torn down (perhaps already leveled at this time), I can tell this little secret. We waited on the mezzanine floor by the revolving door. A few feet down the hall, outside, was a fire exit door. We were going to bring Bill in that way.

We had quite a crowd of security men and helpers, assistants, and Committee members waiting to welcome the captain. Among this illustrious group were Stu Hellinger (in charge of security and already developing an ulcer), Pat O'Neill (Stu's assistant), Manny Moreño, and Ben Yalow. We scrutinized every cab coming down the street. The air buzzed with excitement. It was a miracle that the fans didn't catch on to what we were doing (shades of Leonard Nimoy in 1973).

Suddenly there he was, *walking* up the street to the hotel! We dashed out into the icy February air and stopped him before he reached the revolving doors. As we took him in the secret entrance, I asked him why he was walking.

Bill smiled. "Why take a cab? The subway left me off right near here."

"You took the *subway?!*" Gurgle, choke.

"Sure."

"And no one recognized you?"

This time, he laughed. "No. I just read my book and minded my own business like everyone else. Besides, if you don't act as if you want to be recognized, you won't be, usually."

We took him up the back elevator and into the kitchen just opposite the ballroom. I told him we would wait there until the programing was over in the ballroom (see the floor plan of the Commodore).

Meanwhile, everyone was staring, and the female contingent was sighing. He looked fantastic! Tanned, and rosy-cheeked

William Shatner at the 1975 helpers' party, sipping some soda while greeting all his fans. This was just after he almost went *splatt!* (*Elizabeth Vanier*)

Gene Roddenberry, David Gerrold, Hal Clement, and Isaac Asimov on a writers' panel at the 1975 con. Somebody must have said something funny. *(Jeff Maynard)*

Robert Lansing, Majel Barrett Roddenberry, Gene Roddenberry, William Shatner, and George Takei during the star panel at the 1975 con. *(Jeff Maynard)*

At the Chicago con, William Shatner and Dale Westrate: Dale is wearing a T-shirt saying, "Tomcat Kirk at age 9½." This picture was taken by JoAnne Westrate, Dale's mother, who also made the T-shirt. *(Benjamin M. Yalow)*

A close-up of William Shatner answering one of the questions at the 1975 con. From the expression on his face, it must have been a goodie! *(Jeff Maynard)*

George Takei surrounded by some of the participants in the 1975 Dead Dog Party, a mixture of Committee, helpers, and friends. Don't you just love George's headgear? *(Jeff Maynard)*

from the cold; and slim, as was discovered when he took off his shearling jacket. I handed it to Manny Moreño and told him to guard it well. He did.[2] Some people asked for and got autographs.

Before we left, Bill handed me the shoulder bag he was carrying and asked me to take care of it for him.

"Joanie, hold onto this for me, will you?"

"Of course," I said. "I'll take good care of your pur- uh, bag."

He laughed. "You can call it a purse. I'm secure."

Then we both laughed.

Someone must have spotted Bill through one of the small windows set in the kitchen doors, because when we left, a huge crowd had formed outside the ballroom—which was overloaded and then some. The security guards and helpers locked arms, and we walked to the ballroom entrance. At least we tried. The crowd surged forward and we got squished. Bill was holding onto my hand, but I got pulled behind him. He tried to make sure I was all right and gave me a big smile. Two girls in the line of smile slowly swayed and toppled over.

I said, "Now look what you've done!"

He laughed. "I'm lethal."

Once we got into the ballroom, he noticed all the people running.

"Where are they going?"

"To do something for those girls."

Bill looked very startled. "You mean they weren't just fooling? They really . . . ?"

"Yup, they really."

That was the first time I ever saw William Shatner gulp!

Elyse said I should introduce Bill, so I started to go up on the stage.

"Where are you going?"

"To introduce you." He was very nervous. And even more so as a half-dozen mikes were hung on him.

"Ladies, gentlemen, and fans. I am very happy to introduce to

[2] Before the weekend was over, Manny was to receive many bids on that coat, including one for $600. Gee, we could have sent Bill home in a blanket. Somehow I think he might have missed that coat, since it was about 20 degrees outside.

you our special guest, Mr. William Shatner." Short and sweet and safe. Bill squared his shoulders, took a deep breath, and strode out onstage.

Pandemonium—and not silent, either.

He commented on how he had spent a lot of money to have his jacket fitted properly and they (meaning the Committee) had hung a half-dozen wires and mikes on him.

"Well," he said, laughing, "now for a rap session. There are a lot of you here, and there seems to be only one of me." Just then, one fan shouted, "That's enough," and the whole ballroom erupted with laughter, including Bill.

"She said, 'That's enough' but I don't know if she was referring to my remarks or my looks. Listen, the only way we can really make this work is by having quiet so I can answer all your questions. You'll be able to hear me, and I'll be able to hear the questions, and I'll try to be as honest as I can about the answers." At this point Bill got a bit impatient with all the wires hung on him, and in removing all but one he also removed his jacket.

"Take it off!!!" a fan screamed, and others joined her. "Take it all off!!!"

Handing me his jacket, Bill started to laugh, "I don't need much encouragement. Now, seriously, if we are going to accomplish any sort of communication between people like yourselves who love 'Star Trek' and a person like myself who loved making it, let's establish some ground rules. The first one is that I will try my damndest to answer your questions as honestly as I can, and if you're quiet, I won't have to yell and I can be more myself. All right. A rap session usually starts with a question. Why doesn't somebody ask me a question, and what I'll do is take off from there and try to amplify the answer a little and maybe I'll tell you something that you don't know. On the other hand, you'll probably tell me something I don't know."

There were many questions asked, and I wish we had the space to print all of them. However, I will attempt to give you some of the more interesting and amusing ones. We did screen the questions to prevent any embarrassing ones. You never know when some fan will get up and say, "How come you got so fat?" or "Why do you look so much older than on 'Star Trek'?" Yes, there are fans out there who would ask those and worse, *much* worse. And you don't pay your guests a lot of money to come thousands of miles to be insulted or upset. By the way, those particular questions were *not* asked of Bill, but they were asked of other stars at *other* conventions. Back to Bill.

LINDA DENEROFF (ballroom assistant): "We have a little boy here."

BILL SHATNER: "Is that the question? Yes, he is a little boy." (laughter)

FAN: "First, I'd like to say I think you're a wonderful actor." (applause and shouting)

BILL SHATNER: "Now . . . there is some question in *my* mind about that."

FAN: "I'd like to ask your advice to young actors."

BILL SHATNER: "And he really means young, too. I don't think that anyone should be an actor unless you're very lucky, very talented, and are willing to roll dice with your life. You know, I'm asked that question sometimes by kids in college who are in drama school. They are in their third year and they say, "Should I become an actor?" By that time they've spent three years in college, where they could have been getting some grounding in some technical skill that would have provided them with a livelihood of some kind, and it's really too late to give them any advice.

"You know, when I used to do a play as an amateur, there was a feeling of love among the cast members. There is the fact that a lot of lonely people gravitate toward the amateur-theater world because there's an entity to which they can belong. So you find people who need other people going into amateur theatrics.

"There are a number of different motivations for becoming an actor. What happens then—after the amateur years are over—is that it becomes a business. An actor has to take roles that he doesn't want to take; he has to do things he doesn't want to do in order to make a living and provide for his family. And the people who are left competing for the roles that you want are people whose very survival is at stake. Now the motivations become different; no longer is it lonely, friendless people clinging to one another, but people who are striving to survive in a very cutthroat world. It's a hard adjustment to make. And it's hard to convey feelings in the competitive professional world. I don't know whether that provides you with any advice, but it's what I feel." (applause)

Bill was then asked several technical questions about special effects and the animated series. Although he explained these very well, I think they have been covered time and again elsewhere.

FAN: "Mr. Shatner, can I see your belly button?"

BILL SHATNER: "See my belly button? [wild laughter] Is that what you said? I've flown nine thousand miles to show you my belly button? [laughter and applause] I'll only take legitimate questions. Next?"

FAN: "In the episode *A Piece of the Action,* when you played the game 'Fizzbin,' did you ad-lib it, or was it written beforehand?"

BILL SHATNER: *A Piece of the Action?*" (puzzled)

FAN: "The Chicago gangster thing."

BILL SHATNER: "Oh, the Chicago gangster thing. I . . . I only remember these things by the girls in them—why didn't you tell me which girl was in it?" (laughter)

FAN: "Because there wasn't any in it!" (cheers and applause)

BILL SHATNER: "There was no girl in it?! No wonder I can't remember! [laughter] Okay. Now, you asked me if I ad-libbed a certain aspect of it? To be perfectly honest with you, I can't remember. I must say there was a minimum of ad-libbing going on, as you've probably seen by that funny film. What do you call it? The blooper reel.

"As you can see, we were very serious on the set. [laughter] I really don't remember the show. Please recall, especially when you look at my face, that— I think we started filming in 1967, so that's a few years ago—'66, was it? I'm getting so old my memory's fading." (There were many shouts of "No" and "You look fabulous," etc.)

FAN: "You have said that you loved doing 'Star Trek.' I'm curious: What episode did you like doing the best?"

BILL SHATNER: "You remember that girl . . . [laughter] I've just described to you the difference between the amateur and the professional world. A synthesis takes place between the amateur and the professional, and you retain some of the love, perhaps more of the love of doing what you do well, as well as the tough professional attitude that's necessary in order to survive.

"I love 'Star Trek' like very little else that I have done in my professional life. [applause and shouting] A lot of you are very young or youngish, and maybe you haven't had the experience of going to a job, coming in, and not really wanting to be there—well, there's school, but school has hope . . . [laughter] . . . not only that you'll get out, but also that you will come out with an education in something that you want to do. But if you are locked into a job as an adult that you really don't care for, and the things that you really care for are outside, after you've finished work, and then you go and do what you really like. . . . Well, I've never been in that position. Mostly, with 90 per cent of what I do, I'm glad to be there.

" 'Star Trek' every morning . . . I lived for a long time out on the beach at Santa Monica—a forty-five minute drive. I had to exercise my dog before I went to work, so I had to get up at 5:00 A.M or 5:30 A.M.—I'm sure you've heard this story from all the other guys who've been here—and finally got to the studio to work twelve, fourteen, sixteen hours a day. I had ten, fourteen pages of dialogue to learn in a day. Sometimes I was faced with problems I didn't know how to solve. I knew that millions of people would be watching, and I knew it was possible that it would be laughable—that's always a terrifying possibility.

"I mean, look—here we are; you're looking at me and I'm looking at you, and it's possible that nothing will happen—that's the potential of a performer. But with rare, rare exceptions, so few that I can't even remember them, every day that I went to work I looked forward to going to work. I was gratified with a day's work, and when it ended, three years later, I was very, very sad. Now, those of you who know what a job is, day in and day out, will know the enormity of what I've just said. Thank you." (applause)

I hated to do it, but Bill's half-hour rap session had already lasted for forty-five minutes, and I didn't want him to think we would take advantage of him. I tapped him on the shoulder and pointed to my watch. He looked a bit startled—he was having a great time, and I think would have kept right on going for another forty-five minutes. I told the fans that that was the last of the questions and that Bill had to leave. (Much shouting of "No, don't go!") "But," I said, "he'll be back at four o'clock on a panel with Mr. Roddenberry, Majel Barrett, George Takei, and Robert Lansing. Okay?" (Fans again shouting and much applause as we left.)

After Bill's appearance, a reporter asked Thom Anderson what he thought was the major difference in the fans' reaction to Bill Shatner and Leonard Nimoy.

"Well," Thom said "when Shatner walks onstage the fans all want a piece of his body. When Nimoy appears its like the Pope is talking. Sexual excitment I can understand; religious fervor is beyond me."

When Bill finished his session, the security squad and I escorted him to his suite on the twenty-second floor.

Remember my telling you of the offers we got for Bill's coat? We were also offered from one fan, if you can believe it, five hundred dollars for his room number and a thousand dollars for the key. But Bill was not staying in the suite overnight; otherwise we could have made a bloody fortune! And that was cash, folks! Besides, all that would have happened is that they would have been greeted by a hairy helper catching a catnap. Well, you can't let two good beds go to waste, and if Bill wasn't going to use them . . .

But he was using it now. He had an hour and fifteen minutes until his press conference, and I thought he'd like to relax. K.C. and some other helpers got us up to the suite. I asked Bill what he'd like to drink, and he said some club soda with lemon or lime. And that's what he got. K.C. made it himself—with both lemon and lime. And you know what? It's good, and very refreshing.

Elyse had gotten some beautiful oranges and apples, and Bill peeled an orange as we talked. I tried to reach the press room to tell them where I was, but no luck. The operators would not ring through even after I told them who I was. "We are not allowed to disturb any interviews that may be taking place," I was told.

Hah! The phone would ring at least twice during every interview. But they wouldn't put *me* through! Okay. Try the worry room. Line's busy. Try registration. Line's busy. I finally sent a helper to the con suite to tell Elyse where I was in case anyone asked. She came down to the suite, and I introduced her to Bill. He thanked her for the fruit.

After she left, he asked if he could call his agent. I dialed and then said I would leave, since he would probably like to be alone.

"Oh no. Stick around. I want to talk to you."

I found out later that while I was trying to get the press room, Ellen was frantically trying to find me. It seems that a young child actor and his entourage (including Mama) had decided to cash in on some of the publicity our con was receiving. They wanted free passes—five of 'em! Ellen had said no. They insisted. Everyone started to look for me. Why it never occurred to anyone to call Bill's suite, I'll never know. Only three-thousand-odd people had seen me leave with him. Sigh. It was finally taken care of, but everyone was miffed at me for not telling them where I was—for all of an hour and fifteen minutes. Another sigh.

Anyway, after Bill had finished talking with Teddy, I talked to him about the people who had requested interviews. Since his time was limited, he decided to limit this to major media. I made the appointments. Then, taking another orange and giving me half, Bill settled back on the couch, and we talked about other cons and fans, fanzines, and fandom. Bill was really interested, and we talked until he was due to go down for his press conference.

At one point, Bill looked at me very seriously and said, "You know that you have been haunting me the last eight or nine months?"

"I . . . what?!" I gasped.

"You've been haunting me. Everywhere I've gone I'd be introduced to someone who'd be sure to say, 'Oh, we have a mutual friend—Joanie Winston!' From Seattle to Philadelphia, Detroit to New York, there was sure to be one person who would say that to me."

"You're kidding! I'm terribly sorry. I . . ."

He laughed. "Oh, I know you had nothing to do with it, but it has really been strange. The topper was the time I was walking down Fifty-seventh Street here in New York with Teddy. I was telling him all about this and he was assuring me that it was all my imagination. Just then, a friend of his came walking up the street toward us. He stopped to say hello, and Teddy introduced us. His friend got 'that look' on his face, and I grabbed Teddy's arm. Smiling, his friend said, 'We have a mutual friend,' and in chorus we both said, 'Joanie Winston.' Teddy and I laughed wildly, and I'm sure his friend thought we'd both been drinking or something. We explained the joke, and his friend's comment was, 'But I do know Joanie!' "

"I have a lot of friends," I said.

"Boy, do you."

Yeah, and ain't it great!

Back to the press conference—and it was a killer. We had so many people guarding Bill you couldn't even see him. We were squirted into the press room like icing out of a pastry tube. What I will never forgive myself for is that I did not see that the so-helpful helpers shoved my press room helpers aside and shut the door in their faces! You can bet I heard about that afterward—and was I mad. I found some of these people later and lit into them. I mean, my kids work hard and almost always miss most of the con. But they do it because they get to see the stars at their interviews, and that makes up for it. But they did not get to see Bill. Please forgive me, Carol, Ruth, Nora, Allyson, Helen, and Marty, it's just that Ellen and I were so busy trying to make order out of the bedlam we didn't notice. In that little room, which was supposed to hold about 150 people, over 200 bodies were squished inside. If there had been rafters, they would have been hanging from them!

As a matter of fact, our lawyer, Bob Harris, made an announcement that if the room did not quiet down, the fire marshals (hi, fellas, nice to see you again) would clear the room.

That didn't work too well. Then Bill tried.

"Quiet down, please. Hang on a second. Don't yell. Why doesn't everyone take one step back, and this gentleman will be happy."

All the while the fans were snapping pictures and shouting questions, and I was tapping Bill on the shoulder motioning for him to give me the mike. I would make them quiet down or die trying.

Bill finally turned to me with a wry grin. "So much for the voice of command."

Then I tried. "Unless you people settle down, the entire room will be cleared and there will be *no press conference*. I WANT TO HEAR SILENCE!!!"

The silence fell like a load of cement, then there was a sudden gust of laughter. I turned and caught Bill making faces behind me, and he saw me and suddenly saluted. Another laugh.

Oh well, at least they were quiet.

Here are some excerpts from the press conference:

FAN: "How does an actor prepare for the part of a man who really doesn't exist in our time and will not exist for many centuries to come?"

BILL SHATNER: "The answer to that came to me when I saw the first pilot. I'm sure you all know that there were two pilots made—one with Jeff Hunter playing the lead, and then mine. And I saw that the first pilot had a kind of 'Look at us, we're sailing a starship in the skies' feeling of self-importance, and it seemed to me that was the major fault in it. If a soldier or a sailor or whatever part of the armed forces an *Enterprise* crew member was a part of had been commissioned to go into space, by that time it would have been as much a part of his or her life as driving a car. For example, a young man asked me in the elevator how I felt about all this, facing all of you and talking, trying to make some sense, and I answered that I didn't even think about it—it was just part of my job. Part of meeting the fans—getting to know you and getting you to know me. I don't think of it as being strange. I don't think of this moment as being anything different or out of the ordinary, although, in fact, it really *is*. It's given to very few people. That's the way I approached playing the part, as though starship duties and adventures were part of everyday affairs. Taking on the Klingons in space would be as normal to Kirk as sailing the seas flying the British flag was to Horatio Hornblower—nothing out of the ordinary. . . . Kirk would be at home on the *Enterprise*, despite his specialized job. And that's how I approached the part. Yes, dear . . ."

FAN: (indistinct)

BILL SHATNER: "The question is: Why do I think 'Star Trek' lives? I . . . I don't know. I can hazard a guess.

"I can only ascribe the popularity of 'Star Trek' to the fact that it appeals on a great many levels: To the kids it's the action and adventure; to the people who are older than kids it probably appeals intellectually as well as on the entertainment level, with the costumes and the action. And then there's a hard-core group, of which I guess we are all members—the science-fiction buffs—and to them it was done well in terms of science fiction. So I think there's no *one* answer to why 'Star Trek' appeals to all you people and continues to over the years. I think it's a complex, multifaceted answer."

FAN: "You've referred to yourself as a science-fiction buff. Were you interested in science fiction before 'Star Trek,' or did 'Star Trek' interest you in science fiction?"

BILL SHATNER: "No, I have read a great deal, and the authors . . . you're going to ask me for the authors . . . Isaac Asimov definitely is one and Theodore Sturgeon and . . . but I can't remember all the authors. Before 'Star Trek' there was more time to read, and I was really into science fiction. [laughter]

"Then 'Star Trek' came along and there were probably unconscious reasons behind my decision to do the pilot. When I was approached and asked if I would like to be in it, and they showed me the first pilot, I had previously made two pilots that hadn't sold, and I was in what I thought to be—and may very well have been—a precarious position. The American position is 'three strikes and you're out,' you know, and I thought if I made another pilot that didn't sell, I might be in some trouble as an actor to get another pilot. I knew I had to choose very carefully, and I think my background in reading science fiction had a great deal to do with the reasons behind my choice. Yes, I was very much a science buff."

FAN: (indistinct)

BILL SHATNER: "I only heard part of that. Did it come naturally to me to . . . to . . ."

JOAN WINSTON: ". . . to use your intuition, as Kirk."

BILL SHATNER: "Oh, as opposed to Spock's logic. [laughter] Well, there's a differentiation in your question. One is what I as an individual could do, and what I was given as an actor to read and interpret within the prescribed lines of the character—which had to be intuitive. But I think, as an individual and as an actor, that I'm more intuitive than logical. I've done a lot of things in my life that, looking back, had no logical basis whatever, and perhaps were mistakes because they were emotionally done. So I would term myself more intuitive and emotional than logical, and so if you're asking me if I identified with those areas of the Kirk character, yes, I did. Yes."

FAN: "At the thought that what you do . . ." (indistinct)

BILL SHATNER: (overlapping) "The thought . . . She's saying, 'Do you recognize that what you do may influence some person?' That's absolutely right. I think that that aspect of a personality's public life is not always taken into consideration by the personality. I don't, for example, indicate publicly what my private views are on a great many subjects, including politics, because of my fear of influencing those who should not be influenced and who should be thinking for themselves."

FAN: "In the 1930s, Buster Crabbe became very famous doing the "Flash Gordon" and the "Buck Rogers" series. In the thirty years in between, when you became perhaps the leading series star in a science-fiction medium on 'Star Trek,' would you say there were many changes that happened to the principal-character concept in those thirty years?"

BILL SHATNER: "Well, certainly between Buster Crabbe . . . certainly between Flash Gordon and Captain Kirk. [laugh-

144 THE MAKING OF THE TREK CONVENTIONS

ter] I think the major difference would be *humanity*. And
perhaps the difference between Mr. Crabbe and myself is
that he was a swimmer and I was an actor to begin with, so
maybe the techniques of approaching the part had something to do with it—I mean, I used the breaststroke and he
used the crawl, you know." (laughter)

FAN: "It's been a long time since you really played Captain
Kirk, and you have done a great deal since then and
presumably have developed as an actor and as a person.
Would you have difficulty going back if you were to play the
role again?"

BILL SHATNER: "That's a very interesting question. I've asked
myself that very same thing: What would I do? And I think
that the most significant thing that happened in the past five
years is that I have learned to *give* more than I did then.

That three-year period—the 'Star Trek' years—was a very
unhappy period in my life. Personally. Things have really
worked out for me on a personal level to such a degree that
I feel, without having trained technically, that my work has
improved because my personal life has improved.[3] And I
feel an openness and a giving—in performing and, I guess,
in relating to you—that I never felt before. I think I would
expose more of Kirk, as a man, as a person, than I did then.

"The relationship between the fictional Captain Kirk and
the real William Shatner is a very intertwined one, and I say
that because in doing a series you don't have time to pre-
tend. By fatigue and just merely becoming accustomed to
the camera being there, it no longer really feels like you're
acting. You're there among friends—playing Charades, almost. Not really, but I'm trying to indicate the warmth that
exists. You almost forget to act; you forget to dissimulate. So
that with any series that has lasted any significant length of
time, what you're seeing is really the actor permeating the
guise of the character he portrays. . . .

"When you would meet an actor associated with a certain
leading-character role, you would probably think, 'Hey, he
really is like his character—it really *is* him!' You're probably
seeing this in me, thinking, "He is Kirk. . . ." It happens—

[3] Mr. Shatner remarried during this period.

the actor has forgotten to control his gestures, his own personality. By this time, he and the character are one. What you saw as Captain Kirk was a very intertwined combination of both myself and the words I was given as an actor to say."

We ended the conference here, as we had to get Bill onstage for his panel with George, Gene, Majel, and Bob Lansing.

Before we continue, I think it only right and proper to describe the rest of the con and not let myself get carried away by Captain Kirk (what a lovely thought!). To give you an idea of all the preparation that goes into putting on one of these cons, why not take a look at the master program Elyse set up for 1975?

All events marked with an asterisk (*) appeared on the printed program given out to the press and fans. Events marked with a dagger (†) are specialized fan activities; they did not appear on the program, but were usually posted around the convention floor. All the rest were to guide us in carrying out the many tasks involved in running the convention smoothly (it should only happen!).

We killed Elyse for that "Rise and shine" at 7:00 A.M. Most of us would not see our beds until three or four in the morning.

My beloved Mike Weisel took care of the films for me, and with the help of the projectionist, Herbie Colt, ran them very well. A pause here for a special thank you to the projectionists' union. They always sent us their best, and that meant a smoothly running film schedule. So thank you Mike Tarr, Wally Olebsky, Herbie Colt, Max Glenn, and Sam Soltan. You were all a joy, and we love you, fellas.

Here's a funny that happened at the 1974 convention. The projectionist, Wally, had been on duty for several hours. I offered to relieve him so he could get a drink, eat, go to the john, or whatever. Without taking his eyes off the screen—he was running *City on the Edge of Forever* at the time—he exclaimed, "I can't leave now. I haven't seen the rest of this episode!"

What makes this so delightful is that he hadn't even heard of "Star Trek" prior to that morning. Wally ended up a full-fledged

MASTER PROGRAM

TIME	EVENT	LOCATION
Wednesday, February 12, 1975		
2:00 P.M.	Committee check-in at hotel	Presidential suite
XXX	Truck Rental and trips	
XXX	Pick up projectors and screens	
	Party for us by hotel (?)	XXX
Thursday, February 13, 1975		
2:00 P.M.	Hotel check-in by assistants and guests	Presidential suite
6:00 P.M.–11:00 P.M.	Art Show set-up	West Ballroom
7:00 P.M.–11:00 P.M.	Dealers' set-up	Windsor complex
7:00 P.M.–10:00 P.M.	Helper registration	
6:00 P.M.	Security begins	
XXX	Guest arrival	
Friday, February 14, 1975		
7:00 A.M.	Rise and shine	
7:30 A.M.– 8:00 A.M.	Breakfast	
8:30 A.M.– 9:00 A.M.	Worry room (con HQ) set-up	Presidential suite
8:30 A.M.– 9:00 A.M.	Registration set-up	Parlor A
9:00 A.M.– 9:30 A.M.	Dealers' set-up	Grand BR foyer
9:00 A.M.– 7:00 P.M.	Registration	Windsor complex
9:00 A.M.– 7:00 P.M.	Worry room (Con HQ)	Grand BR foyer
9:00 A.M.– 7:00 P.M.	Information desk	Parlor A
		Grand BR foyer

TIME	EVENT	LOCATION
9:30 A.M.– 8:00 P.M.	Dealers' room	Windsor complex
10:00 A.M.– 4:00 P.M.	Art Show set-up	West Ballroom
10:00 A.M.– 6:00 P.M.	Press room	Parlor B
11:00 A.M.– 2:00 P.M.	Films*	Grand Ballroom
2:00 P.M.– 3:30 P.M.	Mike McMaster: "Special Effects"**	Grand Ballroom
2:00 P.M.– 3:00 A.M.	Films*	East Ballroom
3:30 P.M.– 5:00 P.M.	Fan Panel*	Grand Ballroom
4:00 P.M.– 6:00 P.M.	Art Show	West Ballroom
4:30 P.M.– 6:00 P.M.	Press party set-up	Presidential suite
5:00 P.M.– 7:30 P.M.	Dinner break*	
6:00 P.M.	Press Room closes	Parlor B
6:00 P.M.	Art Show closes	West Ballroom
6:00 P.M.–10:00 P.M.	Press party	Presidential suite
7:00 P.M.	Registration closes	Grand BR foyer
7:30 P.M.– 8:30 P.M.	"Andromeda Light Show"**	Grand Ballroom
8:00 P.M.	Dealers' room closes	Windsor complex
8:30 P.M.– 3:00 A.M.	Films*	Grand Ballroom
10:00 P.M.–11:00 P.M.	Art Show judging	West Ballroom
3:00 A.M.	Films end	East and Grand ballrooms

Saturday, February 15, 1975

TIME	EVENT	LOCATION
7:00 A.M.	Rise and shine	
7:30 A.M.– 8:00 A.M.	Breakfast—committee and assistants	Presidential suite
8:30 A.M.– 9:00 A.M.	Registration set-up	Grand BR foyer

TIME	EVENT	LOCATION
9:00 A.M.– 9:30 A.M.	Dealers' set-up	Windsor complex
9:00 A.M.– 7:00 P.M.	Registration	Grand BR foyer
9:00 A.M.– 8:00 P.M.	Worry room (con HQ)	Parlor A
9:00 A.M.– 7:00 P.M.	Information desk	Grand BR foyer
9:30 A.M.– 8:00 P.M.	Dealers' room	Windsor complex
10:00 A.M.– 6:00 P.M.	Press room	Parlor B
10:00 A.M.– 6:00 P.M.	Art Show	West Ballroom
10:00 A.M.– 3:00 A.M.	Films*	East Ballroom
10:00 A.M.–12:00 NOON	Fan room: "Star Trek" Federation of Fans† Gee Moaven	Room 107
10:00 A.M.–11:00 A.M.	Panel: "From Script to Seam"* William Theiss, David Gerrold (Dave Simons, Mod.)	Grand Ballroom
11:00 A.M.–12:00 NOON	Hal Clement: "The Peeling of the Apple"*	Grand Ballroom
12:00 NN– 1:00 P.M.	Gene Roddenberry*	Grand Ballroom
1:00 P.M.– 1:30 P.M.	William Shatner: Rap Session*	Grand Ballroom
1:30 P.M.– 2:30 P.M.	Lunch break*	
2:00 P.M.– 4:00 P.M.	Fan room: S.T.A.R. of New York† Germaine Best	Room 107
2:00 P.M.– 4:00 P.M.	Fan room: U.N.I.S.T.A.R.† Geoffry Mandel	Room 108
2:30 P.M.– 4:00 P.M.	Richard C. Hoagland: "From Stonehenge to 'Star Trek' and beyond"*	Grand Ballroom

TIME	EVENT	LOCATION
4:00 P.M.– 5:00 P.M.	Panel: "Aboard the Good Ship *Enterprise*"* William Shatner, George Takei, Gene Roddenberry (David Gerrold, Mod.)	Grand Ballroom
5:00 P.M.– 6:00 P.M.	Majel Barrett Roddenberry*	Grand Ballroom
6:00 P.M.– 7:30 P.M.	Dinner break*	
6:00 P.M.	Press room closes	Parlor B
6:00 P.M.	Art show closes	West Ballroom
7:00 P.M.	Registration closes	Grand BR foyer
7:00 P.M.	Information desk closes	Grand BR foyer
7:00 P.M.– 9:00 P.M.	Helpers' party set-up	Presidential Suite
7:30 P.M.– 8:30 P.M.	"Andromeda Light Show"*	Grand Ballroom
8:00 P.M.	Worry room (con HQ) closes	Parlor A
8:00 P.M.	Dealers' room closes	Windsor complex
8:30 P.M.–12 MDNT	Open house: S.T.A.R.† Germaine Best, Hostess	Room 107
8:30 P.M.–12 MDNT	Open house: "Star Trek" Welcommittee† Allyson Whitfield, Hostess	Room 108
8:30 P.M.– 3:00 A.M.	Films*	Grand Ballroom
9:00 P.M.–12:00 MDNT	Helpers' party	Presidential suite
3:00 A.M.	Films end	East and Grand ballrooms
Sunday, February 16, 1975		
7:00 A.M.	Rise and shine	
7:30 A.M.– 8:00 A.M.	Breakfast for committe and assistants	Presidential suite

TIME	EVENT	LOCATION
8:30 A.M.– 9:00 A.M.	Registration set-up	Grand BR foyer
9:00 A.M.– 9:30 A.M.	Dealers' set-up	Windsor complex
9:00 A.M.– 6:00 P.M.	Art Show	West Ballroom
9:00 A.M.– 7:00 P.M.	Registration	Grand BR foyer
9:00 A.M.– 7:00 P.M.	Information desk	Grand BR foyer
9:00 A.M.– 8:00 P.M.	Worry room (con HQ)	Parlor A
9:30 A.M.– 8:00 P.M.	Dealers' room	Windsor complex
10:00 A.M.– 6:00 P.M.	Press room	Parlor B
10:00 A.M.– 6:00 P.M.	Films*	East Ballroom
10:00 A.M.–12:00 NOON	Art auction No. 1	Grand Ballroom
12:00 NN– 1:00 P.M.	Isaac Asimov*	Grand Ballroom
12:00 NN– 2:00 P.M.	Fan room: Friends of William Shatner† Maxine Broadwater	Room 107
12:00 NN– 2:00 P.M.	Fan room: Senior Citizens' Group† Ethel Andonucci	Room 108
1:00 P.M.– 2:00 P.M.	Lunch break	
2:00 P.M.– 3:00 P.M.	William Shatner	Grand Ballroom
3:00 P.M.– 4:00 P.M.	Writers' panel:* Gene Roddenberry, Isaac Asimov, David Gerrold, Hal Clement (Dave Simons, Mod.)	Grand Ballroom
4:00 P.M.– 6:00 P.M.	William Ware Theiss—costume demonstration	Grand Ballroom
4:00 P.M.– 6:00 P.M.	Fan room: "Star Trek" Welcommittee† Allyson Whitfield	Room 107

TIME	EVENT	LOCATION
4:00 P.M.– 6:00 P.M.	Fan room: Teachers†	Room 108
	Brian McCarthy	
6:00 P.M.– 7:30 P.M.	Dinner break*	
6:00 P.M.	Art Show closes	West Ballroom
6:00 P.M.	Press room closes	Parlor B
6:00 P.M.	Films end	East Ballroom
7:00 P.M.	Registration closes	Grand BR foyer
7:00 P.M.	Information desk closes	Grand BR foyer
7:30 P.M.– 9:00 P.M.	Masquerade prejudging*	East Ballroom
8:00 P.M.	Worry room (con HQ) closes	Parlor A
8:00 P.M.	Dealers' room closes	Windsor complex
9:00 P.M.– 1:00 A.M.	Federation Masquerade*	Grand Ballroom
10:00 P.M.– 3:00 A.M.	Films*	East Ballroom

Monday, February 17, 1975

TIME	EVENT	LOCATION
7:00 A.M.	Rise and shine	
7:30 A.M.– 8:00 A.M.	Breakfast for committee and assistants	Presidential suite
8:30 A.M.– 9:00 A.M.	Registration set-up	Grand BR foyer
9:00 A.M.– 9:30 A.M.	Dealers' set-up	Windsor complex
9:00 A.M.– 3:00 P.M.	Registration	Grand BR foyer
9:00 A.M.– 4:00 P.M.	Information desk	Grand BR foyer
9:00 A.M.– 5:00 P.M.	Worry room (con HQ)	Parlor A
10:00 A.M.– 3:00 P.M.	Press room	Parlor B
10:00 A.M.– 4:00 P.M.	Art Show	West Ballroom

TIME	EVENT	LOCATION
11:00 A.M.– 4:00 P.M.	Films*	East Ballroom
11:00 A.M.– 1:00 P.M.	Art Auction No. 2*	Grand Ballroom (LN)
1:00 P.M.– 2:00 P.M.	Lunch break	
2:00 P.M.– 3:00 P.M.	David Gerrold*	Grand Ballroom
3:00 P.M.– 4:00 P.M.	George Takei*	Grand Ballroom
3:00 P.M.	Press room closes	Parlor B
3:00 P.M.	Registration closes	Grand BR foyer
4:00 P.M.	Information desk closes	Grand BR foyer
4:00 P.M.	Dealers' room closes	Windsor complex
4:00 P.M.	Convention officially ends	
5:00 P.M.	Worry room (con HQ) closes	Parlor A
5:00 P.M.	Security ends	
8:00 P.M.	"Dead Dog" party	Presidential suite

Tuesday, February 18, 1975

4:00 P.M.	Check-out time (extended)	Lobby registration desk

fan, and we got him what he wanted most of all: a "Star Trek" T-shirt, size large.

As usual, I missed most of the programing. We were setting up the press room and arranging interviews and running around a lot. I had promised Jeff Maynard I would see the Light Show this year, but no luck. I heard the fans loved it and promised Jeff I would positively see it the next time. Famous last words!

After Jeff's show, we ran films until 3:00 A.M. (yawn), and there were about five hundred diehards who stayed up to see 'em, too. I saw the last ten minutes of *Where No Man Has Gone Before,* and then helped cart the films and equipment up to the con suite.

7:00 A.M.: Rise and shine, and the thundering horde charged into the con suite, where Devra made them eggs and bacon and goodies.[4] Grand—but they had to pass my door to get to the dining room. I finally put up a sign on the front door that said: "Joanie is sleeping. Keep the noise down to a dull roar or your ass is grass." It helped a little.

My press assistant, Ellen Schlakman, would open up the press room every morning. Bless her curly head. This let me get a few precious extra hours of sleep.

On the way to the press room, I poked my head into the main ballroom to see David Gerrold and Bill Theiss' panel. Everyone seemed to be enjoying themselves, and I was sorry I couldn't stay.

I heard some fans talking about Hal Clement later in the day and realized I had missed him completely. Sigh.

I did manage to hear a bit of Gene Roddenberry's speech before going to pick up Bill Shatner. Lord, but Gene is electric. He holds an audience in the palm of his hand. Gene spoke about the upcoming movie (large standing ovation). Herewith, some excerpts:

"I'll move into the news of the movie right now. And I think the news is good. I had hoped to be able to come here and say we actually had a signed contract, but I think we have the very next best thing to it: The agency says that all of the problems for

[4] By the way, Devra managed this miracle on two hotplates and an electric frypan!

a 'Star Trek' movie, all the major problems and all the hurdles have now been resolved, and Paramount has put on their 1975[5] schedule of information to their stockholders that a 'Star Trek' motion picture will be shot at the studio. (applause)

"The discussions, as I've said to many of you at college and university campuses—the discussions did not go easily. At first they decided that they would recast 'Star Trek' with proven box-office names. They probably had something in mind like perhaps Clint Walker for Captain Kirk and Robert Redford for Mr. Spock [laughter], but the fans, including many of you here, heard about Paramount's attitude—I don't know quite how you heard about it—but you got the news some way, and Paramount was deluged, probably with more mail about this decision than they were about the initial motion picture. It took just about thirty days of that mail for Paramount to capitulate entirely and say, 'We do want the original cast.' [applause]

"I talked to all of the actors involved, and assuming that their schedules are free—assuming that Paramount does not ask them to do it for nothing, which may be close to Paramount's first offer —they have all indicated that, all things being equal, liking the script and so on, that they are interested, they're delighted, and they would like to do it. [applause]

"I think the next question would be, 'What about "Star Trek" afterward?' Discussions with both Paramount and NBC have gone something like this: If the motion picture is successful, one of two things, or perhaps both, could happen. Very possibly it could become a series of theatrically released motion pictures [applause] very much in the way that the first *Planet of the Apes,* and the James Bond series got started. As for television, NBC agrees that if the motion picture is successful, that it is very possible and very likely that we could arrange some sort of return, not in competition with the original show, but something I think would suit all the performers and staff much more—that's to come back each season with a group of 'Star Trek' television movies, specials, either ninety-minute or two-hour [applause] . . . and my discussions at Paramount have been in agreement

[5] As of June 1977, the motion picture has been cancelled and Paramount has announced a new TV version of "Star Trek." What will really happen? Well, your guess is as good as mine. Keep your fingers and toes crossed.

with the idea. And so without saying that anyone is committed to this, this is very much the direction that we are thinking and very much the direction we would like to go. [applause]

After lunch (we always made a point of putting that in the schedule; while we might not have time to eat, at least the fans could grab a bite), Dick Hoagland gave his talk entitled "From Stonehenge to 'Star Trek' and Beyond." Using both NASA and "Star Trek" slides, he gave a fascinating talk on the steps leading up to more voyages into space. Dick is an excellent speaker and also worked on the project to name the space shuttle the *Enterprise*.

We were now on our way from the press room with Bill Shatner, taking him to the main ballroom for the "Aboard the Starship *Enterprise*" panel. Bill had not seen Gene, Majel, and George in many moons—at least since recording the "Star Trek" animated series. He had not seen Bob Lansing since they had done *Assignment: Earth* back in 1967.

Just before this panel we discovered we had lost George. Again. Between the ballroom entrance and the stage. Thom had brought him down and aimed him at Elyse on the stage. She lost him in a swirl of bodies and grew a dozen gray hairs until he was discovered happily signing autographs in the middle of an even happier crowd. Another George story. George loves the fans—he loves to speak to them and really get close to them. George was going to take a turn around the dealers' room, and security and Thom were escorting him. George suddenly ran ahead, and there was Thom calling, "George, George, wait for me, wait for me!" We love you, George, but please don't take such chances!

This entrance was handled much more smoothly. A path had been cleared through the Art Show so that the stars did not have to pass through the main lobby outside the ballroom. This got to be a sore point with Louise Sachter and Wendy Lindboe, who were running the Art Show that year. Some people seemed to think they could shut down the Art Show for almost any reason. A wild-eyed helper would run into the room and shriek, "You have to close off the room because Muggeldy Wump is coming through." They would obediently close down the room and then find out that M.W. had made its entrance somewhere else and no one on the Committee knew anything about the helper or his message. Very strange—and aggravating. This, however, was one of the legal times.

As we walked through, I mentioned Gene's sore hip. Bill had not heard of the accident, and on mounting the stage went immediately to Gene. They greeted each other warmly (cheers from the fans), and Bill asked some very concerned questions about Gene's hip. Gene said it was feeling much better, and Bill reached over and greeted Majel, George, and Bob Lansing.

The fans were in ecstasy. It was the first time Bill and Gene had been together at a convention.

They began, with David Gerrold as moderator and Linda Deneroff handling the question line. For the most part, the questions were intelligent, as were the answers. One fan asked why the bridge was at the top of the ship, an unprotected area, instead of deep within the bowels. Gene answered him by saying that many things were done on the *Enterprise* that were not totally logical, but that the show was being played to a twentieth-century audience. "The great problem in science fiction is to get a sense of identification, a sense that this is really happening. You have to pull back a little because your audience is preconditioned to a certain extent as to what can be done."

Bob Lansing was asked why *Assignment: Earth* was never picked up for a series. Bob passed the ball to Gene, and he thought it was still a good idea and announced that it was going to be re-presented to the networks. The fans greeted this with great joy.

A young fan asked Bill Shatner: "How do you become a star?" Bill gave it some thought and then said: "Well, first of all, you have to twinkle." The audience gave a great roar of laughter, but the young fan looked a bit confused.

One fan asked George Takei what he had been doing since "Star Trek." He spoke of an upcoming special, *Year of the Dragon,* and of his work with the Transportation Board in Los Angeles. (I saw *Year of the Dragon,* and George was brilliant.) Gene added a comment that he would not be surprised if George became a senator one day because of all the good work he had

William Shatner speaking before enthusiastic fans at the 1975 con. This was taken just before the little lost boy was brought onstage. *(Jeff Maynard)*

At the 1975 Masquerade, the judges include a fan, Hal Clement, Joan Winston (hands showing), William Ware Theiss, Robert Lansing, and Diane Duane. In the first now-famous wheelchair is Claire Eddy, with Helen Reed in the other and Val Sussman in between. The sign on Helen's wheelchair says, "Warning, this vehicle cruises at Warp 8!" *(Jeff Maynard)*

William Ware Theiss answering questions during his fashion show at the 1975 con. *(Benjamin M. Yalow)*

Howard Weinstein, author of the animate episode *Pirates of Orion*, making his fir appearance as a guest at the 1976 co *(Benjamin M. Yalow)*

Cyrano Jones, Vina, and Scotty—oops, I mean, Stanley Adams, Susan Oliver, and James Doohan at Bicentennial 10 in 1976. Jimmy's shirt says, "Eric's Dad." Eric is the new edition to the Doohan clan, born just before the con. *(Jeff Maynard)*

Jacqueline Lichtenberg and Gene Roddenberry enjoying a chat at the 1975 press party. *(Linda Deneroff)*

Gene and Majel Roddenberry communicating with all their fans at the 1976 con. *(Linda Deneroff)*

Grace Lee Whitney signing her autograph for pleased fans at Bicentennial 10 in 1976. *(Jeff Maynard)*

been doing in California. One good reason to move to sunny Cal: to be able to vote for George!

Someone asked George about his fencing in *Naked Time*. Bill turned to George after he had answered and asked whether he had continued fencing since that time. George said, "You may not know it, but yes." Bill was very pleased to hear that because on the set George was very enthusiastic: "He cut the cameraman. Gene came down to the set to see what was happening, and he sliced him in half." [loud laughter to both these remarks] During the taping, I had to take the sword away from him and he was impossible to get ahold of. So I grabbed him by the throat and choked him." [laughter and applause] George replied that what the rest of the cast didn't recognize was that an actor has to be prepared. Then he told of constant practicing on the set. Bill pointed out, "Every time the director yelled 'cut'— George did!" [huge roar and applause].

George said, "Touché" [another roar].

Gene was asked if he was going to change anything basic in the "Star Trek" universe. He said that every time he goes to bed with Majel Barrett, he hears she is going to get more and better lines. He laughed and then said he didn't think that any major changes would take place. Turning to Bill, he then asked what changes he would like to see. Bill's reply, tongue firmly in cheek, was "Get rid of George!" George answered, "Yeah, make him the captain." The audience broke up. (I wonder: Is this where the "Sulu for captain" campaign began?) Then Bill, more seriously, said, "I imagine there will obviously be some changes, since we have all grown." George quickly interjected, "The word is 'aged'!"

Someone asked Gene how he could justify the many instances of interference that the *Enterprise* and her crew had made on other planets. Gene replied that the justification was in the area of the story. "The No. 1 rule was that we did not have the right to interfere with the evolvement of other people. Vietnam was getting started at that time, as you remember, and the purpose of one show was to try to sneak in a statement against Vietnam, and I think we were successful. Sometimes we let ourselves get more involved than others—it was a case of trying to keep eighteen million people watching every week."

One question asked of Majel Barrett Roddenberry got a roar of approval from the audience. "How did you enjoy those scenes with Spock?" Majel's answer got another roar—of laughter. "Since he only came into heat every seven years, it really didn't come to much."

Bill was asked, "How does it feel to have the ears on?" He paused for a moment, then said, "Well, logically speaking," and then went into detail telling of Leonard's travails with the "ears." How much earlier he had to report to make-up and how uncomfortable they were. "The one time I had them on [The Enterprise Incident], I sympathized with him for the rest of the series, and felt very sorry for him."

At one point Bill was asked how he liked doing The Trouble with Tribbles by David Gerrold. He said it was one of the cast's favorite shows and everyone had enjoyed themselves. David, who was moderating the panel (and doing a superb job, as usual) said, "Let me just add a note here. Writing lines for the cast of 'Star Trek' can spoil a writer because when you see the lines you've written played that well and that competently— when they bring it to life so brilliantly—you get spoiled and you start expecting it from other actors, too, and it disappoints you when they can't deliver the same quality."

The last question was addressed to both David and Gene. A young man who was very interested in the technical end of the program asked why the space station in the Tribbles episode rotated; it had artificial gravity, so why did it have to rotate? A good question, Gene replied, and quickly passed the ball to David, who said, "Gene should answer it; he produced the show." Gene grinned and shook his head. David then answered that he had not done that; all he had written was that there was a space station and "somebody else did, it wasn't. . . . You're right, it's a mistake." This honest statement was greeted with loud laughter and applause.

The panelists made a quick exit except for Majel and Bob. It was supposed to be a solo for Majel, but she made Bob stay, and they both enjoyed it. During the talk she related the story of how she and Gene got married. It is absolutely delightful, and I will tell it in Majel's own words; I only hope you can imagine the style and charm in which she told the story.

"Gene was doing a picture in Japan for MGM. I got a call from him one night saying that I should come to Japan immediately and we would get married. 'Hop on the next plane,' was the way he put it. There was one problem: I didn't have a passport, and it takes, usually, ten days to get a passport.

"I went over to the passport office and spoke to a very nice man. Well, actually, I cried at him. He was the one who told me it took ten days. I said, 'But that's impossible. I have to leave tomorrow (sob) to get married (sob, sniff),'" and I think he got me the passport just to prevent his office from being flooded. [laughter]

"I got on the plane, I don't remember what airline I was so hysterical at that point, and we went flying off into the wild blue yonder. The pilot comes on and says, 'Good morning, welcome to flight so-and-so, we'll be flying at an altitude of so-and-so, and we will be coming into Anchorage, Alaska. . . .' ANCHORAGE, ALASKA!!! I screamed—I was on the wrong plane! Anyway, the pilot went on to explain that this was the first stop on our polar flight to the Orient.

"So, I thought, if I have to go through this hell, the least Gene could do is go through part of it, too.

"We got to Anchorage, and it was like a pitstop for refueling, and I asked, 'Where's the telephone?' I called Gene in Japan. It had to be about four or five in the morning. They woke him up and said, 'Mr. Roddenberry, we have a collect call for you from Miss Barrett in Anchorage, Alaska.' He didn't believe what he had heard, but said, 'Who was going to turn down a call like that?' [laugher] So he picked up the phone, and I said, 'Honey, I've gotten on the wrong plane.' There is this dead silence on the other end of the line. He's thinking, 'I'm going to marry an idiot, right?' [laughter] Then in this awful German accent he said, 'All right, vhat you do is you get back on zee plane, go back to Los Angeles, und ztart all ofer again!' [laughter]

"I finally told Gene that actually it was another way to get to Japan—*he* had gone by way of Hawaii—and here I am, in Anchorage, Alaska!

"Anyway, we got married in a Shinto temple, in a shinto ceremony, that's the most important part. We've always felt we were kind of international and it didn't matter where we were, we'd just adopt the customs of the time and place. So we were married in a Shinto shrine with a Shinto ceremony. I had two maidens in attendance, two musicians, two priests—it was just great!

"MGM put the whole thing on 35mm color film and we thought that was marvelous, except we don't have a 35mm projector, so we've never seen it. [laughter] So anyway, we got married, toured Japan for two weeks, and it was a lot of fun."

Majel has pictures of the two of them in their Japanese marriage clothes. It's a gorgeous picture—ask her to show it to you sometime.

I had to leave after this, since I had to check the press room. I was very bad at this con. I let Ellen run it most of the time, and a very good job she did, too.

After that I checked around the con and then went up to bathe and change for the helpers' party. I wanted to grab a quick bite, too, since I had to meet Bill at 8:00 P.M. to take him to an interview I had set up prior to his appearance at the party at 9:00 P.M. (The helpers' party is set up for all the lovely people who work for twelve to sixteen hours a day for nothing but a free pass and peanut butter sandwiches—sometimes with jelly. For many of them this is their only chance to see the stars during the conventions due to the fact that they are chained, er, locked on duty in the film room, Art Show, doorways, con suite, etc.) I took a bath but had no time for a bite—as usual. There was some problem with the smaller film room, which was cleared up just in time to rush down to the mezzanine and pick up Bill.

He had had a lovely dinner and was in a marvelous mood. To get to the freight elevator (You didn't think we would take him up one of the front elevators, with eight thousand fans roaming the halls, did you? That we did on Sunday—a story of epic proportions!), we had to walk up two flights of fire stairs to get to where the freight elevator stopped. As we started up the first flight, Bill took me around the waist and started jogging up the stairs.

"Come on, or is everyone but Joan and me out of condition?"

In our enthusiasm we bounded up *three* flights and almost burst out onto the ballroom floor! Just as Bill started to push the door open I glanced through the window and yelled, "No, no, we can't go out there!"

Bill grabbed me around the waist again and, almost lifting me off the floor, turned and charged through the security squad and fans massed on the stair below us. As he ran, Bill yelled, "Run, run, the bogie man is after us!"

The fans scattered right and left as we ran down the stairs. Breathless, I pointed at the correct door, and we galloped through, with security and the helpers racing after us. We raced to the end of the hall, where Bill suddenly turned and said, "No, no, they're coming that way, too!" and we ran back down the hallway, strewing fans in our wake.

By this time, everyone with breath left was in hysterics. As I leaned against the wall wondering if I'd ever breathe again, Bill walked over to the now-waiting elevator and, hands on hips, looking for all the world like our Captain Kirk, calmly said, "I thought we were going upstairs. Why are you all standing around?"

I'm sure the elevator operator thought we had all misplaced our marbles when we fell into his elevator in wild hysterics. He turned to Bill, the only seemingly sane passenger, and asked, "What floor?"

"Twenty-two," we chorused and collapsed again. Bill wasn't laughing, but he did have a huge grin on his face.

The helpers who were with us for that wild run have never forgotten it—or their very own private adventure with the star of "Star Trek." I left Bill to his interview and went back to my room to take another bath!

I went back to his suite at nine o'clock to pick him up for the helpers' party. The reporter (for a Canadian paper) wasn't quite finished, and we waited for about five minutes.

Bill gave me his coat as we walked into the con suite and took a deep breath. He was really scared this time—I can understand why. He had no stage to act as a buffer. He was surrounded in seconds. Bill backed up and tried to gracefully dodge behind Claire Eddy and her wheelchair, figuring the fans would be careful of Claire. Hah!

I suddenly gasped. Right behind Bill's slowly retreating form was a wide-open window. I had this instant picture of his falling twenty-two stories and *splatt!*

"Stop!!!" I screamed. "Form a line!" I yelled. "Don't push!" I screeched. That was the night I made "Yenta of the Year."

They finally formed a line and slowly filed by shaking Bill's hand, getting autographs, and snapping pictures. He was very gracious to one and all. Scared, but gracious.

We finally left, and as we took him down the hallway, all the fans who could not get to the helpers' party waved and called out to him. He waved back until we entered the elevator. As we rode down we double-checked the time for his appearance the next day. When we got out of the elevator, Ben realized we were on the lobby floor. We forgot that the freight elevator didn't stop on the mezzanine. I suggested we go up one flight, but Bill said no, he would walk through the lobby.

Ben and I exchanged horrified glances. Riot time. But Bill pulled his sheepskin collar up to his ears and started across the lobby floor. Ben sped after him, pausing every few feet to let the fans bounce off his back. Bill's long legs carried him down the stairs leading to the entrance two at a time. He hopped into a waiting (how lucky can you get?) cab and sped away. As Ben breathed a huge sigh of relief, a large group of screaming fans burst through the doors.

"Where is he?"

"Which way did he go?"

Ben glanced skyward and said, "He just beamed up."

For one moment there the fans believed him. While their eyes were directed elsewhere, Ben quickly disappeared. He's not known as the Gray Eminence for nothing, you know.

I staggered back to the con suite at about four that morning to finally say hello to my bed—which I felt had forgotten what I looked like. I heard the sound of running water. Walking into the kitchen, I found Elyse up to her elbows in soapy water, endeavoring to wash out four hundred dirty glasses. She had walked into the kitchen before going to bed just to get a glass of water and found every available surface covered with dirty glasses. She guessed that everybody thought everybody else would do them, and, as a result, nobody did. Not wanting that sight to greet her in the morning, she started washing. I grabbed a sponge and joined her in the soap suds. We finished at about six o'clock. Elyse had said that if she finished before six she'd go to bed; if she finished after six she might as well stay up. She made it by five minutes.

We held the first art auction on Sunday, and David Gerrold was the auctioneer. We liked to think he enjoyed doing this, as he did it so well. His quick wit and easy banter made the two hours whiz by and, as a side effect, usually made the artists lots of money. Of course, it didn't hurt that our art show attracted some of the best artists in ST fandom. People like Jennifer Reid, Connie Faddis, Monica Miller, Gee Moaven, George Richard (Hal Clement), Signe Landon, Joni Wagner, Alice Jones, Pat O'Neill, Pat and Judy Molnar, Gayle Feyrer, Charlene Taylor, Gordon Carlton, etc.

Devra had worked out the Art Show rules based on the ones Bjo Trimble had set up for the World Science-fiction Convention Art Show. They were as follows:

ART SHOW RULES

(Based on those of the International SF Art Exhibit, courtesy of Bjo Trimble)

1. These rules apply to all entries. Any exceptions are entirely at the discretion of the director.
2. All art must be original work on a "Star Trek," science-fiction, or fantasy theme.
3. The full name and address of the artist, title, and minimum bid or "Not for Sale," *printed,* must be on the back of each piece.
4. All entries must be mounted, matted, framed, or otherwise finished for display.
5. Artwork may be in any medium, including photography and 3-D items.
6. The Art Show collects a 15 per cent entry fee per piece of displayed art work.
7. There will be a $.50 entry fee per each piece of displayed work.
8. There will *not* be a sketch table this year. *Only* display pieces and portfolios may be entered.
9. Each artist may display only *ten* (10) pieces of art.

10. Only one copy of a multiple print run may be hung. Other copies will be held at the control desk. The $.50 fee per design includes display fee.

11. Entries will not be returned by mail unless postage has been sent.

12. Packaging, insurance, and copyrighting, if desired, are the artist's responsibilities. We cannot accept any liability.

13. Unsold work without return postage that is not picked up by the artist or an agent will be donated to the next convention, to be sold on its terms.

14. Entry fees *must* be included with all mailings. Art will not be hung unless fees have been paid.

15. *No one* will be paid at the con. Checks will be mailed to the artists *after* the con.

16. Each display item must have a bid sheet and a receipt, properly filled out.

17. No untitled works will be accepted. This includes works called "Untitled No. 4."

18. We reserve the right to reject any entries that do not meet the standards of the show, or comply with the rules.

19. Do *not* sent art without the proper forms, or forms without art!!!!

20. Any flag-contest entries copied from the *"Star Trek" Technical Manual* will automatically be disqualified.

To digress for a moment, here is a story about two fans, one unhappy, one happy. Carole Kabrin is from Southfield, Michigan, where she works as the newsroom artist for the local NBC affiliate, WWJ-TV. She spent over three hundred dollars to come to New York and attend the 1975 Con—three hundred dollars she could ill afford at the time. She really wanted to met Bill Shatner and give him a charcoal portrait she had done as an expression of her admiration.

It was handed to me just as Bill went onstage for his first "rap session." He was a bit nervous at this time, so he gave it just a quick glance, smiled, said, "How nice," and kept on going. Poor Carole.

However, when he was getting into the cab to catch his plane, clutching the two plants one of the helpers had gotten him to give to his Brooklyn hostess, I asked what he wanted to do with the drawing. It was a beautiful portrait and a handsome likeness. If he didn't want it, I sure did!

"Oh, yes, of course I want it. It's really good, and Marcy will love it. Take care of it and send it out to me, will you, Joan?"

So it went into Bill Theiss' trunk and sent out to sunny California. And Carole—Bill told me later that Marcy did love it.

So there, feel better?

Then there was Valerie Sussman, a librarian at Intermediate School 88 in Brooklyn, New York—and an inveterate "Star Trek" fan!

While at the 1974 convention, Val bought a large black-and-white poster of the entire *Enterprise* crew. Her ambition? To get all of their signatures and hang it in the library at school. In 1974 she managed to get De Kelley, Nichelle Nichols, George Takei, and Walter Koenig by the end of the con.

She brought the poster to our 1975 con, and while she was on the registration line someone appropriated the poster—out of her bag. But that did not deter our Val. She bought another poster and started all over again. I had played a small part in getting some of the signatures on the old (stolen) poster, and I helped her out this time, too. However, it was Steve Rosenstein who got the poster to Bill this time. Bill did not just scrawl those marvelously illegible rolling loops but wrote, and I quote, "To the Students of I.S. 88K, Take Care, William Shatner."

Val was so overcome she forgot all her twenty-odd years of dignity and reverted to age six. She ran up to the stage where Bill was speaking, holding up the poster and grinning wildly from ear to ear. Bill looked a bit bewildered at first; then, recognizing the poster, he gave her a big grin in return.

Val and I have become fast friends, and she informed me the other day that *the* poster, now laminated with all the signatures intact, hangs in a place of honor in the library. And although the student body has been known to "rip off" anything not chained to the walls, *the* poster has remained inviolate. Students from visiting schools stand slack-jawed in wonder and envy when touring the library of I.S. 88 in Brooklyn, New York.

At noon our own Isaac Asimov spoke to a full house. The fans loved Isaac, and he loved the fans. Running back and forth from the press room to the film room, I would peek in and hear snatches of his talk.

In the dealers' room Stu Grossman was suddenly aware that something was terribly wrong—with the air conditioning. There was an awful smell, as if several dead bodies were decomposing all at once, and it was getting worse. The room, which was jammed with fans and buyers, cleared in twenty seconds. Later it was discovered that one of the dealers had brought a small portable stove and had been cooking his lunch—cheese fondue (My, aren't we fancy. Tuna fish isn't good enough?)—when he got involved with a customer and let the fondue burn. The air conditioning, instead of removing the odor, just spread it evenly around the room. Thank heavens that was *not* one of the times the fire marshals picked to pay a call.

Bill was due back at the hotel at a little before one o'clock. He was doing a television interview prior to his last appearance at two that afternoon. He was supposed to be a judge at the Masquerade that evening, but since the last plane for Mexico City (his picture was shooting in Mexico) left at 7:00 P.M. he was unable to attend.

A problem. Well, we were certainly used to those. We had a slight shortage of professional security men. At the time Bill was expected, Gene and Majel were going out to lunch, George would be leaving the press room, and Isaac would be finishing in the ballroom.

And that is why only one large security guard, Sondra Marshak, and I were meeting Bill Shatner at the mezzanine entrance. We kept looking out the door, but no Bill. I had just sent the guard off to make sure that the special elevator was ready and waiting to whisk us up to the twenty-second floor when I was tapped on the shoulder and a cheery, familiar voice declared, "I'm here."

I turned to see a jovially grinning Bill Shatner. Startled, I said, "How did you get into the hotel?"

"Oh, I just walked through the lobby."

"YOU WALKED THROUGH THE LOBBY?!!?" And before I could stop, my arm flashed out and hit Bill on the shoulder.

He laughed and turned to Sondra, "She's always hitting me."

"Only when you do something like that! What do you think would have happened if you had been recognized?" I replied.

"Well, nobody did. I just kept my collar up and walked very fast."

I sent instructions to my palpitating heart to slow down and began to breathe once more. "Okay. Now we have to get to the last elevator over there," I pointed. "We will keep walking, and we will not stop for anything. Let's go."

Sondra and I each took an arm and started to walk. Just then the programing must have come to an end in the main ballroom and in the film room because hundreds of fans began to stream down the stairs leading to the mezzanine.

We kept on walking. Two young girls stopped dead in our path and went white. As we came up to them they parted like the Red Sea, one to each side—thud to the left, thud to the right.

Bill grabbed our arms and in an awful German accent said, "Ve vill keep valking, ve vill step over ze fainting bodies, and ve vill not schtop for anyvone."[6]

Suddenly Bill and I started chanting that, awful accent and all. By the time we got to the end of the hall we were laughing wildly and almost fell into the elevator.

Bill told me later he had felt very secure at our convention. I'm glad, but we certainly had a few hairy moments.

Jeff Maynard told this next one, and I admit I was very flattered.

We had just finished an interview and were walking out of the room. The group consisted of Bill, Sondra, Myrna Culbreath, Jeff, myself, and the security people and helpers. We were walking down the hallway to the back elevator when I suddenly remembered I had left my camera on the bed in the room. I ran back to retrieve it.

This is what Jeff told me later: Bill suddenly looked around and asked, "Where's Joanie?"

Nobody seemed to know. Bill (and these are Jeff's exact words) "dug his heels into the carpet and stated, 'I don't move without Joanie. I won't go anywhere without her. Where is she?'"

Just then I came racing into view, and Bill relaxed and got

[6] Did Bill Shatner learn it from Gene Roddenberry or vice versa?

into the elevator. I think I know the reason behind Bill's feelings. He is, I think, a shy man and is not really comfortable among large crowds of people. The only person he knew at all at our con was me. I was the one familiar face in that huge mass of people, and he liked to know I was around. But I must admit, I reveled in it, especially since I actually got to see some programing, because Bill wanted me to escort him. As a matter of fact, it was the most programing I have ever seen at one of our cons.

Back to the rap session. Most of the questions were much like those of the day before. One I do remember was a fan asking Bill, "How did you meet your wife?" and Bill's quick riposte, "Which one?" which got a huge laugh.

He then told us that he met Marcy Lafferty when he was doing *The Andersonville Trial*. She was working as scriptgirl for the production. She is an actress and a very good one, but she was helping out the director (Or was it the producer? I forget.). Anyway, that's how it all started.

When I announced this time that Bill was leaving, there was a huge roar of disappointment. You must remember that this was only the second convention he had ever appeared at, and the fans could not get their fill of him.

With Bill in the middle of a phalanx of guards, we got through the Art Show room (there we go again) and down the service stairs. We had a cab waiting, and we loaded Bill into the cab and waved good-bye as he drove off.

I then ran like blazes to the con suite. I was one of the models in Bill Theiss' Fashion Show. These were copies of clothes he had designed for various films and television shows. The other models were already collecting their costumes. I grabbed mine and followed. There were Joyce Yasner, Adrienne LeVine, Anne Neiworth, Louise Shaffer, Kathryn Kors, and myself. We dashed into the elevator, carefully keeping the beautiful costumes from touching the floor.

We were to make up and dress in a room on the ballroom floor opposite the press room. Elyse was helping iron the costumes so they would look fresh and new. The ironing board had caused a bit of a problem—like we could not find one in the hotel. Since some of the costumes were made of delicate materials, Bill did not think a bureau drawer would do a proper job. We were getting a bit desperate when the head waiter came to our rescue. The waiters kept a small portable ironing board to freshen up their shirts, and they would let us use it. See what I mean about the Commodore Hotel? Everyone, and I mean *everyone*, helped us.

We all helped each other with our hair and make-up. When you're appearing onstage, you have to exaggerate—your eyes and mouth, etc.—so you don't look like a colorless blur from the back row of the ballroom.

Before each costume made its appearance, Bill would explain who had worn it. There were many questions from interested fans in the audience. They asked about materials, patterns, where Bill got his ideas, and how much the script had to do with his work.

Everyone was fascinated and very attentive. Several of the costumes were in the famous Thiess "Look, Ma, no hardly anything" mode. Joyce got one of those, and with a judicious use of double-backed Scotch tape she managed to get through the show without incident. She really looked grand. Kathryn Kors wore a dress slit up both sides, and you can bet she walked very carefully. The trick, as Bill told us, was a small strip of material attaching the front and back panels, which went between the model's legs. This kept the dress from being too revealing. That was one model who didn't rush across the stage.

The show finished at about six o'clock, and I ran up to my room to take a quick shower and get ready for the Masquerade. Dana had done me the honor of asking me to be a judge. I hadn't eaten since the morning, but before I could rectify that, there was Ellen coming up to the room after closing the press room. If you look at my schedule for the day, you can see I did not get to see much of the press room. Thank heavens they knew what they were doing.

Most of the fans, however, had gotten something to eat. I had gotten together a one-page guide to all the "cheapie" eating places in the area, and they were given out at the information desk by Regina Gottesman. There was a little take-out sandwich place in Grand Central Station that made great sandwiches and also eleven thousand dollars in three days during this con! Howard Johnson's didn't believe us in 1973 when we told them to put

on extra waiters and order extra supplies. Did you ever hear of a
Howard Johnson's running out of ice cream? Or coffee? This one
did. They remembered in 1975 and 1976. It still took some time
to get waited on, but the gorgeous ice-cream sodas were worth
it.

I came down to the ballroom floor at seven-thirty for the
prejudging of the contestants. The lines outside the main
ballroom were already enormous.

Claire Eddy with her wheelchair and a gorgeous young man
named Bill made sure that the fans did not enter the ballroom
till the ballroom was ready for them. The reason the ballroom
was not ready was that all the chairs had to be stacked and removed so we could use the long stage on the side of the room. It
takes a bit of time when you are removing twenty-two hundred
chairs. The hotel staff did this several times during the convention. They did quickly, they did it quietly, and they did it well.
Bless you, guys, wherever you are.

The prejudging took place in the East Ballroom. I was seated
between Bob Lansing and Bill Theiss, a very happy sandwich.
We were all very serious and carefully inspecting the workman-
ship of each of the costumes and, boy, there were a lot of costumes—almost two hundred that year.

Back in the main ballroom, the fans were starting to get a bit
restless, and Dana decided to start the show before we had seen
quite all the costumes. It would have taken at least another hour
—which would have made the Masquerade much later than it
already was.

There were many great costumes that year, and we judges
went quietly nuts. I had a hard time telling the difference between "Most Authentic" and "Best Alien." I usually peeked at
Hal Clement's list and kept myself straight that way. Hal was on
my right, and next to him was a fan selected from the audience.
On my left, going down the line, were Bill Theiss, Bob Lansing,
Majel Barrett, Diane Duane (an excellent artist and even better
nurse), and David Gerrold. David should not have been there.
He was feeling awful and running a fever—even *before* Angelique Trouvere appeared in what there was of her costume.

That's David, though. Another time his back was killing him,
and he just got it taped up and held the art auction anyway.

So there we all were, sipping water and ginger ale, watching Dana and our dear Allan Asherman announce the contestants for several hours, trying to make up our minds. One of the main bones of contention (or should I say "bodies") was "Most Beautiful." The two favorites were Connie Faddis, in a dress and cape she had designed and created as a Kraith pilgrimage outfit. (There is a picture of it somewhere in this book.) The other was Angelique Trouvere. Most of the costume was on her head—lots of plumes, ribbons, and beads. The rest was some sort of panel arrangement fore and aft that displayed a lot of Angelique.

I love both girls, but I also love Kraith. This is one of the "Star Trek" "alternate universes," which was created by Jackie Lichtenberg. Both costumes were beautifully made and presented, but I had definite Kraith leanings. The males on the panel, however, after they retrieved their eyeballs from across the room, decided on Angelique.

Besides deciding "Most Beautiful," we had to make up our minds on the winners of "Most Authentic," "Best Alien," "Best Costume for Children Under 12 Years of Age," "Most Humorous," "Best Presentation," "Best 'Star Trek' Costume," "Best Un-'Trek' Costume," "Best 'Star Trek'-Related," and "Most Original."

Puff, puff, pant, pant. All of the above took *five* hours! Aslosh with ginger ale and water, I raced up to the con suite. I was ready for *food!* As I walked in the door, I ran into Joyce. We turned to one another and—in unison—said, "Did you eat today?" We could barely hear each other over the noisy rumblings of our deprived stomachs. I remembered having two gulps of Sanka around 8:30 A.M.; Joyce was ahead of me by three sips of juice. Nothing in the con suite fridge suited our fancy—we were particular, yet. So we took a cab up to the Chinese take-out place around the corner from my apartment. We brought back all sorts of goodies to the hotel and settled down in my rooms to have a feast. One problem: The Committee members have better noses than bloodhounds when it comes to Chinese food. Oh well, sharing is good for the soul, they say. And I wish "they" would mind their own business!

I didn't hear about this particular catastrophe until way after it happened. Wendy Lindboe and Louise Sachter had planned to attend the Masquerade, but they didn't make it. They were in charge of the Art Show, and they saw very little of anything during the day but the West Ballroom, which is where the art show was. (Except, as we mentioned before, an occasional star being smuggled through.)

The night of the Masquerade they closed the room at about 6:00 P.M., but Wendy and Louise stayed until about ten o'clock putting back up all the stuff that had fallen off the walls that day. Masking tape is very unreliable, but that's all the hotel would let them use. Tacks and sticky tape were *verboten*. When they finally finished, they staggered up to the con suite to get something to eat and collapse for a while. The phone rang, and it was Stu Hellinger telling them, "It's raining in the art show!"

They raced back downstairs—excuse me, they had hysterics *first*, then they raced downstairs. They found that Charlie Gilbert and Stu had planted huge trash cans underneath the lighting fixtures, which had all become very efficient showers. This was caused by a pipe that had burst on the floor above. Louise and Wendy ran and got plastic dropcloths to spread over the display tables. Miracle of miracles, nothing was damaged. The leak had been discovered just after it had happened, and Charlie had gotten Stu, and they had been able to move everything out of the way in time.

It was now twelve midnight and the Masquerade was over and Louise and Wendy felt the only thing they wanted to see at that point were their beds.

Monday dawned. Well, it must have, since it was there when I got up. Why is it that Mondays are always a kind of blur at our cons? Could it be that an average of two hours' sleep a night, meals at odd hours (if at all), and a vast amount of running hither and yon (especially yon) can get a Committee down?

Yup!

I remember! This was the day Leonard Nimoy was not coming! Mr. Nimoy had very kindly appeared at our two previous conventions and the fans seemed to expect him to make his usual unannounced, unscheduled surprise appearance. But not this year. Try to convince the fans of that! And that is exactly what we did that whole day—right up to the end: We tried to convince them. I mean, he wasn't even in the New York area.

All our Mondays were famous for one thing: *It was the last day of the con!!!!* Most of the fans felt kind of sad and dreaded the approach of four o'clock. On the other hand, the Committee, assistants, helpers, and hotel staff were watching the clock with increasing glee!

Regina Gottesman manned, uh, womaned, er, personed (?) the information desk through the 1975 and 1976 conventions. Through all the programing changes and all the mix-ups and delays in the film schedule, she coped and kept her cool. You really need someone with a tremendous sense of responsibility for this type of job, and we were very lucky to find Regina. I'm very lucky to be able to call her a friend.

The information desk, the dealers' room, and the whole *magilla* shut down at 4:00 P.M. Another yippee? You got it. The worry room and security did not close down till 5:00 P.M. Many of the fans did not want to admit the con had ended and kind of milled around for a few hours just discussing the events of the weekend.

I was talking to some fans in the main ballroom when Stu Grossman came in, trailing a dozen or so dealers in his wake. Stu was in charge of the dealers' room for both the 1975 and 1976 cons. He had a problem. Well, it wasn't exactly a problem—it's just that he didn't know what to do since it had never happened to him before. It seems these dealers wanted to give Stu money for tables at next year's con. They didn't care that we had no idea what those tables were going to cost. "I'll give you $$ per table, and if they end up costing more, send me a letter, and I'll send you a check. This was a great con for both the fans and the dealers, and I want to make sure I don't miss out next year."

Suddenly the fans who had been hanging around the stage darted forward and said they also wanted to pay for next year's con. Right now. We were offered $$ by hundreds of people for memberships to the 1976 convention. My goodness.

After a hasty conference, we decided to take the dealers' money (there were only a couple of dozen of them). To the hundreds of fans we promised that we would send out our fliers with all the information very early in the year, and they could send in their money then. If they wanted, they could leave their names and addresses, and we would make sure they were on our mailing list. They all signed up. I guess they just didn't want to take a chance on missing the next con, especially since we had announced that it was to be our last.

From what I heard later, this was the first time this had ever happened at a convention. We were stunned and very pleased, because this meant that they came to the cons for the con and not just for the guests, films, or exhibits. I guess all you have to do is build up a reputation for giving the fans what they want, and they will come to your cons. This made up for a lot of the bad times.

Meanwhile, up in the con suite people were sprawled around in various positions of pooped. After a while of just luxuriating in not having to do anything, somebody mentioned the magic word: *Food!*

At our cons, food usually meant Chinese or Japanese—because we liked that stuff, that's why. Some of the Committee went out to dinner, and a lot of us ordered some Chinese food sent in to the hotel. Well, actually it was snuck in—in lots of plain brown-paper bags that smelled delicious (the food, not the bags!). During and after this monster munch, fans and guests drifted in for the famous (or infamous) Dead Dog Party. Why is it called that? Well, I guess it's kind of a tradition that the last hangers-on make dead dogs out of any bottles that happen to be lying around. Or maybe because you are dog tired? Our group was not a drinking group, unless you count Pepsi-Cola, so we just finished up all the soda and munchies hanging around so we would not have to cart them home. We usually doubled what we thought we'd use so the Dead Dog Party would be a gasser, and 1975 was no exception.

We had a very busy group in the living room that evening. Pieces of paper were being passed around with lyrics scribbled across them, bursts of song (some even on key) dribbled out, and it meant that the Committee, assistants, and helpers, including Steve Hartman, David Gerrold (well, he *was* family), and others were all making up rhymes and editing lyrics for yet another filksing.[7]

[7] Filksing: To sing filksongs, words set to familiar music, usually about science fiction, fantasy, or "Star Trek." It's fannish for "folksong." And actually is the result of a typo.

I was sitting in my room with Elyse and Bill Theiss when Steve Hartman came in and asked to borrow my reel-to-to-reel recorder. All of the above (plus others) had written a song to commemorate the 1975 "Star Trek" convention. It is called "The Battle Hymn of the Helpers," sung to, surprise, surprise, "The Battle Hymn of the Republic."

BATTLE HYMN OF THE HELPERS[8]

Mine eyes have seen the glory of the ending of the con.
They were trampled on the carpet when the movies were not on,
They were tearing down the walls the guests had rested hands upon,
Praise Ghu,[9] they are all gone!

[*Chorus* (repeated after each verse)]
Glory, Glory Roddenberry,
Glory, Glory Roddenberry,
Glory, Glory Roddenberry,
Praise Ghu, they are all gone!

They were lurking in the corridors where Gene and Majel lived,
Our security arrangements were as leaky as a sieve.
Room numbers Committee didn't know, the Trekkies would gladly
      give.
Praise Ghu, they are all gone!

Bill Shatner owes his life to fen[10] whose names he'll never know,
They are placing their frail bodies where the Trekkies want to go,
And we all are deeply thankful Leonard Nimoy did not show.
Praise Ghu, they are all gone!

Our guests were wont to wander where our helpers feared to go,
Dear George once tried to roam around and thought no one would
      know,
We picked up what was left of him and put him in the show.
Praise Ghu, they are all gone!

Ike Asimov made speeches where he told all he did know.
Jeff Maynard set up six days to put on his light show.
Robert Lansing gave us extra work, he knows where he can go.
Praise Ghu, they are all gone!

[8] Copyright © 1975, Tellurian Enterprises, Inc.
[9] Ghu: Just so no one is offended, in fannish circles this takes the place of "God."
[10] Fen: plural for "fan."

There wasn't much of Destiny her costume didn't show,
The Vulcan hooker Patia matched against her blow for blow,
But helpers didn't notice: they were busy clearing rows.
Praise Ghu, they are all gone!

Dave Gerrold brought some fur with him, a tribble it was called
Dick Hoagland gave his speech on the space program, now stalled.
And Bill Theiss showed us some costumes that we all thought would
    fall.
Praise Ghu, they are all gone!

Hal Clement fixed the science errors that Gene's writers made.
And reshaped worlds to be those where the *Enterprise* had stayed
This year he told of the world where to Vaal men prayed.
Praise Ghu, they are all gone!

Bob Lansing, Gene, and Majel were all talking in the Suite,
The Committee and assistants were all nursing blistered feet,
We'll discuss our plans for next year's con, but *not* before we eat!
Praise Ghu, they are all gone!

If some of the above lines do not quite scan, remember these
were put together by a pretty pooped group.

That song has been sung at "Star Trek" and science-fiction
conventions all over the United States and Canada at this point.
Who knows? Tomorrow the world!

It was Tuesday and *no* rise and shine, thank you very much.
Oh, the sybaritic luxury of sleeping late. I love it. I mean, I know
there are people out there who actually love to get up at
outlandish times like seven or eight or nine o'clock *on purpose!*
Without any reason, just because they like to! Makes no sense to
me at all. Of course, there are also those people who poop out at
ten-thirty at night, too, while people like me are still going
strong at 2 in the A.M.—which is why we like to sleep late in the
first place.

CREATIVE WHEELCHAIR WRAPPING: 101

As I mentioned earlier, Gene Roddenberry brought a rented
wheelchair to the 1975 con. He had hurt his hip on one of his
speaking tours, and this was the only way he could come to the

con. We were all delighted that he thought that much of us and our convention to go through all the pain and aggravation.

Gene was leaving on a college speaking tour directly after the con. His hip was better, and he asked if we would please send the wheelchair home for him. We readily agreed, not knowing what we were letting ourselves in for.

Patia Von Sternberg (pip of a name for a helper, eh?) and I walked around the wheelchair for a while. We had set it up in the spacious elegant hallway of the presidential suite. It was Tuesday, February 18, the con had ended yesterday, and we had all gotten our first good night's sleep in I don't know how long. We would need it.

Patia and I couldn't find any wrapping paper, so we gathered up several copies of the New York *Times* and a huge roll of four-inch paper tape. This was the tape you have to wet with a sponge. That was our *first* mistake. There were many more to come.

We laid the chair on its side and proceeded to wrap it. It *sounds* so easy, *but*. First we had to use the tape to join several layers of the newspaper together until we got a strip about ten feet long; then we tried to wrap the wheelchair. It's all in that verb, "tried." All the hysterics, aggravation, paper cuts, and headaches.

I would now like to announce to one and all that the New York *Times* makes for crummy wrapping paper. It tore and fell apart every chance it got, and I admit there were many. The hallway became a battlefield and the enemy dead, huge, torn piles of newspaper. We put ten layers of that *※!? paper over "it," as we had christened the wheelchair. But handles, seats, and footrests are not convenient shapes to work with; they have pointed edges that love to tear through newspaper and did so at every opportunity.

After two hours, three sponges, and almost all the tape (about two hundred feet!), we gazed proudly at our handiwork. Patia and I turned and shook hands. Then we heard this terrible crash. "It" had toppled over, and handles and footrests were poking through the paper. We aaarghed, and then we aaarghed again. We had used so much tape our hands were stuck together!

After a session with the hot water in the john, we once again approached our problem. Suddenly I remembered something I had seen in the kitchen. It was a half-dozen huge green trash bags. We first padded the offensive areas (well, they *were* offensive to us), and then stuffed the wheelchair into the bags.

We finally finished and stood back to admire our masterpiece and got hysterical. Dana ran out of her room and broke up. The way it was wrapped, the corner of one of the bags pointed up and slightly to the rear of this monstrous form. It looked just like a gigantic Vulcan ear!

CREATIVE WHEELCHAIR WRAPPING: 102

On Wednesday we discovered that the post awful would not accept the package as wrapped. We still can't figure out why. We began to feel as if an albatross had been hung around our necks.

On Thursday, Patia had gone home and Dana, good-hearted soul, volunteered to help me. We took "it," or the ※°$!?, as we now called it, down to the convention storage room on the first floor of the hotel. The hotel had reclaimed the con suite, and it was, once again, the plain old Presidential Suite. We pushed back all the cartons and piles of program books, pocket programs, shopping bags, trivia contests, and assorted articles left over from the con to make room to wrap.

Dave Simons had bought us rolls and rolls of *real* wrapping paper and a huge roll of six-inch-wide sticky tape (Hooray! No water and no sponges!) and we set to work. The first thing we discovered was the sticky tape has its disadvantages also—like sticking to everything, including us. At one point of the proceedings, the titanic roll of tape got away from **us** as we were rolling it around the ※°$!? thing for the umpty-umpth time. It skittered and scuttled across the littered floor. By the time it circled the room, it had collected two trivia contests, four fliers, a shopping bag, and my cigarettes.

Dana and I actually leaped upon it and rode that tape like a bucking bronco. As we cut off the offending litter, it decided, all of its own accord, mind you, to coil itself in my hair. It's a good thing Dana gives a good haircut, as well as running the best Masquerade in fandom.

After catching our breath, we continued to tuck corners, trim edges, and put layer after layer of paper and tape on the thing. We must have added ten pounds to its total weight. When we finally finished, it looked as if there might be a body sitting in the damn thing!

But the albatross still clung. We had to find a freight company to accept this monster we had created, plus the assorted stuff we were sending to Los Angeles for Bill Theiss. Did you know that Railway Express was out of business? We found out that day. After much finger-walking through the Yellow Pages, we finally got someone who would come to the Commodore loading dock and pick it up. We left the money for the freight charges with one of the guys from the Banquet Sales Department. Then Dana and I went on our merry but totally wiped-out way.

But that was not the finish. Remember, I jokingly called it an albatross. It seemed determined to prove me right.

When the freight company arrived to pick up the wheelchair, it had disappeared. Who would walk off with such a monster, you ask? So did we. It was found a week later underneath a tarpaulin in the back of the loading area. No one knew how it got there. Gremlins? Gorns? Your guess is as good as ours. We strung it with good-luck amulets and once again sent it on its way.

Evidently the amulets didn't do any good. Somewhere between New York and Los Angeles "it" faded into a sort of limbo. I would get these plaintive calls from Gene's secretary, Susan Sackett, asking, "Joan, when did you say the wheelchair had been shipped?" I had a strange feeling that instead of using amulets I should have plunged a stake through its seat!

We had the shipping company put a tracer on it and kept on calling them to ask "Where is it?" every few days. Then one day, like magic—black or white, take your pick—it appeared on the Roddenberry doorstep. With all wrappings intact—well, I should hope so! We heard it took almost thirty minutes to *unwrap* it.

I still say it was gremlins!

"STAR TREK" TRIVIA CONTEST QUESTIONNAIRE
THE "STAR TREK" CONVENTION, 1975

1. The rocket base in *Assignment: Earth* was called
   A. Omaha   B. McKinley   C. Cape Canaveral

2. In *All Our Yesterdays,* the star about to nova was
   A. Tau Ceti   B. Beta Lyrae   C. Beta Niobe

3. A peace treaty between the Federation and the Klingon Empire was imposed on the planet
   A. Triskelion   B. Organia   C. Eminiar VII

4. The first episode (in air-date order) to feature Romulans was
   A. *Balance of Terror*   B. *The Enterprise Incident*
   C. *Deadly Years*

5. In *A Private Little War,* Kirk's native friend was
   A. Nona   B. Tyree   C. Rael

6. In *A Piece of the Action,* two of the warring gang leaders were
   A. Oxmyx and Bele   B. Oxmyx and Korax   C. Oxmyx and Krako

7. In *Devil in the Dark,* the miners were most concerned about
   A. Dilithium   B. Pergium   C. Neutronium

8. In which episode did Kirk *not* beam down with the *first* landing party?
   A. *Shore Leave*   B. *Operation: Annihilate*   C. *Arena*

9. What was the Federation's cut in *A Piece of the Action?*
   A. 60 per cent   B. 25 per cent   C. 40 per cent

10. Spock distinguishes between "fascinating" and "interesting" in
    A. *Balance of Terror*   B. *Galileo 7*   C. *Squire of Gothos*

11. Lieutenant Kevin Riley drank poisoned
    A. Water   B. Milk   C. Coffee

12. Who shot Chekov in *Specter of the Gun?*
    A. Morgan Earp   B. Wyatt Earp   C. Virgil Earp

13. A Tricorder was overloaded in
    A. *That Which Survives*   B. *Arena*   C. *Alternative Factor*

14. Janet Wallace married a man named
    A. James   B. Roger   C. Theodore

15. In which episode do we see a waterfall?
    A. *The Apple*   B. *The Paradise Syndrome*   C. *A Private Little War*

16. Marlena's last name was
    A. McGivers   B. Moreau   C. Masters

17. How many life-support canisters were there originally on board the S.S. *Botany Bay?*
    A. 72   B. 80   C. 84

18. Which one of Kloog's eyes was the weakest?
    A. Right   B. Left   C. Middle

19. The "givers of pain and delight" were the
    A. Eymorgs   B. Vians   C. Morgs

Jeff Maynard, whip in hand, ready to hold off all comers as an Orion slave girl, played by Chris Lundi, lounges seductively atop his dealer's table at the 1975 con. *(Jeff Maynard)*

William Ware Theiss, Joan Winston, and Robert Lansing judging the 1975 Masquerade. *(Benjamin M. Yalow)*

nica Miller in her alternate-universe
ss uniform at the 1976 con. *(Connie
ddis)*

Vicki Mandel in her dress uniform at the
1976 con. *(Connie Faddis)*

ce Yasner as Surak of Vulcan at the 1972
; her outfit is completely hand-crocheted.
ice the committee badge on hip.

Angelique Trouvere wearing her idea of
what an inhabitant of Wriggley's pleasure
planet would wear, at the 1975 con. *(Jeff
Maynard)*

Hal Clement and David Gerrold as judges at the 1976 Masquerade. Behind them are Dave Simons, Diane Duane, and Lee Smoire discussing the current catastrophe. There is *always* a catastrophe. *(Benjamin M. Yalow)*

Christine Bunt as "Flutter Fantasy" at B centennial 10 in 1976. *(Jeff Maynard)*

20. Who did Scotty say was "mad enough to chew neutronium"?
    A. Ambassador Fox   B. Gary Seven   C. Krako

21. In which episode did Kirk enter into his log the notation "Star date: Armageddon"?
    A. *Day of the Dove*   B. *Let That Be Your Last Battlefield*
    C. *A Taste of Armageddon*

22. Who was *not* an android?
    A. Andrea   B. Drea   C. Rayna

23. Who never served as *Enterprise* communications officer?
    A. Alden   B. Boyce   C. Palmer

24. William B. Harrison was the flight officer of the ship
    A. *Beagle*   B. *Antares*   C. *Horizon*

25. Warp drive came into use around the year
    A. 2018   B. 2038   C. 2058

26. The hardest substance known to Federation science was
    A. Duranium   B. Rodinium   C. Pergium

27. Which newspaper ran the story "FDR Confers with Slum-area 'Angel'"?
    A. *Star-Dispatch*   B. *World Tribune*   C. *Daily Sun*

28. Who asked Spock his first name?
    A. Miramanee   B. Leila   C. Droxine

29. What was the *Enterprise* looking for when it entered the Sigma Draconis system?
    A. The Gorn ship   B. The stolen shuttlecraft   C. Spock's brain

30. In which episode (in air-date order) did McCoy first say "He's dead, Jim"?
    A. *Where No Man Has Gone Before*   B. *Man Trap*
    C. *Naked Time*

31. What did Nancy Crater use as a nickname for McCoy?
    A. Bones   B. Dink   C. Plum

32. What was the name of the space vessel stolen by the Kzinti?
    A. *The Traitor's Claw*   B. *Revenge*   C. *The Court Jester*

33. What was the only function of the slaver weapon that was beyond the capabilities of the Federation?
    A. A more powerful phaser   B. A new space drive   C. A total conversion of matter to energy

34. What name was the "Jack the Ripper" entity *not* known as?
    A. Kesla   B. Beratis   C. Isak

35. How much did Edith Keeler offer to pay Kirk and Spock for working at the mission?
    A. 10 cents an hour, five hours a day   B. 15 cents an hour, ten hours a day   C. 22 cents an hour, ten hours a day

36. According to *Bread and Circuses,* how many people will die in Earth's Third World War?
    A. 3 billion   B. 7 million   C. 37 million
37. In what episode did Spock call Bones "Captain McCoy"?
    A. *The Immunity Syndrome*   B. *I, Mudd*   C. *The Tholian Web*
38. Who said, "I don't trust men who smile too much"?
    A. Spock   B. Krass   C. Kor
39. In the episode *Miri,* in the doctor's office, there hangs a sign on the wall. It reads
    A. No Smoking   B. Exit   C. Quiet, Please
40. In "Star Trek's" third season, at the end of the credits, at the end of the show, what picture is shown?
    A. Balok   B. Stars   C. Vina
41. Which of the following peoples share common ancestral roots?
    A. Klingons and Romulans   B. Romulans and Vulcans   C. Vulcans and Klingons
42. In *Court-martial,* how did Spock discover that the computer had been tampered with?
    A. By beating it at chess   B. By getting an incorrect answer   C. By Finney's confession
43. Miramanee was
    A. A high priestess   B. Daughter of the chief   C. Dohlman of Elaas
44. In *Mirror, Mirror,* who hit the alternate Spock on the head with a skull?
    A. Kirk   B. Scotty   C. Uhura
45. The "life prolongation" disease was first apparent on Kirk's
    A. Face   B. Hand   C. Leg
46. What did Charlie Evans offer Yeoman Rand?
    A. A vial of perfume   B. A necklace   C. A bouquet
47. Landru was found in
    A. The Hall of Audiences   B. The Vault of Tomorrow   C. The Oracle Room
48. Marta's dancing reminded Spock of
    A. The Vulcan marriage ritual   B. Vulcan children in a nursery school   C. A Vulcan dance of combat
49. Once the *Enterprise*'s self-destruct system is activated, no command can stop it after
    A. Kirk gives his code sequence   B. The thirty-second countdown begins   C. The thirty-second countdown reaches five

50. The "other" part of Nomad was
   A. Ton-Rad   B. Tan-Ru   C. Ty-Ree
51. The Horta uses —— to bore through rock.
   A. Corrosive acid   B. Heat   C. Teeth
52. In *The Tholian Web*, —— was used to counteract the effects of interspace.
   A. Masiform-D   B. A theragin derivative   C. Stokaline
53. Who wrote *Nightengale's Woman?*
   A. Phineas Tarbold   B. Samuel T. Cogley   C. Stephen Kandel
54. Puppeteer Shari Lewis helped to write which of the following episodes?
   A. *Plato's Stepchildren*   B. *Slaver Weapon*   C. *Lights of Zetar*
55. On Ekos, Spock used —— to help him and Kirk escape from jail.
   A. Transmuter   B. Transceiver   C. Transponder
56. In which episode did Uhura *not* appear out of uniform?
   A. *Plato's Stepchildren*   B. *Charlie X*   C. *Tholian Web*
57. What is the only way to locate a stasis box?
   A. By using another stasis box   B. By using a tricorder   C. By using the last setting of the slaver weapon
58. Who said, "And I never believed in little green men"?
   A. John Christopher   B. Roberta Lincoln   C. Colonel Fellini
59. The Kzinti are
   A. Gorn-like creatures   B. Intelligent cats   C. An offshoot of the Klingon race
60. Whom did Scotty call a popinjay?
   A. Under Secretary Baris   B. Harry Mudd   C. Ambassador Fox
61. In Romulan terminology, the equivalent of a Federation starship captain is
   A. Commander   B. Subcommander   C. Lieutenant Commander
62. In which episode did Spock say, "Logic is a wreath of pretty flowers that smell bad"?
   A. *Amok Time*   B. *I, Mudd*   C. *This Side of Paradise*
63. The first thing Cyrano Jones tried to sell the bartender was
   A. Spican flame gems   B. Antarian glow-water   C. Tribbles
64. How long was Norman on board the *Enterprise* before he took over?
   A. 1 week   B. 72 hours   C. 24 hours

65. The man in charge of Deep Space Station K-7 was
    A. Nilz Baris   B. Cyrano Jones   C. Mr. Lurry
66. Where were the unit components of the *Enterprise* designed?
    A. San Diego   B. San Francisco   C. Santa Barbara
67. Who was particularly fond of Lewis Carroll's work?
    A. Tonia Barrows   B. Uhura   C. Amanda
68. Gary Seven's office was located at
    A. 68 West 81st Street   B. 811 East 68th Street   C. 118
    East 68th Street
69. Who said, "Behind every great man there's a woman urging
    him on"?
    A. Captain Kirk   B. Harry Mudd   C. Cyrano Jones
70. What overwhelmed Scotty in *Return to Tomorrow*?
    A. The idea of engines the size of a walnut   B. The
    androids   C. The abilities of the preservers
71. Commodore Mendez's first two initials were
    A. J.I.   B. J.L.   C. J.S.
72. We have seen a phaser cannon, a phaser rifle, and a phaser
    bore. In which episode did we see a phaser cannon?
    A. *Once upon a Planet*   B. *The Menagerie*   C. *Where No
    Man Has Gone Before*
73. On what planet is the penalty for fraud "Death by hanging,
    death by electrocution, death by phaser . . ."?
    A. Deneb IV   B. Deneb V   C. Deneb VI
74. In what episode did Kirk pose the question, "Is there anyone
    on this ship who even remotely resembles Satan"?
    A. *The Apple*   B. *This Side of Paradise*   C. *Catspaw*
75. Robert Fox was a(n)
    A. Galactic high commissioner   B. Special ambassador for
    the UFP   C. Assistant Federation commissioner
76. The two men killed by the Vians were
    A. Ozaba and Thann   B. Linc and Marvick   C. Ozaba and
    Linc
77. The show *Arena* was written by Gene L. Coon. Who wrote
    the story on which it was based?
    A. Murray Leinster   B. Fredric Brown   C. William Rostler
78. In which episode did Scotty wear his kilts?
    A. *The Savage Curtain*   B. *Journey to Babel*   C. *Amok
    Time*
79. Larry Marvick was in love with
    A. Mira Romaine   B. Miranda Jones   C. Marlena Moreau
80. M-5 killed the crew of the
    A. U.S.S. *Excalibur*   B. U.S.S. *Exeter*   C. U.S.S. *Yorktown*

81. Kollos was a(n)
    A. Klingon   B. Archon   C. Medusan
82. Who was *not* in the landing party of *Day of the Dove?*
    A. McCoy   B. Scott   C. Chekov
83. "Four thousand throats may be cut in one night by a running man" is from
    A. *Friday's Child*   B. *Space Seed*   C. *Day of the Dove*
84. What is the name of the former commodore who is now governor of Mantilles?
    A. Wesley   B. Mendez   C. Stone
85. How many tribbles fell on Kirk from the storage compartment?
    A. 1,771,651   B. 1,771,561   C. 1,771,156
86. What was the root placed on Kirk's shoulder in *A Private Little War?*
    A. Mako   B. Mugato   C. Melenex
87. In which episode is it established that Vulcan has no moon?
    A. *Amok Time*   B. *Man Trap*   C. *Cloud Minders*
88. How did the vampire cloud enter the *Enterprise?*
    A. By passing through the hull   B. Via the transporter
    C. Through the No. 2 impulse vent
89. The Clark Gable movie Edith Keeler wanted to see was playing at the
    A. Strand   B. Orpheum   C. Lyceum
90. Who was Kodos the Executioner posing as in *Conscience of the King?*
    A. Anton Karidan   B. Arthur Karidan   C. Arthur Leighton
91. The Organians caused all instruments of violence to radiate with a heat of
    A. 250° F   B. 350° F   C. 450° F

MATCHING: For each of Dr. McCoy's occupational disclaimers, indicate the letter for the matching episode:

92. "I'm a doctor, not a coal miner"   A. *The Deadly Years*
93. "I'm a doctor, not an escalator"   B. *Mirror, Mirror*
94. "I'm a doctor, not a bricklayer"   C. *The Devil in the Dark*
95. "I'm a doctor, not an engineer"   D. *All Our Yesterdays*
96. "I'm a doctor, not a mechanic"   E. *The Doomsday Machine*
97. "I'm a doctor, not a Moon shut-   F. *Return to Tomorrow*
    tle conductor"   G. *Friday's Child*
98. "I'm a doctor, not a psychia-   H. *Metamorphosis*
    trist"   I. *Corbomite Maneuver*

99. "I'm not a magician, Spock, just an old country doctor."
100. "I will not peddle flesh. I'm a physician."

J. *The Tholian Web*
K. *The City on the Edge of Forever*
L. *Empath*

OTHER STAR TREK CONVENTIONS;
OR,
YES, VIRGINIA, THERE ARE PEOPLE OUT THERE
AS CRAZY AS WE ARE!

In the midst of running around and helping to organize the Committee cons, I actually got the chance to attend other people's "Star Trek" conventions. I was invited as a speaker to some, and others I attend as a fan. Unfortunately, I cannot attend every convention, much as I would like to do so.

The first August party in 1975 was a big event for me. It was the very first time I was asked to speak at a convention. Of course, anyone who knows me knows that I *speak* at cons (ol' Motormouth, that's me), but I mean on the dais—in front of an audience. The chairman, Rich Kolker, called me a month or three prior to the con. They were using facilities at the University of Maryland and expected a few hundred people. They ended up with about eleven hundred.

Rich picked me up at the train station that Friday much the worse for wear. Amtrak had lost its cool, literally—the air conditioning on the train pooped out as we left Grand Central Station. It was in the midnineties, and by the time we reached the station my clothes were dripping—but not dry. But since everybody else was in the same condition, I didn't feel so bad.

We got to the student hall just in time for the big event of the con. Rich couldn't afford any of the stars, but he had arranged for Gene Roddenberry to speak via a telephone hook-up. Gene spoke for about twenty minutes, and the fans could hear him over the loudspeakers. They really enjoyed it.

I wasn't due to speak until the next day, but I stayed quite late, talking to a lot of the fans. If I started mentioning names, they would fill this entire book—well, that's one way out! Anyway, we talked "Star Trek" into the late hours, and it was heaven —a very hot and humid heaven, since there was no air conditioning. The only chance I got to cool off was in my motel room at night.

The next day, I took time out from selling *Star Trek Lives!* and signing autographs (don't stop, I love it; can't believe it, but love it), to appear before a large crowd that I am delighted to say filled the hall. No speech; I just answered questions about the stars, the conventions, the Committee, the movie, and other assorted "Star Trek" stuff.

Here's a funny, I think. Later that evening, the man bringing some films got lost or something, and I filled in onstage for a while. As I fielded the questions from the audience and the fans seated on and around the stage, I felt a tug on my Levi's. I looked down; a young man looked up at me quizzically and asked, "Who *are* you?" What do you do in a case like that? Underwhelm him with, "I'm Joanie Winston"? I could hear him saying, in a loud, clear voice, "So what?" Fear being the better part of valor, I asked him, "How long have you been at the convention?" hoping he would say he had just arrived. No such luck. He had been there the whole day. "Oh," I said, "well, why don't you ask someone to tell you? I'm too embarrassed. Next question." Well, after all, *Star Trek Lives!* had only been out a month, and he probably had never heard of the Committe or our cons. I'm glad it happened, though. If the Winston head was about to expand, that young man put a quick stop to it—because no matter what happens, I am a fan first, and proud of it.

August was a busy month for me, conwise. Jackie Lichtenberg and I went to the 1975 Chicago "Star Trek" convention to sell our book, see old friends, and meet new ones. I also went because it would be one of the rare times I was not working on the convention (little did she know, folks). As it turned out I ended up being press liaison for Bill Shatner, which is not the worst thing that can happen to one, but it did put a crimp in our sales. Besides, most of the fans already had our book, so we ended up signing all their copies—even the one that belonged to the kid who when he found out who I was, said, "Geez, after reading your chapters I thought you were fourteen years old and crazy." Well, one out of two's not bad.

However, I figured I wouldn't be up on the con floor too much since Bill was only to appear twice on Saturday and once on Sunday. Famous last words. The program schedule was a bit "off." Look, it was their first con, and unless you have them on a leash or they have a broken leg (which Shatner was just recovering from, by the way; he had broken it while doing a stunt on his "Barbary Coast" set, and it happened just four weeks prior to the con), guests tend to wander. I would be told to be ready to take Bill to the main ballroom at a certain time, only to discover that I would have to wait because they couldn't find someone, or somebody had taken more than their allotted fifteen or twenty minutes. So they would ask me to tell Bill that things were running a bit late. Several times. I told them that since he is a very bright man, he would realize that when I didn't come to get him, he wasn't going anywhere. They insisted. Sigh.

Bill was in a bit of pain during that time. While onstage that morning he had picked a little boy up onto the stage and hurt his leg. I guess he couldn't resist because the boy, Dale Westrate, was wearing a mama-made T-shirt that said "JAMES 'TOMCAT' KIRK AT AGE 9½." The boy was thrilled, and Mama was in ecstasy (see picture).

Later that afternoon, while waiting to make his second appearance of the day, a reporter asked Bill for an interview. One of her questions was, "Is this fun?" Bill looked at her, then at the smudged tile walls of the waiting area, and said, "*This* isn't fun." Pointing through the window in the kitchen door to all the fans listening blissfully to Leonard Nimoy, Bill said, "*That's* fun!" I think she got the idea.

That's very true; the fans are what make it fun. And it was fun to many fans for whom this was their first convention. The great idea of having the helper security guards dressed as Klingons. That was fun—and it worked. How could you get mad when a Klingon with a scowl and a gruff voice told you to "clear the way"?

Bill, looking fantastic despite his discomfort, allowing the fans to see who Bill Shatner really is—that was great.

Leonard Nimoy, who took his life and those precious bones in his hands, making a tour of the dealer's area. That was fun. Just to watch the fans' faces as he unexpectedly passed by. A gas. And I got the feeling he rather enjoyed it himself.

Jimmy Doohan, running a circuit of the ballroom and touching outstretched, happy hands. That was fun.

Nichelle Nichols, charming everyone is sight with her beauty and bright intelligence. That was lovely.

DeForest Kelley, just being himself, which is enough, because there is no one nicer. That was fun.

George being George, grinning, always a joy.

Walter Koenig, shy almost, but the fans eating it up.

David Gerrold and Bjo Trimble, who were host and hostess in the programing room. They were superb, untiring (at least they never showed it), good-natured, and kept the whole ball of wax from falling apart.

The parties. Like the one Nichelle's fan club gave, hosted by Virginia Walker, President, and the one Laura Scarsdale, Melinda Shreve, and Mary Lou Dodge had in their room. They publish *Delta Triad*, a really fine fanzine. Those were four A.M. fun.

The Dead Dog Party that Joyce and I gave because the neophyte Committee didn't know about them. We collected all the fans we saw and bought dozens of sodas from those coin-happy hotel machines. Then I ran down to the drugstore and got some candy and stuff. That was fun.

Now that I've said what *was* fun, let's get to what wasn't. I have no idea what trouble the Committee had with the hotel, but the hotel sure got even when they gave them a place for the dealers. It was all open, with staircases at either end, and almost impossible to keep pilferproof. Tony Anello, who was in charge, went up the wall trying to work with those arrangements.

The Costume Ball. The prejudging went on at—are you ready?—*nine in the morning!!* I spoke to one of the more visible Committee members, and she said that after much discussion, just prior to the con they had decided that the ball wasn't that important. Yipe. It was to some of the fans who had to get up at four in the morning to get their make-up and costume together! Not too many people other than those entered showed up

—no wonder (mumble, grumble), at *nine in the morning!!* Then some of the fans had to walk around in their costumes till the final judging at—you still with me?—*six in the evening!!* That would make even Spock's ears wilt.

One also had a hard time finding a Committee person. As a matter of fact, I asked the chairperson about this. She said she stayed mostly in the con suite so people could find her. The others were around but didn't wear a special badge or anything. Most cons, both "Star Trek" and science-fiction, have their committee members sporting big badges with COMMITTEE on them in bold letters, and/or a room somewhere on the main floor of the convention for the fans to be able to find a Committee member to talk to, cry to, or complain to. I really think that's a must.

As I have said, this was a first con, and most of the fans had a good time, but if you want to read a behind-the-scenes description of the helpers' plight at this and the New York Hilton convention run by much the same group, there is a booklet called *The Chicago and New York Strektaculars!* written and drawn by Phil Foglio, with lyrics by Ann Passovoy and published by boojums press.

Star Con 4 in Detroit was a bit of a disaster. The chairman had his hotel swept out from underneath him because of nonpayment of *their* electric bill. He had three weeks to find another location. Because of this, most fans thought the con had been canceled and did not go. As a consequence, the con did not take in anywhere near the money they had expected and had to cancel two of their three guests, Bill Shatner and DeForest Kelley. George Takei did come and was a delight, as usual.

The chairman, because of having to cancel some of his stars, reduced the entry fee. That was very nice. What wasn't so nice was that the press got the idea that the actors canceled out and that that was why the con went down the drain. Some not-so-nice things were written, and the people at the con were very shocked by the whole matter.

My friends and I had a lovely time and got to meet some of the midwestern fans, like Josie Williams. We had a lot of parties, and that helps make a good con.

Toronto is one of my favorites cities, and when Chairperson

Elizabeth Pearse asked me to be a guest, I was delighted. Jackie was to be one, too, and this doubled my pleasure.

This was my introduction to the Dorsai. They had run security at the 1975 Chicago con, but I really got to *know* some of them at Toronto. The Dorsai get their name from Gordie (Gordon R.) Dickson's well-known science-fiction series about this corps of soldiers.

I had already known Larry Propp from some southern cons I had attended. But here I got to meet Zilch, Manfred, Storyteller, and the one-and-only Sharon Ferraro, who is now Mrs. Story-teller (Mike Short). Nice folk. Crazy, but nice. Also the Passovoys, Doc and Ann. Not only do the Dorsai do security, but they also hold the grandest filksings your heart ever heard.

Filksings? Well, them's folksongs set to well-known tunes with fan-written lyrics, usually on SF, fantasy, or "Star Trek" topics, some of which can be printed in a "G"-rated volume. Some are very funny. Some are very sad, and some, especially the way Ann Passovoy and Juanita Coulson sing them, are very beautiful.

This was also the con where I finally got to meet Phil Foglio. He is an Artist, with a capital A—bright, funny and extremely talented. His cartoon books, derived from "Star Trek" and its characters, are something of underground classics.

This was a lovely con, well-run and lots of fun. Jackie and I got some ego-boo out of it, too. On the last day, Sunday, we were called early (oh lord!) in the morning and asked to introduce the guests scheduled for that day. Bjo and John Trimble had been doing it up to then and beautifully, but they were pooped, so Jackie and I tried to fill their place. All the stars were very co-operative and patient. Valerie and Ralph Carnes were running the programing, and they were extremely helpful.

Ralph told me he was going to introduce Nichelle Nichols because they were going to play a little joke on her. One of the papers had called her "staggeringly beautiful." He wanted all the fans to stand up when he started to introduce her, and as she walked onstage he would announce the "Staggeringly Beautiful" Nichelle Nichols, and everyone was to stagger back and collapse in their seats. The fans loved the idea, and everything went according to plan, including Nichelle's shock and then laughter.

This was also the con when I met Grace Lee Whitney. Talk about beautiful—a silvery blonde with a gorgeous tan and a figure to match. A really nice person. The fans adored her. She would sign autographs and pose for pictures by the hour. Well, it *was* one of her first cons!

By the way, the stage was fitted out with a beautiful replica of the *Enterprise* bridge. Elan "Lani" Litt had come up to Toronto with me. We were talking to Mark (pant, pant, pounce, pounce) Lenard in the con suite. Lani had just given him a copy of Jean Lorrah's *Night of the Twin Moons*, a Sarek- and Amanda-based fanzine. She and Jean thought he might like to see it, having played Sarek. Just then a Dorsai marched in and asked if anyone could weld. Lani's eyes lit up, and she dashed out with him. That was the last I saw of her till eight-thirty the next morning. She had been helping the Dorsai put the bridge together the whole night!

It was a beauty. And the lights and buttons and stuff worked, too. That's what took so long. Well . . . I got to know the bridge, too. No, I didn't weld, I unscrewed. (Watch it there, fellas.) I unscrewed a lot of screws, Phillips and otherwise, for about two hours before we had to go to the airport. Had a great time. Kill me, I like to unscrew screws!

As I said, it was a lovely con. It's a shame Elizabeth lost so much money. A lot of cons started going to the cleaner's around this time, usually because of bad planning, or not realizing that their area will support a small con but not one set up for five thousand or more. Since Elizabeth had planned hers very well, it must have been because of the summer weekend when the Olympics were in Montreal or that Toronto just did not have more than the four thousand-odd (and some were *very* odd) fans who came. I prefer to believe the former.

One that was successful was the ST and Space-science con in Oakland, California. I was invited but had already committed myself to a small con in Richmond, Virginia. Oakland had everyone, and it was very successful. They must have had over ten thousand fans attend. They had Len on Saturday and Bill on Sunday and were hanging fans from the rafters. Now, wait. Oakland did *not* have everyone. Nichelle Nichols was the guest of honor at the Richmond Con. This of course was much smaller, and was originally planned for Norfolk, but the hotel washed out, so they moved it. They only got a little over a thousand, but everyone had a ball—except for the woman with her son who was furious that they had programed films opposite the speeches. Pat Kelly, the co-chairman with John Upton, tried to explain counterprograming to her, but she just wanted her money back. She got it.

The happiest people besides the attendees were the dealers. Many of them sold out just about everything they brought with them. Before the con a lot of them were bemoaning the fact that they could not afford to go to Oakland. After the con was over and they carted their vastly depleted stock to their cars, they were jubilant. Even more so later, when they heard that a lot of the dealers in Oakland had not done well at all.

In Richmond, the dealers were on the same floor as the rest of the con. In Oakland, they were on an upper floor in a small, stuffy room, although some selected dealers were on the programing floor. No, I don't know why. Also, the Oakland fans have a "Star Trek" store in their area, The Federation Trading Post (we have one in New York, too), so the fans seemed to be more interested in seeing the programing than in buying. The Richmond fan, on the other hand, had no such convenience. This was, for many, their first convention and their first eyeball at all that lovely "Trek" merchandise. Picture a swarm of locusts clearing up a corn field. You got it.

But the Richmond convention was noted for something else: Nichelle Nichols. There is one beautiful lady. Talk about enchanting a roomful of people. I saw it with my own big browns. One session Jackie and I will never forget. We were just finishing a joint appearance when someone poked me in the back from behind the curtain. They whispered, "Don't either of you leave the stage after you introduce Nichelle. Okay?" I was a bit startled but nodded my head.

After her welcoming ovation she told us all she thought the women guests should share the stage at least once during the convention. She then told a little bit about Jackie and me, making us blush, the stinker. Nichelle answered questions, including one that was coming up with great frequency, she told us later.

"Was Uhura having an affair with Captain Kirk?"

"Of course not," she would say, with a huge grin and her expressive eyes and brows wigwagging an affirmative. The audience ate it up.

Every gathering always requested a song, and this was no exception. It was usually "Beyond Antares" from *Conscience of the King*, and Nichelle does it beautifully. But this time she said she would prefer to do a favorite of hers, Gershwin's "Summertime."

Jackie and I sat on the table next to Nichelle as she sang. I have heard "Summertime" many times but never sung before with such feeling, power, or beauty. By the time she finished we and some of the audience were openly crying. There was a most deserved standing ovation when she ended that last glorious note.

Nichelle turned to me, her face aglow, and her eyes widened as she reached over and wiped away one of my tears.

"You lousy——!" I sobbed and we both gave her tearful hugs and kisses.

I will never forget that lady or Richmond, Virginia.

Okay, Joan, wipe your eyes and blow your nose. What was the next con? I guess Bi-Centennial 10 in New York. I was not able to attend, as I was going to the World Science-fiction con in Kansas City, but I understand the fans had a great time. A lot of our own con helpers and assistants were there, and they pitched in and helped out. A first con always has problems, but if it's a good con, the fans are not aware of it.

This con was most noted for one event: Bill Shatner walked down into the audience and spoke to the fans from there. Star security was in cardiac arrest, but Bill quieted the fans with one sentence that went something like this: "I'd like to come down there if it's okay with you and you're going to be cool."

The whole room was glued to the floor. I got this from Carol Frisbee, who was one of those who enjoyed the view.

They had the whole crew except for Leonard, who had a prior commitment in California. The way I heard it:

Bill was beautiful.

De was a doll.

Jimmy was just marvelous.

Nichelle was a knockout.

George was great.

Walter was wonderful.

Grace Lee was gorgeous.

Susan Oliver was swell.

Kathryn Hays was a gem.

Stanley Adams was adorable.

And David Gerrold was indispensable, as usual.

The last con I'll mention is one that is part of a coming trend. What I think is, so many of the two- and three-day cons have lost money and even cost people their homes (yes, isn't that awful!) that people are following in the footsteps of some New York fans and having "Mini-'Trek'" cons—one-day affairs with either one or two guests, a dealers' room, some films, and charging a nominal admission, anywhere from $2.00 to $5.00, depending on their hotel expenses. The bigger the city the more expensive the hotels tend to be.

I was invited to speak at one run by Ray Stevens and John Ellis in Alexandria, Virginia. Jesco von Puttkamer from NASA was the other speaker. I had met him at Toronto, and he is a very impressive-looking man. We nicknamed him the Silver Flash. He has this glorious mane of silver-white hair. More on Jesco later.

The Committee had planned a small con. They needed 250 attendees to clear expenses. They charged $2.00 for children and $2.50 for adults. By three in the afternoon, they had passed the 900 mark! Everyone seemed to be having a ball except for some dealers. *This* time they were crying because they had not brought enough merchandise and were already sold out of much of their stock.

My talks went fairly well, but a lot of the people did not know who I was. Many of them had not read *Star Trek Lives!* The dealers were happy about that because that sold out fast! Even the ones I didn't get around to signing.

Before I had to leave, Jesco and I had a lovely talk. He told me some fascinating stories, but this is the best one.

The first con he ever appeared at was Chicago 1975. It was the big press conference, and most of the stars were present. Jesco said he knew that some one of the reporters would ask why a NASA representative was at a "Star Trek" con.

Sure enough, one of the reporters asked that very question.

Jesco gave it some thought and finally said, very seriously, "I had to come, you see, because I love Nichelle Nichols' legs!" That kind of put a stop to anyone else asking him any questions.

I have one one more Nichelle story to tell. This is one that her manager, Harry Friedenberg, told me. Nichelle was appearing at the Playboy Club in Great Gorge, New Jersey, the same week-end as the Playboy Science-fiction convention was taking place. Jackie, C. L. Moore, Theodore Sturgeon, Fred Pohl, Nichelle, I, and lots of other people were there that weekend. Because Nichelle was there, a lot of us got to see her do her act. This was not singing without music at a con—this was the real thing! She has a great act, with many little "Star Trek" touches. One num-ber is called "If the Crew Could See Me Now," and another one is a love song dedicated to "The Captain."

That afternoon, before her show, according to Harry, they were in Nichelle's dressing room, and Harry said, "Honey, why do you try for that high note? You know, sometimes you can't make it."

Nichelle looked at him. "When my voice decides it wants to go that high, Harry, it goes that high."

Harry looked back. "Just remember, honey, Yma Sumac you ain't."

That evening Nichelle did her show in the Playboy lounge, and I am a witness, she hit that note and hit it beautifully. In the midst of the applause she walked over to where Harry was sit-ting and said, triumphantly, "Yma Sumac, eat your heart out!" The whole room rocked with laughter, and so did Harry.

There are a lot of conventions planned for 1977, most of them small affairs, but a few large ones. I wish them all success and I'll probably be at most of them, if not as a guest, then as a fan. If you see me there please come over and say hello and let's have some good "Trek" talk.

CHAPTER VIII

WE FINALLY GOT IT RIGHT,
AND WE'RE GONNA QUIT WHILE WE'RE AHEAD!
(The 1976 "Star Trek" Convention, February 12–16, 1976, the Commodore Hotel, New York, New York)

"STAR TREK" TRIVIA CONTEST QUESTIONNAIRE
THE "STAR TREK" CONVENTION, 1976

1. On which three starships has James T. Kirk served?
   A. *Enterprise, Constellation, Farragut* B. *Enterprise, Farragut, Republic* C. *Enterprise, Valiant, Constitution*
2. What is the megatonnage of the fusion explosion that will result when an impulse engine is overloaded?
   A. 97.361 B. 97.183 C. 97.835
3. Last year we asked you for Gary Seven's address; now we want to know his apartment number. It is
   A. 3C B. 12B C. 11A
4. On what planet did Kodos commit genocide?
   A. Tarsus IV B. Eminiar VII C. Talos IV
5. What was the name of Flint's planet?
   A. M-113 B. Theta Cygni 12 C. Holberg 917-G
6. Many times Spock has been accused of being mechanized and inhuman, but who accused Captain Kirk of being "mechanized, electronized, and not really human"?
   A. Marlena Moreau B. Anton Karidan C. Flint
7. Rojan was a(n)
   A. Kelvan B. Ekosian C. Platonian
8. How many times in three seasons of "Star Trek" did James Kirk use the corbomite bluff?
   A. Once B. Twice C. Thrice
9. In *The Menagerie*, Commodore Mendez said the only death

penalty on the books was General Order Seven. But in *Turnabout Intruder,* Sulu claims that the death penalty was General Order

    A. Four   B. Five   C. Six

10. In *Patterns of Force,* Spock and Kirk used the crystals in their transponders to burn out the lock of their jail cell. These crystals were made of

    A. Dilithium   B. Pergium   C. Rodinium

11. Shaun Geoffrey Christopher will head the first Earth———probe.

    A. Jupiter   B. Ganymede   C. Saturn

12. What food had Captain Kirk ordered before he realized that the tribbles were in the food processors?

    A. Turkey sandwich and coffee   B. Chicken sandwich and coffee   C. Ham sandwich and coffee

13. In *Specter of the Gun,* the Melkotians "sent" Kirk and Company to Tombstone. What was the "date" on which they appeared there?

    A. April 12, 1871   B. October 26, 1881   C. September 8, 1861

14. John Christopher's serial number was

    A. 8457293   B. 4859723   C. 4857932

15. In boasting of the accuracy of the sensor web she wears to see, Miranda Jones states that she is standing precisely how far away from the door?

    A. One meter, one centimeter   B. One meter, four centimeters   C. One meter, seven centimeters

16. In what episode did Dr. McCoy put Captain Kirk on a diet?

    A. *The Corbomite Maneuver*   B. *The Enemy Within*   C. *Charlie X*

17. In *And the Children Shall Lead,* Stevie was disappointed with his coconut and vanilla ice cream. So he selected again. What did he receive the second time?

    A. Chocolate marble with pistachio and peach   B. Strawberry and apricot and peach   C. Chocolate pecan and pistachio

18. In *Charlie X,* Captain Kirk referred to UESPA (he pronounced it "You-spa"). In what episode did we find out that those initials stood for United Earth Space Probe Agency?

    A. *Where No Man Has Gone Before*   B. *Tomorrow Is Yesterday*   C. *Assignment: Earth*

19. After the vain attempt to end M-5's control over the *Enter-*

prise, Spock directed Chekov to go over to the bridge's engineering section and check on which of the following:

A. The H-279 elements and the G-95 systems   B. The H-95 elements and the T-279 systems   C. The H-95 elements and the G-279 systems

20. The planet Organia was listed as —— on the Federation's cultural scale.

A. Class D-minus   B. Class C-minus   C. Early medieval

21. Which one is *not* one of Captain Kirk's medals or commendations?

A. Silver palm with cluster   B. Legion of Honor   C. Star Fleet Citation for Gallantry

22. In which episode did Spock *not* get slapped across the face?

A. *Journey to Babel*   B. *Amok Time*   C. *The* Enterprise *Incident*

23. In which episode *did* Spock's nerve pinch work?

A. *Patterns of Force*   B. *I, Mudd*   C. *Assignment: Earth*

24. Geologist D'Amato was featured in which episode?

A. *Devil in the Dark*   B. *The Apple*   C. *That Which Survives*

25. In *Operation: Annihilate,* Kirk's brother, Sam, had only one son. But in *What Are Little Girls Made Of?* the android Kirk claimed that his brother had —— sons.

A. Two   B. Three   C. Four

26. The director of the Tantulus prison colony was

A. Dr. Piper   B. Dr. Corey   C. Dr. Adams

27. The American Continent Institute is mentioned in which episode?

A. *The Menagerie*   B. *Tomorrow Is Yesterday*   C. *Dagger of the Mind*

28. Dr. Roger Korby discovered important immunization techniques on what planet?

A. Ekos   B. Orion   C. Exo III

29. Who was the flight officer on the S.S. *Beagle?*

A. William B. Harrison   B. John Farrel   C. John Daily

30. Whose dressmaker did Spock pay compliments to?

A. Natira   B. Miranda   C. Droxine

31. For the invention of duotronics, Richard Daystrom received what two prizes?

A. Nobel and Majorska   B. Majorska and Z-Magnees   C. Nobel and Z-Magnees

32. In which episode did McCoy *not* say "He's dead, Jim"?

A. *Is There in Truth No Beauty?*   B. *The Changeling*   C. *Balance of Terror*

33. In three seasons of "Star Trek," two directors directed the most (and equal) number of episodes. They were:
    A. Marc Daniels and Vincent McEveety   B. Vincent McEveety and Joseph Pevney   C. Joseph Pevney and Marc Daniels

34. Anan 7 offered Captain Kirk a drink of
    A. Tranya   B. Trova   C. Antarean brandy

35. Uletta, before she was killed, was to be married to
    A. Eneg   B. Isak   C. Davod

36. The technique of synaptic fusion was used to
    A. Create an android duplicate of Captain Kirk   B. Restore Spock's brain   C. Impress human engrams onto the circuits of a computer

37. In *The City on the Edge of Forever*, what did Captain Kirk buy himself to eat?
    A. Ham on rye sandwich   B. Bologna and a hard roll   C. Mixed vegetables

38. Who was *not* a Klingon?
    A. Kryton   B. Krell   C. Kahless

39. In which episode is Spock topless?
    A. *Amok Time* B. *This Side of Paradise*   C. *Patterns of Force*

40. In which episode is Kirk *not* topless?
    A. *Charlie X*   B. *The Naked Time*   C. *The Corbomite Maneuver*

41. How often do ore ships call at Delta Vega?
    A. Every 20 years   B. Every 25 years   C. Every 30 years

42. In what state did Captain Christopher's plane crash?
    A. Colorado   B. Nebraska   C. Arizona

43. When Scotty was asked to lie, how old did he say he was?
    A. 35   B. 42   C. 22

44. In which episode does Dr. M'Benga *not* appear?
    A. *A Private Little War*   B. *That Which Survives*   C. *The Ultimate Computer*

45. Gary Mitchell liked
    A. Kafarian apples   B. Saurian brandy   C. Plomeek soup

46. McCoy used a —— to rouse Kirk from the Vulcan death grip.
    A. Psychostimulator   B. Physiostimulator   C. Cardiostimulator

47. What was the date of the news article, "FDR Confers with Slum-area 'Angel'" as shown on Mr. Spock's tricorder?
    A. February 21, 1932   B. February 23, 1936   C. February 22, 1934

48. In *The Paradise Syndrome*, the Indian tribe was composed of three Earth tribes. They were
    A. Sioux, Apache, and Seminole B. Mohawk, Algonquin, and Navajo C. Navajo, Mohican, and Delaware

49. What class ship was the S.S. *Botany Bay?*
    A. DY-100 B. DY-300 C. DY-500

50. In *The Doomsday Machine*, under which Star Fleet regulation was Commodore Decker able to take command of the *Enterprise?*
    A. Star Fleet Order 104, Section B B. Star Fleet Order 114, Section C C. Star Fleet Order 124, Section A

51. In return, Spock wrested command from Decker under which Star Fleet regulation?
    A. Star Fleet Order 141, Section B B. Star Fleet Order 104, Section C C. Star Fleet Order 114, Section A

52. The original home of the Platonians was
    A. Sundara B. Earth C. Platonia

53. In which episode did Spock refer to himself as "second officer" while making a log report?
    A. *The Man Trap* B. *The Enemy Within* C. *The Naked Time*

54. Captain Pike lived near
    A. Mojave B. Denver C. White Sands

55. Flint's residence bears a striking resemblence to a structure on which other planet?
    A. Deneva B. Rigel 7 C. Talos IV

56. Mira Romaine was born on
    A. Earth Colony 5 B. Martian Colony 3 C. Rigel 4

57. The salt vampire's true appearance was revealed to us in *The Man Trap* when she died. In what other episode did it appear as a prop?
    A. *The Devil in the Dark* B. *The Menagerie* C. *The Squire of Gothos*

58. Mark Lenard played both a Romulan and a Vulcan. Who is the only other person who has played both?
    A. Jack Donner B. Barry Atwater C. Lawrence Montaigne

59. According to the episode credits, who wrote the Brahms paraphrase that Spock played in *Requiem for Methuselah?*
    A. Ivan Ditmars B. George Duning C. Alexander Courage

60. John Lormer was the only actor to play three different roles in three different episodes. He was in *For the World Is*

Hollow and I Have Touched the Sky. He also appeared in:
A. *The Return of the Archons* and *The Menagerie* B. *The Return of the Archons* and *The Deadly Years* C. *The Return of the Archons* and *All Our Yesterdays*

MATCHING: Match each medication with the letter next to the show in which it was mentioned. (An episode may be repeated more than once.)

61. Benjisidrine   A. *By Any Other Name*
62. Ryetalyn   B. *Miri*
63. Hyronalin   C. *Plato's Stepchildren*
64. Cordrazine   D. *The Tholian Web*
65. Stokaline   E. *The Naked Time*
66. Masiform D   F. *The Deadly Years*
67. Theragin derivative G. *Journey to Babel*
68. Formazine   H. *The City on the Edge of Forever*
69. Kironide   I. *The Apple*
70. Tri-ox compound   J. *Requiem for Methuselah*
                         K. *The Cloud Minders*

MATCHING: Match the quotation with the letter next to the show in which it was said. (An episode may be repeated more than once.)

71. "My son, the doctor."   A. *A Private Little War*
72. "Sir, there is a multilegged   B. *The Galileo Seven*
    creature crawling on your   C. *A Taste of Armageddon*
    shoulder."   D. *The Man Trap*
73. "Well, then thank pitchforks   E. *The Omega Glory*
    and pointed ears."   F. *Where No Man Has*
74. "That which is ours is ours   *Gone Before*
    again. It will never be taken   G. *The Naked Time*
    from us again."   H. *What Are Little Girls*
75. "Rig up a cord and send down   *Made Of?*
    a pot of coffee."   I. *The Savage Curtain*
76. SPOCK: "Doctor, you're a sen-   J. *The Lights of Zetar*
    sualist."   K. *The Corbomite Maneu-*
    MCCOY: "You bet your pointed   *ver*
    ears I am."   L. *The* Enterprise *Incident*
77. "Get out of my way, Saw-   M. *The City on the Edge of*
    bones."   *Forever*
78. "Take D'Artagnan here to sick   N. *Balance of Terror*
    bay."   O. *The Gamesters of Tris-*
79. "I don't make house calls."   *kelion*
80. "Command and compassion   P. *The Changeling*
    are a fool's mixture."   Q. *This Side of Paradise*

81. "I am a Vulcan, bred to peace."
82. "We're very tired, Mr. Spock. Beam us up home."
83. "Mr. Spock, I'm sick of your half-breed interference."
84. "Picturesque descriptions will not mend broken circuits, Mr. Scott."
85. "By golly, Jim, I'm beginning to think I can cure a rainy day."
86. "They're come to pay their respects to Alvin."
87. "I'm not *that* green, sir."
88. "The haggis is in the fire for sure."
89. "In a different reality, I could have called you 'friend.'"
90. "Scotty, inform Star Fleet Command. Disengage nacelles; jettison if possible."
91. "I used a hand phaser, and ZAP!—hot coffee."
92. "Biped, small. Good cranial development; no doubt with considerable human ancestry."
93. "May the Great Bird of the Galaxy bless your planet."
94. "Mr. Sulu, if I'd wanted a Russian history lesson, I'd have brought Mr. Chekov."
95. "There will be a formal dance in the bowling alley at 1900 hours tonight."
96. "Gentlemen, human beings have characteristics, just as inanimate objects do."
97. "I don't know what's causing it —virus, bacteria or evil spirits —but I'm working on it."

R. *The Alternative Factor*
S. *Catspaw*
T. *That Which Survives*
U. *A Piece of the Action*
V. *Court-martial*
W. *The Deadly Years*
X. *The Enemy Within*
Y. *Spock's Brain*
Z. *Arena*
AA. *Friday's Child*
BB. *The Devil in the Dark*
CC. *Obsession*
DD. *Bread and Circuses*
EE. *Mirror, Mirror*

Chris Lundi as a bird of paradise at the 1976 con. *(Linda Deneroff)*

Connie Faddis in her Pre-Reform Vulcan Warrior Queen outfit, made of hand-worked copper, at the 1976 con. *(Benjamin M. Yalow)*

Helen Wood and Mark Gilray at the 1975 con. Helen is in her *Mirror, Mirror* universe costume, and Mark is Spock's right ear!?! *(Jeff Maynard)*

Majel Barrett Roddenberry and Gene Roddenberry joyfully joining fingers in a Vulcan love gesture after a three-hour autograph session at the 1972 con. On awakening the next morning, Gene reached over to give Majel a kiss, and she murmured, "Don't touch me, I'm a star!"

Gene Roddenberry speaking to an attentive, standing-room-only audience of about eighteen hundred at the 1972 con.

98. "The term 'half-breed' is some-
    what applicable, but 'com-
    puterized' is inaccurate."
99. "Fool me once, shame on you.
    Fool me twice, shame on
    me."
100. "I know the time; I don't need
     a blooming cuckoo clock."

Why is it that I have such a difficult time getting to my own
conventions?

This was Thursday, and the Con had opened today at 2:00
P.M. I had hoped to arrive by four o'clock, but no luck. I phoned
the con suite and left a message that I would be late because I
had to finish a special report. Suddenly at six o'clock I remembered that I had theater tickets for De Kelley in my purse. He
had wanted to see *Chicago,* and I had gotten him two down-
front seats through some friends. At this time I was still under
the impression that his lovely wife, Carolyn, was accompanying
him.

I called the con suite again. All the lines were busy. Par for
the course. I then tried to reach De's room. The operator would
not connect me. I told her who I was—still no. Every fifteen
minutes I would try the con suite, registration, and the worry
room; all lines were busy.

And there I sat with thirty dollars' worth of *Chicago* burning a
hole in my purse.

I finally got to the Commodore at about seven-thirty that evening. The curtain had just gone up on *Chicago.* De was not in
his room, and no one seemed to know where he was. I was in my
room unpacking when I heard this commotion outside my window. Even though I was twenty-two stories up I could hear the
following conversation as if I were five feet away. "*He's* here!
He's here!" Somebody leaned out of a tenth-story window,
"Who's here?" "The Great Bird!" They shouted up. And that's
how I found out that Gene Roddenberry had arrived. Someone
called to say that Gene wanted to see me in his suite. So I
trundled over.

Gene and Majel were on the opposite side of the hotel. They
had wanted a suite with two bedrooms, and that was the only

TIME	GRAND BALLROOM	EAST BALLROOM	TUDOR ROOM	TIME
Thursday, February 12, 1976				
10 A.M.	Films			10 A.M.
12 NOON		Films		12 NOON
2 P.M.	David Gerrold		Films	2 P.M.
3	George Takei	James Doohan		3
4	Howard Weinstein	William Theiss		4
5	Dinner	Films		5
6				6
8	Films	Autograph and Photograph Sessions—First Floor		8
1 A.M.				1 A.M.
Friday, February 13, 1976				
10 A.M.	Films	Films		10 A.M.
11				11
12 NOON	George Takei		Films	12 NOON
1 P.M.	Nichelle Nichols	David Gerrold		1 P.M.
2	Gene Roddenberry	Isaac Asimov		2
3	Science-Fiction Editors' Panel	Films		3
4	James Doohan		Nichelle Nichols	4
5	Dinner		Films	5
8	Allan Asherman's Slide Show	Autograph and Photograph Sessions—First Floor		8
9	Fashion Show			9
10	Films			10
12 MDNT.				12 MDNT.
1 A.M.				1 A.M.
Saturday, February 14, 1976				
10 A.M.	DeForest Kelley	James Doohan	Films	10 A.M.
11	Hal Clement: "The Ecology of Regulus V"	Nichelle Nichols and Majel Barrett		11
	David Gerrold	George Takei	"Space Colonies Now!" D. McHugh and L. Abdulezer	
12 NOON		Films	Films	1 P.M.

Saturday (continued)

Making of a Star Trek Novel
Cogswell, Spano, and Pohl
Roddenberry and Barrett
Films
Autograph and Photograph Sessions—First Floor

Time		
3		Fan Panel: Costume Design — Dana L. F. Anderson
4	Gerrold and Weinstein [Animation]; Nichelle Nichols	Films
5	Dinner	
6	"Trek-A-Star"	Autograph and Photograph Sessions—First Floor
8	Song Contest / Songfest	
9	Films	
10		
12 MDNT.		
1 A.M.		

Sunday, February 15, 1976

Time		
10 A.M.	Art Show Auction	Films
11		
12 NOON	Lunch	
1 P.M.	Stars' Panel; Isaac Asimov	Hal Clement "How to Write the 'Star Trek' Story (or Please Don't Make Him Say That!)"
2	Joan Winston	Films
3	Nichelle Nichols; George Takei	
4	DeForest Kelley; William Theiss	
5	Dinner	
6:30	Autograph and Photograph Sessions—First Floor; Masquerade Prejudging (Contestants Only)	Autograph and Photograph Sessions—First Floor
7:30		
9	Federation Masquerade	Films
12 MDNT.		

Monday, February 16, 1976

Time		
10 A.M.	Art Show Auction	Films
11		
12 NOON	Lunch	
1 P.M.	George Takei; David Gerrold	Gordon Dickson
2	Science-Fiction Writers' Panel; James Doohan	Films
3	Nichelle Nichols; Films	
4	Star Trek Lives! — J. Lichtenberg and J. Winston; Malcolm Klein Animation	

one available on the floor. The extra room was for the baby, Gene Jr., (Rod) and his nurse. When I got to the suite Gene told me that Majel was not there. The baby was ill, and until he was better she would not think of leaving him. The extra bedroom was being used by someone who worked for Lincoln Enterprises and was selling behind their table in the dealers' room.

As I was talking to Gene, who should knock at the door but De Kelley. He had come to have a drink with Gene prior to the press party. I told him about the tickets and he offered to pay for them anyway, but I wouldn't permit it.

Just a few weeks before, when De was a guest at Lisa Boynton's con at the New York Hilton, he had asked me to get him tickets to A Chorus Line. They were the hardest tickets to get, but I got them. As it turned out, he was due onstage at the time the matinee was to begin that Saturday. He told me this when he came over to my ABC office for a visit. At about that same time a New York Daily News photographer was due to arrive to take pictures for an article they were doing on the "Star Trek" cons. (I know, I couldn't believe it either!)

She was delighted to find De there, and while I entertained Carolyn, the photographer got all the secretaries together and took pictures of them surrounding De in an adoring fashion. None of them found this hard to do. My secretary, Christine Accardi, was right in the front line. She thought he was delightful. Bright girl.

When De came back to my office he told me of his problem and asked me to please go to the theater with Carolyn. "She will enjoy it much more sitting next to someone she knows."

I was delighted since I had not had a chance to see A Chorus Line and offered to pay for the ticket. De refused because, he said, "You're doing us a favor."

And that was why I would not permit him to pay for the Chicago tickets.

Gene, De, and I were talking awhile when the phone rang. It was Majel. After speaking for a few moments, Gene handed me the phone.

"Hi, Majel, how is little Rod feeling?"

"Oh Joanie, he is much better, and if his temperature stays normal, the doctor says I can come to the convention tomorrow."

"Great, we are all looking forward to your arrival."

She asked how the con was going, and I told her very well. We had decided to have the membership completely preregistered. That meant all 6,000 tickets to be sold prior to the con and *none* at the door.

Joyce Yasner was registration director this year, and it was quite a job. By the February 1 deadline, we had received 5,250. This was a fantastic amount, but not the 6,000 we had hoped for. To Joyce's dismay, we voted at a meeting to sell tickets at the hotel on Tuesday and Wednesday. That still left about 400 unsold memberships. We could have advertised, but let's face it, we would have gotten 4,000 fans for 400 tickets, which equals a riot in anybody's language. No thanks, we'd take the loss. (Actually, we sold quite a few tickets in the worry room during the con—people who pleaded on hands and knees, press people who, after seeing one day of the con, decided to bring their children, a husband who came with his wife, at the last minute, from Milwaukee, people like that there. One of our lawyers, Sandi Harris, told me of a very nice priest who asked to buy a ticket. Sandi explained that we were not selling tickets at the door, but thought we could manage one for him. Looking concerned, he said, "But there are 53 more of us outside." We sold them tickets!)

Majel said that she would let us know what flight she was coming on if she could make it, and I handed the phone back to Gene. De mentioned that he and Gene had been rehashing old times and, in particular, an old TV pilot Gene had written that they had worked on, *Police Story*. It had been years ahead of its time, and it had an important fact: De had played a doctor; a police doctor, to be sure, but a doctor just the same. Funny how things work out, isn't it?

We talked for a while; then there was a knock at the door. It was Lise Eisenberg and Karina Girsdanski, come to collect us for the Committee-Guest party. Gene and De were once more deep in old reminiscenses, and it took me about ten minutes to get them out of the room and down to the con suite. I was greeted with cheers and applause, but I'm no fool. I was walking between "The Creator" and "The Doctor," and delighted to be in such handsome company.

Gene headed for his favorite room, the den off the gigantic liv-

ing room. This room was smaller, more intimate, and we all
would gather at his feet and just drink him in.

Have I ever described the con suite? Well, it's the Presidential
Suite of the Commodore Hotel, so called because it's where Ei-
senhower ran his 1956 campaign from. First there are large double doors leading into a large hall with two more big doors.
Along this hallway are three doors. One is a closet, and the other
two lead into the bedroom and sitting room of the small junior
suite that I occupied during the 1975 con. This was called 22B.
The rest of the suite is called 22A. Through the next double
doors, we see an even larger hall. On the right are three doors,
one a large closet and two leading into huge master bedrooms
with adjoining dressing rooms and baths. On the left are four
doors; the first leads into the large kitchen with many, many cab-
inets, two double sinks, a refrigerator, and a two-burner hotplate.
This is where Devra made breakfast for the thundering horde,
otherwise known as the Committee (those who got up at "Rise
and Shine"—7:00 A.M.!), various assistants and helpers, and occasionally a Jimmy Doohan or a Nichelle Nichols or a David Gerrold would join them for corn flakes and coffee.

The second door led to a really fancy powder room. That
made four bathrooms in the suite, and don't think that didn't
come in handy! Then you come to two sliding doors, which lead
to the formal dining room, which sat twelve. Well, when we used
it, it fed more like twenty. The last two sliding doors and you
were in what the hotel called "The Grand Salon." We called it
the living room. They had removed the grand piano (!), but this
forty-by-twenty-foot room had two couches, half a dozen chairs
and tables, a fireplace, and wasn't crowded in the least.

If you'll go back to the hall straight ahead, you will see two
more doors; those lead into the den, which is right next to the living room, and all the doors can be left open so that a huge area
is available. Off the den, in an alcove, is a wet bar. That means
that there is a sink and a small fridge.

The den was a large, friendly room. There were a big desk, a
couch, and several assorted armchairs and tables. There was also
a huge color TV (that made four in the suite!). We were not to
discover until the very end of this con that the couch opened up
into a huge double bed. But the thing that caught everyone's eye

was a big world globe in the corner. It lit up! All I could think of
when I first saw it was: Is it as big as the one Nero Wolfe had in
his office?

As you can imagine, this was one grand place to hold a party.
It was like old home week. All of the guests, with the exception
of Howard Weinstein, had been to previous cons, and it was
catching-up-on-news time.

Nichelle Nichols was not coming in until Friday night, and we
hoped fervently that little Rod would be better so Majel could
come.

This was really going to be a "party con." Besides tonight's
affair, there was to be a press party on Friday night and a party
for the helpers on Saturday night. Well, since this was to be our
last convention, we figured we might as well have a rip-roaring
time.

On Friday, we opened the press room. We were not happy.
We were situated in the Dartmouth Suite, located on the mezzanine floor. On Sunday, somebody vandalized the area and pulled
out all the phones. (Not fans, we're sure.) Even with this lack of
communication, they would not let me have one of the CB units.
Hell, I was not only in charge of press and films, I was also vice
chairperson. I sulked for about six seconds and then said . . .
Well, what I said could not be printed here.

We had changed our rules this year. Before, we had given free
press passes to anyone who could show an affiliation with a
school or college newspaper, magazine, radio, or TV station. We
had received over six hundred requests for the previous year's
con. Less than 10 per cent of them ever wrote stories. We know
because we had asked them to send us copies, and they had to
clear the pictures through us. (See the copy of the 1975 Pocket
Program, printed at the beginning of Chapter VI.) It finally
dawned on us that a lot of these kids were just out to get free
passes—especially since I had overheard some of them brag to
their friends of this very fact. Soooo . . .

Our progress report went out in October, and in it we stated
that while we would continue to honor the school and college
press people with admission into the press conferences, they
would now have to pay for their press tickets. The number of
requests dropped to forty! How do you like that?

Of course, the professional media people had no problem. They just had to show their identification, usually a police card, or in some instances, where they had called or written in advance and we could verify it, a letter from their editor. While the press were very co-operative, we saw very little in the papers or on TV. They told me their editors wanted news of riots and overcrowding. (Shades of the Hilton convention!)

A for-instance: Thom Anderson was our chairman that year, and he was in the worry room taking care of lost kids, lost wallets, lost badges, etc., various cut fingers, mashed toes (we had two nurses in attendance)—the usual stuff. Suddenly this beautiful young woman confronted him.

"I'm —— from the '——Show.' Where's the riot?"

Thom looked up, a little startled, then said, "I'm sorry, but we're not having one today," and turned to his next problem. His assistants, Alina Chu, Michael Spence, and our two dear lawyers, Bob and Sandi Harris, just stared at her.

She swept out and went into the programing room, crowded but well-behaved; then the film room, crowded but well-behaved; then the dealers' room, crowded but well-behaved. Then she started to buttonhole fans.

"What's wrong with this convention?" she asked, eagerly.

"Nothing," the fan would stammer. "It's great. I'm having a ball."

After half an hour of this, she finally left in disgust. She should have waited for Saturday night's autograph session, but that comes much later.

We had four press interviews set for that afternoon: first George at one o'clock, then David at two, Jimmy Doohan at five, and just before charming Jimmy, three science-fiction editors— Fred Pohl of Bantam Books, Pat LoBrutto of Ace Books, and Jim Baen of *Galaxy* magazine. Pat and Fred you have met in Chapter V.

I didn't get to see much of the programing (as usual), just glimpses here and there as I raced by: Nichelle Nichols singing, Gene and Majel charming one and all, Howard Weinstein speaking, George being George, and Jimmy Doohan singing! It was a musical convention!

Howard Weinstein—that name was familiar. Elyse knew she had heard or seen that name somewhere. Of course, he had written a "Star Trek" animated episode called *Pirates of Orion*. Well, he had also written a request for a ticket to our con. Elyse wrote back and asked if he would come to the con as a guest and speak to the fans. He sure would.

Howie (as we now call him) walked into the Commodore and realized he did not know where he was going. The lobby was very crowded with fans, but Howie spotted two young men with red Committee badges walking toward the elevators.

Hoping they were going where he wanted to go, he followed them. They were Ben Yalow and Dave Simons. They got off on the twenty-second floor and headed for the con suite. Following behind them, Howie said, "You don't know me, but I'm a guest of the convention, and I hope your leading me to the con suite."

Ben and Dave turned and in unison said, "You're Howard Weinstein." Howie's jaw dropped and he said, "How did you know?"

"Well," they said, "we know everybody else, so you had to be Howard Weinstein."

That's why they're on the Committee, Howie.

During the Dead Dog Party, Howie was to be immortalized in verse, and here it is:

> Howie Weinstein, Howie Weinstein,
> Who are you? Who are you?
> Wrote an animated, wrote an animated,
> Just for you, just for you.
> [To the tune of "Frère Jacque"]

Isaac Asmiov did not make his speech and was replaced by films (hardly an equal exchange). But Isaac's daughter had been in an auto accident. He called Elyse to tell her he would not be able to come to the con until he was sure his daughter was all right.

During that afternoon's interviews, Ellen came over and told me that some men from *Time* magazine were asking if they could set up in an empty room in our area. They wanted to interview fans and take some pictures. I went over to see them and noticed they were taking pictures of some young, uh, chubby, uh, large (forget it) fans with funny hats and covered with buttons and patches. I called him over and said, "Am I fat?" He looked startled. I pointed to my helpers. "Are they fat?" He gulped and finally spoke.

"No."

"Then," I said, "why are you taking pictures like that and calling them, as I know you will, 'typical "Star Trek" fans'? Because if that's all you see at this con and that's the kind of coverage you mean to do, you can leave right now."

I was mad. Good and mad. I was sick and tired of being pictured as a freak and a nut and a weirdo because of the biased and narrow-minded media coverage. This was our last con, and I could take off the kid gloves. I let him have it.

He quickly assured me that was not the story he was looking for. His editor wanted him to cover the convention from a pro angle since he, the editor, was a closet Trekkie. I winced. I do not care for the word "Trekkie." It brings to mind little kids running down the aisle shrieking "Spoooooooock" or "Kirrrrrrk." We talked for a while and I introduced him to several of the fans just hanging around. He admitted later he found them all intelligent and articulate and *not* fat.

The photographer came over at that time, and I suggested they come back that night and see the Fashion Show and perhaps even the masquerade on Sunday. Of course, they had to check it all out with Dana, since she was in charge of both these events. The photographer did come back for both of these and, as a matter of fact, he searched me out after the Masquerade on Sunday to say how gorgeous the costumes were and how glad he was that I had suggested it.

Don't get excited. You didn't miss the issue the picture and article were in. Time never printed them. And they have no reason they will give, at least not to me. Sigh, again.

Oops, the press party. The last one, how about that? I raced up to my room to get dressed. (Why am I always running?) I wasn't in the con suite this year. I decided I couldn't take the "thundering horde." This year, I had a large junior suite down the hall just past the elevators. It had a king-size bed plus a

couch and two armchairs and a big table and four chairs. It was
a big room.

The first two nights a friend from Washington, Avedon Carol,
shared it with me. Well, to be truthful, she crashed. Then the
last night I convinced Daphne Hamilton to stay over for the
Dead Dog Party and . . .

Anyway, a little late, I got to the party. I went around greeting
guests and making sure everything was taken care of. I took one
look at the buffet and died. We had gotten 10 pounds of bologna
and salami plus about 7 pounds of assorted cheeses. There were
a couple of chunks of bologna left, but no cheese.

Jill Wallach, who was in charge of the con suite, told me that
the cheese had disappeared about five minutes after hitting the
platter. We quickly sent someone out to the deli for more. That
was the party where we went through three hundred dollars'
worth of booze in four and a half hours.

But I had to run, again. I was due onstage as moderator for
the Fashion Show. It was to start at eight-thirty, and I still had
to get into my sari. That's easier said than done. It had been so
long, I forgot how. After three tries, I finally got it draped right
and, that's right, ran to the elevators. If you think it's easy to run
in a sari, try it sometime. It's like trying to run with a straitjacket
around your knees!

A little note here: This was around the time of the Victoria flu.
Originally we had twenty-four entrants for the Fashion Show.
The flu knocked out seventeen of them. We got Joyce Yasner
and Linda Deneroff to take the place of two of the flu-filled entrants. William Ware Theiss, the constume designer of "Star
Trek" was the judge. He really had a hard time; the designs were
really gorgeous.

The ABC News cameramen were there and the *Time* photographer, too. He had to set up in one of the display rooms and
was in ecstasy. At least that's what he said. After the show was
finished, Dana and Bill joined me, and we went upstairs to find
the party still in full swing.

I guess it was a good party. No one wanted to leave, but we
had Gene, Majel, De, George, Nichelle, Bill Theiss, David Gerrold, Fred Pohl, and Jackie Lichtenberg to keep things swinging
while I was gone. At about ten-thirty, we decided that was *it*,

and we suddenly ran out of liquor. You'd be surprised how quickly that can end a party.

After the press had left, the guests, Committee, assistants, and helpers settled down to a nice, long talkfest. It was lovely.

Saturday had just started, and we still had Sunday and Monday to get through. This had ended up being a five-day con. You see, we usually held it on Washington's Birthday weekend, and this year, Lincloln's Birthday fell on the Thursday just prior to that weekend. So, in a moment of midwinter madness, we decided on a five-day con.

I had a feeling that I would still end up on the local community farm for the definitely bewildered. It would just take one day longer this year. I hope they did the padding in my room over. I hate that shade of blue.

We opened the con on Saturday with De and Jimmy—the fans went nuts, as you can see by the program (which got changed several times by unforeseen circumstances). Each day was different. Elyse thought long and hard about the program, and this one ended up giving her fits. We had to work together to schedule the films in the different rooms so that the two union projectionists had time to eat, take care of natural functions, and not run into themselves coming and going. At times it was a *very* close thing; the guys were great! And so was my faithful Mike Weisel.

There was the usual trouble with the projectors breaking down, and bulbs going dim, and film breaking, and somebody almost falling through the three-hundred-dollar screen, and somebody else having an epileptic seizure in the middle of *Mirror, Mirror*—all in a day's (and night's) work for Michael. Very rarely did I hear about those things from him. He just took them in stride and did his usual magnificent job. I was so lucky to find him.

We had three press conferences due for Saturday: De at twelve noon, Gene and Majel at 1:00 P.M., and Bill Theiss at 3:00 P.M. I was flitting in and out, and Ellen took care of a lot of this. I don't remember exactly what I was doing (running around a lot, probably). I was vice chairperson, as everyone kept reminding me, and got stopped for many things.

One time a young girl had lost her badge and said that she

just could not afford to pay the money to get a new one. I took her to the worry room and talked Bob Harris into giving her a new one. She had an ID, and she was on our list. We had the rule that if you lost your badge, you had to pay for a new one because otherwise it would be so easy to give your badge to a friend who hadn't paid and get a new one for yourself. After all, there was your name on our list. Everyone got very good at judging who the deadbeats were—and I didn't think she was one of them and, I guess, neither did Bob.

Perhaps one attendee should have bought two memberships, just in case. Joyce was on duty at registration on Friday when this very, very pregnant lady walked in. As she got her badge Joyce asked when the baby was due. Very calmly, the woman smiled and answered, "Yesterday."

Everybody's eyes snapped wide open, and we had a helper follow the woman with a chair all through the con. She seemed to have a great time. She told everybody she just would not give birth until after the con was over. I understand the baby was born on Tuesday. Talk about timing—and determination!

In the worry room, Thom was taking care of three things at once, as usual, when a "lady" walked—or should I say undulated —in. Thom was pointed out to her as the chairman, and she told him what she wanted. What she wanted was a "room to entertain in." Thom stared at her blankly for about six seconds and then got her drift. He decided to play the innocent—it's easy for him with those big baby blues. As she was going into more detail, her fees, and the convention "cut," about a dozen ten- and twelve-year-olds ran into the room.

Thom looked at her and said, "Since most of the attendees are in that age range, you can see that your 'special' services would not be required."

The woman stared at the kids and back at Thom who, along with Alina, Mike, and the Harrises, was having a terrible time trying to keep a straight face. She mumbled something unintelligible and left.

Just as she turned the corner, they all collapsed in hysterics. They would need to remember that laugh, later.

There was trouble, right here in Convention City. On the schedule it said that there were to be autograph and photo sessions on the first floor at six o'clock. Well, that's not quite what happened. One of the assistants was supposed to take the Roddenberrys out to dinner—on the convention. We loved them, and we wanted to do something extra. When he found them, they were in the New York, New York bar in the hotel lobby with George, Nichelle, and Jimmy. So they all ended up going. That was okay.

But . . . It seems they went to a restaurant rather far away and did not get waited on for an hour. By the time they finished eating, it was one hour past the autograph and photo sessions. Thom and I went down to calm the crowds—and make no mistake, there was a *crowd!* Thom says I saved his life. I don't know about that, but I did tell a big lie, and I hope the fans there will forgive me.

I told them that everybody had gone to dinner with some people from Paramount to talk about the picture and they would be back soon, and we would reschedule the session. They were all very good about it—*then.*

However, when the stars still hadn't appeared at the newly scheduled time, there was panic. We sent a helper down. She was all of five-one, and when she saw this crowd of impatient, starting-to-be-angry people (and they had cause), she just yelled, "It's been canceled again," and ran for her life.

Well, —— —— of the "—— Show," you should have come today. You would have seen our first and, thank Ghu, last riot. Stu Hellinger told me later that it never really got to "riot" proportions. It was slowly and quietly dispersed by Dave, Manny, Pat, Stu, and Ghu knows how many helpers. First they started cutting the lengths of all the lines and slowly started shifting people out, apologizing all the while. I was on an elevator on my way to check the Tudor Room on the lobby floor to make sure our quiet riot had not spread. The elevator doors opened onto the first floor, and a very harassed helper held out his arms and said, "Nobody off on this floor!" Everybody stared at him and behind him. All you could see (he was rather large) were heads and arms and wide-open eyes and mouths all going at once. We all stared, mesmerized until the elevator doors closed.

However, the Tudor Room was orderly, and the films were

being quietly enjoyed. Thank heavens. Then—are you all paying attention?—I went out to dinner.

A friend, Mike McQuown said, "You've got to eat!" Yes, but not usually at conventions. It's just not done, like sleeping. There are so many other things to do. But Mike insisted, and I had an hour and twenty minutes of peace and quiet. It was very *refreshing*.

I got back in time to change for *Trek-a-Star*. This is a hilarious musical spoof of "Star Trek." *H.M.S. Trek-A-Star* was first performed at the twentieth West Coast Science-fantasy Conference in 1967. Bjo and John Trimble were crew members, and Dorothy Jones sang the lead, Yeoman Rand. The music is taken from Gilbert and Sullivan's *H.M.S. Pinafore* rearranged by Dorothy Jones and Felice Rolfe with special lyrics by Karen and Astrid Anderson and Dorothy Jones, with Poul Anderson, Jerry Jacks, Joe Rolfe, Felice Rolfe, and Thomas Cobley.

The story is a simple one, with Yeoman Rand in love with Kirk, and Kirk in love with his ship. They pick up a castaway who looks like a haystack, called Stackstraw. He immediately falls in love with Rand, and it becomes a round robin. When Spock relieves Stackstraw of his covering, we discover Kirk's old nemesis, Finnigan, who had been under an evil spell. Anyway, it all ends well except that Spock comments, "This is basically irrational." Maybe, but it is also a lot of fun, and the songs are great.

Barbara Wenk had contacted a goup of students in Toms River, New Jersey, who had a Gilbert and Sullivan club in their high school. They agreed to do the show for us for free passes and a night's lodging. Actually we got a call from the Parks Department in Dover Township, and they asked if the students could give a preview performance in a park before doing our show. If we would agree, they would supply a bus (!) to take the kids to and from Tom's River. We agreed. You betcha! A bus!

The line of fans stretched around the area outside the ballroom like a snake. Inside they were setting up the scenery, and the "actors" were getting made up. As the fans filed in they were handed a program for *Trek-a-Star* and a song sheet for the Song Contest/Songfest that followed.

The Committee and assistants had reserved seats up in the balcony. When we arrived, we found a lot of fans in our seats. Politely (and some not so politely), they were asked to leave.

The show began, and almost three thousand people, most of whom had never heard of *Trek-a-Star*, let alone seen it, went out of their gourds—with joy! They loved it. The students ranged in age from fourteen to eighteen years of age. Spock was played by a fourteen-year-old. And he was *good!* So was everyone else in the show.

After the show, Dana got up on the stage with her guitar and led the wildly enthusiastic audience in a series of wildly unlikely songs. You'll find one in the chapter on the 1974 con and another in the chapter on the 1975 con.

At one point, if you can believe it, Devra, Joyce, Linda and I did a hora (that's a kind of Jewish reel) to "There's an Amoeba," which is set to the music of "Hava Nagila." That none of us broke a leg during his demonstration proves that God looks after all fools.

While this madness was going on, a woman went up to one of the security people and rather hysterically reported the loss of her wallet. It had all her rent money in it, and she wanted to know if anyone could have found it and turned it in to lost and found. No one had. The Committee, which had been notified, was ready to take some money out of petty cash for her. Just then a helper walked up and handed in a wallet—*the* wallet. With all the rent money intact. It made everyone feel really good —especially the woman. P.S.: She offered the helper a reward, but he wouldn't take it. Nice.

Dana was still going strong in the ballroom, and she did all the songs twice, and the fans still wanted more. And more. And more. Finally, Dana's voice gave out and she ended the session to a well-deserved standing ovation.

Devra went with the *Trek-a-Star* performers up to the twenty-second floor. As they all got off the elevator, the hallway was jampacked with people. The performers walked single file, and as the first cast member was recognized, the crowd broke into applause. Then the crowd started to sing "We Boldly Go Where Men Have Never Gone Before Us." The rest of the cast and Committee picked it up, and the halls rang all the way to the helpers' party—stopping only when the lead person walked into Gene Roddenberry's chest. All the people in the hall who were not invited to the party (it was just for the helpers, assistants, and guests) clapped and laughed delightedly.

It was a great helpers' party. Elyse, Devra, and Wendy had baked for days to make the cakes, cookies, and Elyse's famous brownies. We also served, coffee, tea, milk, and soda—not necessarily together—although one helper mixed milk and Pepsi. (Ugh!)

De Kelley came in and spent some time with us, along with Jimmy and Nichelle. The kids went bonkers. Many of them had been unable to see any of the programing because they were on duty on staircases, in the film room, or in the Art Show. Now was *their* time.

We had planned a little surprise. Tellurean Enterprises, and Devra and Nova Enterprises had contributed assorted "Star Trek" merchandise, from fanzines, and buttons to T-shirts, for us to give out to the helpers. George Takei picked the winning numbers out of a bowl. About fifty gifts were handed out.

The Roddenberrys stopped by before retiring to their suite. We surprised them by serenading them with "The Battle Hymn of the Helpers." Gene's reaction was stunned astonishment, but Majel joined right in and gracefully kneeled at the feet of "The Creator." We all roared and then we bowed and kneeled also— and sang it all over again and *Louder!!!* As we sang, Gene backed into a corner, expressions of disbelief and amazement flitting across his face.

It was one of the most exciting and satisfying moments of any convention. We were showing two of our favorite people just how much we love them. You could have built a pathway to the stars with all the love in that room—which made the shock all the greater when they called from their suite after they had returned to tell us they had been robbed!

It was the Committee's turn to be stunned—by horror now, not joy. It was not till much later that we were to discover that over a dozen other robberies had taken place that night— dealers, fans, Committee, and regular guests of the hotel, some while in their rooms. Three girls had been asleep in their beds as the thief or thieves had taken their purses. They didn't discover it till the next morning. One man just thought it was the maid and was locked in a closet while his room was stripped of his possessions.

We managed to keep the knowledge of this major catastrophe to ourselves. The police were very good about being unobtrusive, and we wish to thank them now. We had kept all this from the fans at the party because we did not want to spoil their good time. Of course, some of them noticed our white faces and asked what was wrong. We said that someone had been robbed and just left out the name. So the party continued for another hour or so.

It finally broke up when Devra, who with Barbara was occupying the 22B suite that I had had the year before, decided to end it. Devra appeared attired in a white flannel nightgown and slippers and went over to everyone and said "It was so nice to have you. Thanks so much for coming. I hope you *had* a good time." They got the hint.

The Committee, including our attorneys the Harrises, David Gerrold, and Bill Theiss, gathered in the con suite for an emergency meeting. While waiting for everyone to get together, I helped Steve Whitmore wash glasses in the kitchen. Well, I had to do something. Washing glasses is constructive; screaming and banging your head against the wall are not. We all decided that the fans would have to be told, and finally at about three in the morning we decided upon the words and that David would make the announcement the next day. I also wrote one to deliver to the press.

David delivered it simply and sincerely. The fans were shocked and promised to keep clear of any restricted areas. They were wonderful. David, I know we thanked you then, but I'd like to thank you again now. For everything.

I went to visit the Roddenberrys that morning. The thief had taken all their money and also Majel's clothes. Majel and Gene (God bless them) are so marvelous, they even had a funny story to tell me. It seems that Gene coincidentally had been teasing Majel about her clothes being stolen. He took a shower that morning, and in his robe went to the closet to get a suit.

"Oh ——!" Gene yelled. Majel came running and started to laugh. The closet was bare!

But it really wasn't funny. Gene was not going straight home. He was going on a two-week college tour, and all he had to wear were the slacks, jacket, shirt, and tie he had worn the night before.

That was when I ran around the con mentally sizing up every man I met. Was he Gene's size? While I was out of the room, a young man named Howard Greenwald came to the rescue. He had just come to give Majel a gift of a lovely pin and earrings made in the shape of the command insignia. Anyway, he sped to his room and brought back a couple of shirts that, luckily, fit Gene—and they were drip-dry, too!

Just recently, I met Howard at a talk I gave at the Port Washington Library. He told me that the shirts were returned to him a while later, freshly laundered, with a beautiful letter and a flight-deck certificate. The best part was that this joyful package arrived on Howard's birthday.

After getting Gene settled, shirtwise, I collected Jackie, and we rushed down to the press room. We had a press conference. We also had a problem. Jackie was just coming down with a bad cold (which later turned out to be the flu, along with a massive ear infection), and she also had laryngitis. It was at this meeting with the press that I introduced her as "The Whisperer."

The first thing I did was make the announcement about the robbers. I did not mention the Roddenberrys, and perhaps that's why the media did not publish anything. As we were answering questions, out of the corner of my eye I saw my "coup" enter and take a seat in the back of the room.

It was Anne Meara and her two children, Amy and Ben Stiller and their cousin, Matthew Fenton. Let's backtrack to about a month prior to the con. One day, in the office, I got a call from Miss Meara. She wanted to get some tickets to the convention. She remembered meeting me at Paramount when she was shooting a special film for the U. S. Treasury Department that my old friend Howard Rayfiel was producing. I had always admired the act that she and her husband, Jerry Stiller, did, and told her so. She was currently appearing as the star of the "Kate McShane" series. (Unfortunately, not even Anne's great talent could save the series.) Anyway, I told her I wouldn't think of taking her money. I would give her the three tickets. She replied "I always sing for my supper."

"Well," I said, "if you insist, you can sing for your supper by appearing as a surprise guest."

"I'd love to."

"Great! What day do you want me to come down?"

"Um, why don't we make it for Sunday afternoon—okay?"

While Jackie was whispering all about the "Star Trek" Wel-committee (see Chapter IX for information), I walked over to welcome Anne and her two children and their cousin. Ellen had given them gold press badges because they had the blue guest badges in the worry room.

After the interview was finished, I took Anne and the children up to the main ballroom. The star panel was about to begin, and I wanted her to give Gene and Majel their plaques. What plaques? Well we, the Committee, had decided, since it was our last convention, to give all our beloved guests something to commemorate the occasion—hence the plaques. They were shield-shaped, about five-by-seven inches, with a brass plate engraved with the recipient's name, the date, the convention, and a few words of love.

Anne and I waited backstage while the three children sat on the floor in front of the stage—the best seats in the house. I unwrapped the plaques and almost died. Anne looked over my shoulder and got hysterical. Instead of "Gene Roddenberry" it said "Gene Robbenderry!"

Majel's was correct. But what could we do about Gene's? Well, I hoped in the emotion of the moment he wouldn't notice and we would get it from them later and have it corrected. And that's what happened. Whew!

I introduced Anne to the audience, and they went wild.

"We always try to have a surprise or two for you during the convention. On two occasions it was Leonard Nimoy [roars and screams]. Last year it was Robert Lansing [roars and screams]. This year we have someone you all know, but she has no real connection with 'Star Trek' except that she and her family love it as much as we do.

"Ladies and gentlemen, the star of the new CBS series 'Kate McShane,' Miss Anne Meara."

Screams, yells, and a standing ovation.

Anne told me later that she was completely stunned by her reception. She said a few words, telling the fans of her family's love of "Star Trek," and then presented the Roddenberrys with their plaques. She was gracious, charming, and lovely.

We stayed and watched the panel for a while, one of the few times I saw programing during that convention. There were the usual questions, and I wished the fans would be a little more original in their thinking. I mean, if Jimmy Doohan was asked once, he was asked twenty times, "How did the matter-antimatter engines work?" I mean, really, kids.

It's a good thing Jimmy is a quick thinker. Each time he would relate "the Theory of Concupicity." You know, he was so good, a lot of the fans believed him.

Jimmy was a good boy today. But earlier in the con he had given Linda Deneroff, the assistant in charge of the ballroom, actual palpitations. It was this way: Jimmy loves people, and people love Jimmy. And sometimes this love so overwhelms him that he just has to let it out. He walked onto the stage in the main ballroom, and Linda introduced him. The crowd roared their love, and Jimmy, without giving Linda any warning, leaped off the stage and started shaking hands with hysterically joyous fans. As he got farther and farther into the crowd, Linda got paler and paler. By the time he made a full circuit of the ballroom, *including the balcony*, Linda was the color of this sheet of paper.

When he realized how upset she was, he said he was sorry he had caused her to worry. When a man is as charming as James Doohan, you forgive him anything.

Whoops, I had to leave. I was due in the East Ballroom for my first onstage appearance at the con. Anne and the kids toddled along with me. They actually went to hear me talk! How about that?

The films had just ended, and a lot of the kids had left to go to the dealers' room, to the Art Show, to see Isaac Asimov in the main ballroom, or to go to the john—or so Carol McFeeley, who was the assistant in charge of the East Ballroom, told me.

We set up the mike, and I started to talk. First I introduced myself. Then, spotting Jackie in the audience (a loyal friend and true), I introduced her. I also introduced Anne Meara. Equal time for everybody. I even introduced Ben Yalow, who doesn't like *anybody* to know who he is. Then I answered questions about the cons, about *Star Trek Lives!*, about ABC, and about television in general. While I spoke I noticed the room filling up. How nice, I thought. Then I thought, idiot, they're coming in early to get a good seat for Nichelle Nichols. (She was right after me.)

I got a nice hand when I finished, and that pleased me. Nichelle asked me to introduce her and that gave me a thrill. I said, "Ladies and gentlemen, I have the honor to introduce someone who needs no introduction. She is beloved by us all for her beauty, charm, and talent: Miss Nichelle Nichols."

We couldn't stay to hear all of Nichelle's talk because the kids had to go to the john; Anne and I saw it as an opportunity to have a smoke. The two of us were about to have a nicotine fit. Anne had run out of cigarettes, so one of the helpers ran down and got some for her and we sat and talked and smoked till it was time for Anne to give De Kelley his plaque.

I found out later that when several people heard we were in the ladies' room smoking, they thought we were "smoking." Sorry, folks, just the ordinary kind of cigarette.

We were sitting on the edge of the stage waiting for De to make his entrance when Anne suddenly turned to me and said, "What should I say to Mr. Kelley?"

"Well, why not ask him if he makes house calls, or something?"

She laughed, "Say, do you write situation comedies?"

I introduced Anne, and the crowd went wild again. She presented the plaque to De amid laughter and applause. De was his usual gracious and charming self. You know something, I've never seen him when he hasn't been.

We stayed to watch De for a while, but then Anne had to call her sister-in-law to come to pick her up. We walked into the con suite, and all the helpers looked and looked again. The buzzing started. And the little pieces of paper appeared like magic. After she gave the autographs she agreed to do a tape interview with a gentleman of the press, who was thanking his lucky stars that he happened to be in the con suite at that moment.

I know I seem to be thanking people all over the place, but what's right is right. Anne, thank you for giving us so much of your time. If that's the way you sing for your supper, I'll spring for a meal for you any day!

Before she left, Anne stopped to thank the two helpers who had kept a collective eye on the children. Debbie Myers and Michael Scholnick were prime examples of what helpers should be: bright, efficient, and well-mannered. Thanks, kids.

Before leaving, I went over to Claire Eddy to see how she was feeling. You remember Claire: At the 1975 Con she had sprained her ankle and ended up in a wheelchair. This year, not to be out-done, she got a glorious case of the Victoria "A" flu. On Friday morning she was in the con suite living room preparing to go downstairs and join the fray when she suddenly felt sick and dizzy. Diane Duane, who was a nurse as well as a fine assistant, took one look and said, "You'd better lie down before you fall down."

Claire lay down. She ended up running the helper horde from the couch in the con suite. Oh, didn't I tell you? Claire had become a member of the Committee and was in charge of the helpers. She, with her assistant Steve Whitmore, did a beautiful job. With a two-way radio unit at her side and a permanent path cleared to the john, she handled all the problems with dispatch—and a fever of 102 degrees. A bravo, please.

Remember my mentioning the vandalism that took place in the press room? Well, they had torn out all the phones and stolen some blank cards and pens. My crew was going nuts. With no phones there was no way to keep track of and arrange the comings and goings of the stars for their interviews. We got some extra helpers and set up a runner system. As usual, even in their most insane moments, my kids handled themselves like pros. As a matter of fact, several of them have headed the press rooms at other conventions.

We had a problem. Well, we always had problems, but this was a biggee. The Masquerade did not begin until nine o'clock. What to do with all those fans until then? We had films in the Tudor Room until twelve midnight and in the East Ballroom until seven-thirty, when the prejudging for the Masquerade began, and then films again till midnight. The main ballroom had to have all the chairs taken out between five o'clock and seven-thirty so we could seat everyone. Steve Rosenstein and the hotel staff were setting up the side stage for the Masquerade. That way if everyone was seated on the floor we would have enough room, we hoped.

But you can't have several thousand people sitting and twiddling their thumbs for almost two hours. What to do?

David to the rescue! Bad back and all. David had hurt his back and had been taped up by the house doctor and was still in a bit of pain. Did I say he was in a *bit* of pain? He did not tell us till later that he was in agony. But when he heard of our problem, he volunteered to keep the fans entertained. He was supposed to be "on" from about seven-thirty to eight-fifteen, when I was to relieve him. When I got down there, he was having such a good time, I ended up just sitting and enjoying—except for the times I had to tell some fans to pull in their legs so other people could have room to sit down. I'm afraid I yelled a bit. But, by George—uh, Joan—they moved, and fast. Thanks, fellas.

While David answered questions, a young soldier got up and announced that he had come all the way from Fort Polk, Louisiana, because he had heard that this was our last convention and he would not miss it. David asked if he was having a good time, and the soldier said it would have been worth it if he had had to walk the whole way.

The Masquerade started on time, and David was a judge along with Bill Theiss and Hal Clement. Instead of being seated in the audience, the judges were seated behind a table at the end of the stage. It worked out very well.

As usual, there were many gorgeous costumes, some of which you will see in the picture sections. Connie Faddis had a costume made largely of copper, which she herself tooled. She was the Romulan praetor, and she was magnificent. So was Monica Miller, in her blue silk and diamonds. And so were many others —too many to mention. It was our last Masquerade and in some ways our best.

It finished about 12:30 A.M., and the Committee and guests wended their way up to the con suite. We talked for a while, and somebody decided at about two o'clock to make spaghetti and sauce. We all thought that was a flash of genius. And delicious, too.

Monday. Mondays always seem to have their own particular problems built in. This, the last of our con Mondays, was no different. George had informed Elyse that he had to leave Sunday night because he was shooting a pilot on Monday. George was scheduled for 1:00 P.M. Elyse quickly moved Mal Klein from the East Ballroom at three o'clock to George's time. We'd replace Mal with films. Mal was giving a talk on the "Star Trek" animation.

Then Nichelle went to Elyse. Nichelle had been fighting a battle against the flu during the whole con, and she finally lost. She asked if it would be all right with us if she left on Sunday night. So Elyse replaced Nichelle with Jackie and me—only it turned out that the hotel had double-booked the East Ballroom (a mistake and how) and we had to schedule the films in "B" and "C," where we had been holding the book exhibit. So we ended up in the Tudor Room following Gordon Dickson, whom I would follow any day—and have.

They were swinging from the rafters when we entered. Gordie was telling them all about the Dorsai, and they were lapping it all up.

Gordie had arrived the night before from Boston. He had been at another convention and had left early so he could appear at ours. Wasn't that great? We always tried to have a kind of subliminal-science fiction convention going on the same time as the regular con. That way fans would get to know the science-fiction writers and be turned on to their work.

Isaac Asimov said that the sales of his books have risen greatly since he started speaking at "Star Trek" cons. And it didn't hurt when Bill Shatner said his favorite authors (the two he could think of at the moment, anyway) were Isaac and Theodore Sturgeon. Within half an hour of those words leaving Bill's lips, there was not a book by either of those gentlemen to be found in the dealers' room!

When Gordie finished his speech, "The Whisperer" and I took over. It was mostly a question-and-answer session. Jackie answered questions about "Kraith" and the "Star Trek" Welcommittee, which she started. She now has a stable of about fifty writers working on "Kraith" stories. I think you would call that being an inspiration. I fielded a lot of questions about being on

the "Star Trek" set, what the actors were like, and what went
into putting on a convention. Many of the fans were upset that
the committee was not going to do any more. I tried to explain
how much work went into a con and that we just could not
spend that much time, effort, and life force any more—at least
not without getting a bit more than "fun" out of it. One fan got
up and said that this was her very first convention. She had read
about the cons in *Star Trek Lives!* and hated to think that this
was the last of The Committee Cons. This last statement brought
a large burst of applause.

A lot of people must have felt that way because, since Sunday,
everyone wearing a red Committee badge was stopped every
other step by concerned fans pleading for this not to be our last
con. We found out later that there were actually six petitions
floating around the con asking us to please put on more conventions. One of them was from the dealers! It gave us all a very
warm feeling. It meant the fans came to our cons because they
knew they'd get a good, fun con. It almost didn't matter who the
guests were (I said, "almost").

When we finished our bit, we signed autographs for a while. I
always get a big kick out of this. I mean, I love to get people's
signatures and to have some fan want mine—it's a big thrill.

I stopped by the worry room with Joyce Yasner after the auto-
graph session. We met the science-fiction panel there. I knew
Fred Pohl, but I had never met Ted Cogswell or Charles Spano.
Fred mentioned that Messrs. Spano and Cogswell were writing a
"Star Trek" novel called *Spock Messiah*. On hearing the title,
Joyce and I made very impolite noises. They looked a bit disconcerted—but not disconcerted enough, since they kept the title.
I'd better not make any further comments. Except—I just don't
understand why they don't get some of the people who were
connected with the show to write a "Star Trek" novel, or even
publish one of the excellent fan-written novels by fans like Connie Faddis, the Basta sisters, Leslie Fish, Carolyn Meredith, and
many, many others.

Jimmy Doohan was the last speaker of the day. He sang, he
joked, and he and the fans had a ball. By the way, don't you just
love Jimmy's beard? I hope they let him keep it for the movie. If

"they" don't, we may have to start another letter campaign. Are
you listening, Paramount?

We closed the press room for the last time and said good-bye
to a lot of the fans. We arrived in the con suite just in time to
hear Barbara Wenk as she answered the telephone.

"'Star Trek' con. We have retired. The con is over, and we are
not having any more. Can I help you?"

She said she heard a gulp at the other end of the phone, then a
sigh, and then the person hung up.

That kind of set the tone for the rest of the evening. Most of
the guests and many of the fans had already scattered to the
winds; only the diehards were left. Val Sussman, Linda Deneroff,
Elan Litt, Diane Duane, David Gerrold (I told you he was family), Pat O'Neill, Wayne Smith, Janet Ingber, and others were
writing filksongs and munching Freihoeffer's. Oh, the Freihoeffer's? They are the munchiest, chewiest chocolate-chip cookies
you have ever flung a tooth around. Barbara Wenk's father had
driven down from Poughkeepsie (no less) with one hundred
boxes. You read right, one hundred boxes. Then her mother
brought down another sixty, Listen, that's all some of the Committee survived on, Freihoeffer's. We thought they were all gone
by Saturday but someone found a hidden cache of eight boxes
under the kitchen sink. Munch, munch. After the Freihoeffer's,
we were in the mood for some serious eating. So we sent out for
—all together now—*Chinese food!*

Janet Ingber came over to tell me a lovely story about David.
Here it is in her own words:

"On Friday afternoon at the 1976 con, I attended David Gerrold's press conference. It was excellent. Everyone enjoyed talking and listening to David. He was open and honest with the
press and showed a genuine interest in what we were writing.

"The next time I got to talk to David was Saturday night in, of
all places, an elevator. He began the conversation by saying that
he had seen me in the press room and various other places
around the convention. I must admit I was a little surprised that
he remembered me.

"He then asked me if he could ask me a personal question.
Call it instinct, intuition, whatever, I knew what he was going to
ask even before he began. He asked me if I had a vision prob-

lem: specifically if I were blind or legally blind. His question didn't bother me. He approached the situation in a nice way. He then went on to say that he had done a lot of work with the blind and that he thought my navigation was fantastic. At this point I was shocked. I thought it was really nice for him to take the time to notice, and that he thought enough of my ability to ask his question without my getting mad or defensive. The next day I bought an 'I Like David Gerrold' button." (P.S.: Janet is legally blind.)

Since Janet is one of my special friends, thank you, David.

Besides the songwriting, fans were gathered in the den talking while others, still flu-filled, were zonked out on various couches and chairs. For once I was feeling fine—a little tired, but otherwise, fine. Maybe it was because I tried to get at least five hours' sleep a night and eat two meals a day. Hmmm, maybe that was it.

I was not the only one feeling "fine." In the corner of the dining room was a huge, and I mean *huge* plastic bag filled with those little plastic fragments one uses to pack fragile packages. You know, they look like corn doodles. I don't remember how they got there, but I sure remember how they left!

The Plastic Doodle War started very innocently. David asked Elyse, "What is it?" Elyse told him, and he took one out and tossed it to Lee Smoire, saying, "Don't say I never gave you anything."

Then Elyse playfully tossed a few at David, whereupon he picked up the huge bag and held it upside down over Elyse's head. It had a loose tie around the mouth, and only a small drizzle of doodles fell. Then Elyse grabbed the bag away from David, and all mayhem broke loose, along with the tie on the bag.

That did it! Everybody started throwing handfuls at everybody else till the floors of both the dining and living rooms were inches deep. All during this, Wilma Fisher was sitting watching all the fun and drinking her tea. David felt she should join in the fun. So he dropped a few doodles in her tea. Wilma looked at David, and then she looked in her cup. Four "things" were floating around in her freshly brewed tea. Before Wilma could retaliate, our hotel man, Charlie Gilbert, walked in. He took one horrified look at what was once the staid, dignified Presidential Suite and threw a fit! (I think he was just tired and on edge, because he knew the hotel would be closing down and wasn't sure where he would end up. I'm glad to say he's now at the Biltmore, and they are extremely fortunate to have someone of Charlie's caliber.)

Anyway, he threatened us with expulsion from the hotel if we didn't clean up the mess right away. Everyone fell to, and while my blind friend Andy Jadelskyj held the big plastic bag, all of us threw handfuls of the ding-blasted doodles into it. We cleaned up every bit in about twelve minutes.

Charlie had calmed down by then and was only teasing us. Pretending to be oh so serious, he made a full tour of the suite and pronounced it a job well done. Whew!

You'd have thought with the riot and the robberies there would have been enough excitement for our last convention. Nope: The powers-that-be were not finished with us yet.

Jeff Maynard said it happened about 9:00 A.M. on Tuesday morning after the con. He smelled something funny and opened his room door to see clouds of smoke filling the hallway. He dashed out of the room and peered down the hall toward the elevators and couldn't even make them out in the murkiness. Talk about panic! He ran back in his room and frantically called the hotel operator, visions of *The Towering Inferno* dancing in his head. As she answered, he yelped, "There's smoke on the twenty-second floor—lots of smoke!!"

Calmly, she answered, "Yes, sir, we know about it. Everything is all right. The fire is on the third floor."

"Oh," said Jeff. And hung up. *On the third floor!* Then what's the smoke doing all the way up here?

He rushed out into the hall again just in time to see some firemen loom out of the gloom. "What's happening?"

"It's all under control; we're just checking the rest of the hotel."

Heaving a sigh of relief, Jeff returned to his room, and stuffing towels under the door to keep out the worst of the smoke, he went back to bed.

Meanwhile, Joyce smelled the smoke and ran down twenty-two flights of stairs. I always knew she was in good condition.

234   THE MAKING OF THE TREK CONVENTIONS

Where was I? *I* never even woke up. Yup, I slept through the whole thing. The fire engines, the shouting, and the general sound and fury did not disturb the Winston slumber.

Tuesday was for cleaning up. We straightened up the con suite (Charlie always said we left the maids very little to do), distributed all the leftover food, loaded as much as we could on the truck and the rest was put in the storage room. This was all the remaining programs, trivia contests, badges, etc., and would be picked up at a more convenient time. Stu Grossman, Ben Yalow, and I packed up all the films we had borrowed from Paramount. Ben and I took a cab over to the Post Office and after parting with about fifty dollars they promised to send the films off for us. Thank you, Paramount, for five years of episodes. Thank you.

At about this time the Committee decided to go out to dinner in a genuine restaurant. We talked of many things, mostly how well the con had gone. How happy the fans had seemed. The one thing we didn't discuss was next year—because there wasn't going to be any next year. And that was strange, very strange. As a matter of fact, when "our" weekend in February rolled around in 1977, we all kinda panicked. What are we gonna do? Where are we gonna go? Well, we—or most of us, anyway—decided to go to a science-fiction con in Boston. It is usually a rather small con, but for some reason (?) it got a lot of new fans, "Star Trek" fans, that year. It was a good con and had some dear, familiar faces around—Isaac Asimov and Hal Clement and David Gerrold, to mention a few. Many of us got together and held a kind of minicon in the midst of the other con. We gathered in the lobby and our rooms and talked "Star Trek" till the wee hours. It was great!

There is a kind of epilogue to all this. Our beloved Commodore Hotel is gone. There were rumors all over the place before and after our con. At one point we heard that they were closing on January 20, 1976. Our con was taking place the weekend of February 12. We really did not need rumors like that one, not with two other cons taking place just the month before ours. One was Al Schuster's at the Statler-Hilton in the beginning of January. That was okay, because many of the fans went to both.

But the one due at the New York Hilton in the middle of January—*they* were spending $$,$$$ on publicity *and* calling themselves "Star Trek" Con 1976, which was a bit too close to what our con was called.

A lot of people got confused. Oh, the letters and phone calls.

"Why didn't you tell us you had changed your dates from February to January?"

We hadn't.

"How come you're at the Hilton this year and not the Commodore?"

We weren't.

"I thought you said Leonard Nimoy wasn't coming."

He wasn't. We thought he was for a while, but there was a mix-up—and he wasn't.

Here's a funny: The weekend of the New York Hilton convention we were at the Commodore with our assistants and helpers stuffing the old shopping bags. Suddenly the phone rang.

"What's your film schedule for tonight?"

??????

"What's the matter? Don't you people know what's going on at your own convention?"

"Yes, ma'am, we know what's going on at *our* con, but *our* con is three weeks from now!"

??????

We told her to call the Hilton. She said she already had, and they didn't seem to know anything—so she had called us! She also asked if we were planning to have twenty thousand people, too.

"No," we said, "we're limiting it to six thousand."

She bought two tickets.

Anyway, six thousand was just about right for the ol' Commodore. There might have been more, since that total did not include the dealers, guests, or press. Anyway, six thousand was a good figure because it was not so many that you felt jammed but enough so you felt the excitement.

After three conventions the hotel staff knew us and we knew them. I've spoken about Charlie Gilbert before—he was our man, and anything we wanted, we got—within reason, of course. He and Maureen Edwards would drop into the parties and check to see if everything was all right. Charlie always said if you're having a big con you don't go home at six o'clock. You stay around and look after things. He is a rare, rare type, and we are very grateful to him and all his staff.

Michael Roche was the electrician. He would stroll into the ballroom or the press room or the film room and look around. "Looks like you need another mike (or extension cord) in here." In five minutes we would have it.

The last con to be held at the Commodore was a "Star Trek" minicon with Jimmy Doohan as special guest star. He had been one of our first guests, and now he was the last "Star Trek" star to make an appearance at the hotel.

We felt very much at home at the Commodore; it was "our" hotel. When we got word it was really closing its doors for the last time, we knew we had to do something. We gathered a group together and held a wake. You read right: a wake! It was held in the beautiful New York, New York bar. There were about seventeen of us, including Stu Hellinger, Linda Deneroff, Elan Jane Litt, Val Sussman, Janet Ingber, Thom Anderson, Regina Gottesman, Fern Marder, John Vanible, Pat O'Neill, Mark Marmer, and Ben Yalow.

Elan had made one of her famous carrot cakes. It had black icing, and written in white it was inscribed, "It's Dead, Jim." Joan Lunden of WABC-TV covered for the eleven-o'clock news. There was even a song written to commemorate the sad occasion:

"ODE TO THE COMMODORE"[1]
(or "It's Dead, Jim")
by Foggy MacIntyre, Barbara Peters, Ben Yalow, Linda Deneroff, Elan Litt, Thom Anderson, Stu Hellinger and Cindi Casbey.

O Commodore, O Commodore
O grand hotel that we adore.
O Commodore, O Commodore
O grand hotel that we adore.

You're right near subway, train, and bus
And also Relaxation Plus,
So thanks for no high rates for us
O Commodore so glorious.

[1] To the tune of "O Tannenbaum."

The cons were here and you were nice
But we kept running out of ice.
Our hot parties began to zoom
But maids came in to clean the room.

Your ballroom floor had carpets new
And painted walls of white and blue
And when we left the final con
The furniture was somehow gone.

O Charlie Gilbert, you were fine;
You're never with your wife at nine.
The people who checked in here were
All beating up Stu Hellinger.

New York, New York was fine as such
But Brew Burger just charged too much.
The hotel service, it was fine:
You brought us beer and scotch and wine.

The presidential suite we loved
On Forty-second Street above;
The Hyatt House we want to cuss
Because you are evicting us.

The source from which our pleasure stemmed
Too bad the building is condemned.
O Commodore, you gave your all;
Get ready for the wrecking ball.

Good-bye, old friend; there will never be another like you.

THE LAST "STAR TREK" TRIVIA CONTEST

(Leftover questions that never made it into the previous contests.)

1. Who first noticed that the Talosians had captured Captain Pike?
   A. Dr. Boyce B. Jose Tyler C. Mr. Spock
2. Commissioner Hedford suffered from
   A. Sakuro's disease B. synthococcus novae C. Rigellian fever
3. The planet Deneva was originally colonized as a(n)
   A. freighting-line base B. medical research center C. agrarian commune

4. In which episode did Kirk press a button and then wait for the turbolift to arrive?
    A. *What Are Little Girls Made Of?*　B. *Mirror, Mirror*
    C. *Where No Man Has Gone Before*

5. In *The City on the Edge of Forever,* what was the room number of the "flop" Kirk and Spock shared?
    A. 21　B. 5-G　C. 17

6. Condition Green means:
    A.　Someone is in trouble but no one is to go to his aid
    B.　Under no circumstances approach this planet
    C.　War or invasion is imminent

7. How old was Zefram Cochrane when the Companion found him?
    A.　35　B. 87　C. 62

8. Who were in *Wolf in the Fold?*
    A. Sylvia and Kara　B. Kara and Sybo　C. Sybo and Angela

9. What is Dr. Piper's first name?
    A. Robert　B. Mark　C. Philip

10. Radans are
    A. Dilithium crystals　B. Aliens　C. Rare jewels

11. In *The Immunity Syndrome,* how much of the crew fainted when the first telemetry probe was launched?
    A. One third　B. One fourth　C. One half

12. How many androids were on Mudd's planet?
    A. 207,908　B. 207,809　C. 209,708

13. Mysteries give Captain Kirk
    A. Headaches　B. Bellyaches　C. Goosebumps

14. A megalite survey was made on
    A. the *Enterprise*'s computers.　B. an ion storm　C. Nomad

15. In *The Enemy Within,* what was the first thing the "evil" Captain Kirk did?
    A. Go to Janice Rand's cabin　B. Demand Saurian brandy　C. Punch a crewman

16. Who was Angela Martine marrying?
    A. Andrew Stiles　B. Robert Tomlinson　C. Joe Tormolen

17. The androids of Mudd's planet were made of
    A. beryllium-titanium alloy　B. selenium-tellurian alloy　C. rhenium-neodymium alloy

18. In *Friday's Child,* the *Enterprise* received a false distress call from the freighter
    A. S.S. *Wodan*　B. S.S. *Antares*　C. S.S. *Deidre*

19. What technique was used to take the *Enterprise* into the past in *Assignment: Earth?*
    A. implosion of the engines   B. Guardian of Forever   C. light-speed breakaway factor
20. How many people (crewmen and civilians) had middle names beginning with the initial *T?*
    A. One   B. Two   C. Three
21. Charlene Masters was
    A. an engineering assistant   B. chemist   C. an old friend of Captain Kirk's
22. In *Day of the Dove,* what decks did the Klingons control?
    A. The crew's quarters   B. Deck 6 and Starboard Deck 7
    C. Deck 5, Engineering, and Auxiliary Control
23. Who was captain of the *Astral Queen?*
    A. Tom Nellis   B. William B. Harrison   C. John Daily
24. What was Sam Kirk's private transmitter code?
    A. GSK 783, Subspace Frequency 3   B. GSK 837, Subspace Frequency 4   C. GSK 738, Subspace Frequency 2
25. In *The Doomsday Machine,* what was the name of the security guard assigned to escort Commodore Decker to sick bay?
    A. Montgomery   B. Washburn   C. Elliot
26. In which episode did Uhura speak Swahili?
    A. *The Tholian Web*   B. *The Changeling*   C. *I, Mudd*
27. In what year was Flint born?
    A. 3834 B.C.   B. 3034 B.C.   C. 3384 B.C.
28. Hodgkin's Law of Parallel Planet Development was mentioned in
    A. *Miri*   B. *Bread and Circuses*   C. *A Piece of the Action*
29. Who was the mutual friend of Captain Kirk and Miss Piper?
    A. Areel Shaw   B. Helen Noel   C. Helen Johannsen
30. How old is Ensign Chekov?
    A. 21   B. 22   C. 24
31. How long had it been since Kirk and Areel Shaw had last seen each other?
    A. Four years, two months, and an odd number of days
    B. Four years, seven months, and an odd number of days
    C. Seven years, two months, and an odd number of days
32. The two "attendants" dreamed up by Dr. McCoy in Shore Leave were from
    A. A cabaret on Rigel 2   B. Wrigley's pleasure planet
    C. Orion

33. Who called Spock a "dope"?
    A. Charlie X   B. Bela Oxmyx   C. Harry Mudd
34. What song did Uhura hum in *The Changeling?*
    A. "Nightingale Woman"   B. "Charlie Is Our Darling"
    C. "Beyond Antares"
35. What is the basis for much of the equipment on the *Enterprise?*
    A. Transtator   B. Tricorder   C. Transponder
36. Philana gave Spock
    A. a kithara   B. a scroll   C. shield
37. In what episode was Spock compared to Pan?
    A. *Plato's Stepchildren*   B. *Bread and Circuses*   C. *Who
    Mourns for Adonais?*
38. Who has been called a "walking freezer unit"?
    A. Spock   B. Dr. Dehner   C. Norman
39. In what year will "Nightingale Woman" be written?
    A. 1996   B. 2015   C. 1999
40. On what planet will "Nightingale Woman" be written?
    A. Rigel 4   B. Tarbolde   C. Canopus
Identify who said the following quotations:
41. "You Earth people are a stiff-necked lot, aren't you?"
42. "You are beautiful, more beautiful than any dream of beauty
    I've ever known."
43. "But that's not the way it happened!"
44. "Each kiss is as the first."
45. "That was the equation! Existence! Survival must cancel out
    programing!"
Choices:
A. McCoy   E. Kang   I. Kirk
B. Bela Oxmyx   F. Spock   J. Areel Shaw
C. Edith Keeler G. Ruk   K. Helen Noel
D. Garth   H. Chekov   L. Miramanee
Name the episodes from which the following quotations were taken.
46. "Back to that bed, bucko."
47. "Tell me I'm an attractive young lady or ask me if I've ever
    been in love."
48. "A very interesting game, this poker."
49. "What makes you right and a trained psychologist wrong?"
50. "You should be told the difference between empiricism and
    stubbornness, Doctor."
51. "Have you ever been engaged, Mr. Spock?"
52. "The air is the air."

53. "I understand, Doctor. I'm sure the Captain would simply have said, "'Forget it, Bones.'"
54. "Well, Jim, here's another morsel of agony for you."
55. "I have little to say about it, Captain, except that, for the first time in my life, I was happy."
56. "When in Rome, we'll do as the Romans do."
57. "Only fools fight in a burning house."
58. "My bairns, my poor bairns."
59. "If we let out a yell, I want an armed party down there before the echo dies."
60. "Mr. Spock, you're a stubborn man."

Choices:

A. Where No Man Has Gone Before
B. The Corbomite Maneuver
C. Mudd's Women
D. The Man Trap
E. The Naked Time
F. The Conscience of the King
G. What Are Little Girls Made Of?
H. The Galileo Seven
I. This Side of Paradise
J. Amok Time
K. The Deadly Years
L. Bread and Circuses
M. A Private Little War
N. The Tholian Web
O. All Our Yesterdays
P. The Savage Curtain
Q. Requiem for Methuselah
R. Day of the Dove
S. The Paradise Syndrome
T. Turnabout Intruder
U. The Enemy Within

CHAPTER IX:

THE CONVENTION EXPLOSION;
OR,
WHAT DO YOU MEAN, IT'S ALL OUR FAULT?

Here is a list of all the "Star Trek" cons that took place, including ours, from 1972 through what information I could scrounge about 1977:

January 21–23, 1972	The "Star Trek" Con, New York, New York
October 19–22, 1972	Detroit Triple Fan Fair and Al Schuster's "Star Trek" Con, Detroit, Michigan
November 24–26, 1972	Film-Con 1 (Fantasy Film Fans International), Los Angeles, California
February 16–19, 1973	International "Star Trek" Convention, New York, New York
April 19–22, 1973	Equicon, Los Angeles, California
June 21–24, 1973	VulCon 1, New Orleans, Louisiana
October 4–7, 1973	Star Con 1, Detroit, Michigan
February 15–18, 1974	International "Star Trek" Convention, New York, New York
April 12–14, 1974	Equicon '74, Los Angeles, California
June 20–23, 1974	"Star Trek" '74/HoustonCon, Houston, Texas
July 5–7, 1974	Benecia 1, Atlanta, Georgia
July 19–21, 1974	Star Con 2, Detroit, Michigan
September 28–29, 1974	First British "Star Trek" Convention, Leicester, England
November 1–3, 1974	KWeST-Con, Kalamazoo, Michigan

November 23, 1974	Mini-Con 8, Houston, Texas
January 10–12, 1975	International "Star Trek" Convention, New York, New York
February 14–17, 1975	The "Star Trek" Convention, New York, New York
February 15–16, 1975	Mini-Con 9, Houston, Texas
February 21–23, 1975	Red Hour Festival, San Francisco, California
April 19, 1975	Mini-Con 10, Houston, Texas
May 2–4, 1975	OurCon, East Lansing, Michigan
May 24–26, 1975	Equicon '75, San Diego, California
May 29–June 1, 1975	VulCon 2, New Orleans, Louisiana
June 25–29, 1975	"Star Trek" '75/Houston Con, Houston, Texas
July 4–6, 1975	ReKWeST-Con, Kalamazoo, Michigan
August 1–3, 1975	The August Party, College Park, Maryland
August 1–3, 1975	Tele-Fantasy Con, New York, New York
August 8–11, 1975	Philadelphia International "Star Trek" Convention, Philadelphia, Pennsylvania
August 22–24, 1975	"Star Trek"-Science-fiction Spectacular, Chicago, Illinois
August 30–September 1, 1975	Palm Beach Con 1/Trekon International 1975, Palm Beach, Florida
September 20–21, 1975	Second British "Star Trek" Convention, Leicester, England
September 21, 1975	Mini-Con 11, Houston, Texas
October 9–12, 1975	American "Star Trek" Convention, Dallas, Texas
October 30–November 2, 1975	Star Con 4, Detroit, Michigan
November 8, 1975	A "Star Trek" Fan Conference, Seattle, Washington
November 23, 1975	Mini-Con 12, Houston, Texas
November 23, 1975	Mini-Trek Con I, New York, New York
December 12–14, 1975	Star Trektacular, Pittsburgh, Pennsylvania
January 1–4, 1976	Washington International "Star Trek" Convention, Washington, D.C.

January 3–4, 1976	Houston Mini-Con, Houston, Texas
January 16–19, 1976	International "Star Trek" Convention, New York, New York
January 23–25, 1976	New York "Star Trek" '76, New York, New York
February 12–16, 1976	The "Star Trek" Convention, New York, New York
February 13–14, 1976	"Star Trek" Festival, Colombia, South America
February 21, 1976	"Star Trek" Festival, Sacramento, California
February 27–29, 1976	Star Trekon '76, Kansas City, Missouri
March 11–14, 1976	Star Con '76, Dallas, Texas
March 12, 1976	"Star Trek" Festival, Milwaukee, Wisconsin
March 12–14, 1976	"Star Trek": Houston, Houston, Texas
April 9–11, 1976	SeKWeSTerCon, Kalamazoo, Michigan
April 16–18, 1976	Equicon 1976, Los Angeles, California
April 16–19, 1976	The Boston "Star Trek" Convention, Boston, Massachusetts
May 9, 1976	Mini-Trek Con II, New York, New York
May 29–30, 1976	"Star Trek" Convention, Miami Beach, Florida
June 12, 1976	"Star Trek" Con: San Jose, San Jose, California
June 17–20, 1976	Houston Con '76/"Star Trek" '76, Houston, Texas
June 18–20, 1976	"Star Trek"–SPACE CIRCUS, Chicago, Illinois
July 3, 1976	America's Quintcentennial Celebration, El Cajon, California
July 9–11, 1976	"Star Trek" Expo, Washington, D.C.
July 16–18, 1976	Omnicon, Louisville, Kentucky
July 16–18, 1976	Phoenix Comics and "Star Trek" Con, Phoenix, Arizona
July 23–25, 1976	Toronto "Star Trek" '76, Toronto, Canada

July 30–August 1, 1976	Polaris, San Antonio, Texas
July 30–August 1, 1976	The August Party, College Park, Maryland
August 6–8, 1976	"Star Trek" Con, Richmond, Virginia
August 7–8, 1976	"Star Trek" and Space Science Con, Oakland, California
August 13–15, 1976	Intermountain ST/SF Con, Salt Lake City, Utah
August 20–22, 1976	VulCon 3, New Orleans, Louisiana
September 3–6, 1976	Bicentennial 10, New York, New York
September 17–19, 1976	Star Trekin', Austin, Texas
September 23–25, 1976	Excali-Con 7609, Salt Lake City, Utah
September 25, 1976	"Star Trek" Convention: Sacramento, Sacramento, California
October 16, 1976	Rovacon 1, Roanoke, Virginia
October 22–25, 1976	*Playboy* Science-fiction Convention, Great Gorge, New Jersey
October 28–31, 1976	American "Star Trek" Convention '76, Dallas, Texas
November 13, 1976	Star Con '76, Sacramento, California
November 21, 1976	"Star Trek" Mini-Con, Alexandria, Virginia
December 4, 1976	Imagi-Con, San Francisco, California
January 29–30, 1977	Puget Sound Star Trekkers–Con II, Seattle, Washington
February 11–13, 1977	"Star Trek" and Space Science Con, San Francisco, California
March 19, 1977	Mini-Trek, Alexandria, Virginia
March 26, 1977	Star Trek Mini-Con, Baltimore, Maryland
April 1–3, 1977	Moncon I, Morgantown, West Virginia
May 7–8, 1977	Star Con, Denver, Colorado
May 15, 1977	Mini-Trek Con III, New York, New York
May 28–30, 1977	Phoenix ST, Comic and SF Film Con, Phoenix, Arizona
June 10–12, 1977	VulCon 4, New Orleans, Louisiana

June 18–19, 1977	Space Con 4, Los Angeles, California
June 22–26, 1977	Houston Con '77/Star Trek '77, Houston, Texas
June 24–26, 1977	"Star Trek" Con 1977, Kanas City, Missouri
July 7–10, 1977	Dallas Con, Dallas, Texas
July 15–18, 1977	"Star Trek" Philadelphia, Philadelphia, Pennsylvania
July 22–23, 1977	Infinite Star, 77 Milwaukee, Wisconsin
July 30, 1977	Okon, Tulsa, Oklahoma
September 2–5, 1977	"Star Trek" America, New York, New York
September 30–October 2, 1977	Star Con, San Diego, California
October 14–15, 1977	Salt Con, Salt Lake City, Utah

As you can see, we went from three conventions in 1972 to forty in 1976. There are only twenty-one definite cons planned so far for 1977—but this is only the middle of 1977 as I am writing this, and I know that will change. This list gives just the known and listed cons. I got this list from Helen Young and Allyson Whitfield of the "Star Trek" Welcommittee (STW). If you ever have any questions about anything to do with "Star Trek," write to:

"STAR TREK" WELCOMMITTEE
P. O. Box 207
Saranac, Mich. 48881

Include a stamped, self-addressed envelope (SASE), or you'll get put on the bottom of the pile—and it's a big pile!

If you want the *"Star Trek" Directory* to tell you what's going on where with fandom, fan clubs, fanzines, etc., send $1.50 and a SASE to:

Directory Sales Department
P. O. Box 206
New Rochelle, N.Y. 10804

It's "Star Trek's" Yellow Pages. The people who make up STW network do it out of love and a strange form of insanity, because they make no profit out of this. Also a wish to tell all the people who think they are alone about fan clubs in their area, where to buy fanzines and patches. How to form a fan club for their favorite star. What books have been or are now being written about "Star Trek" and "Star Trek"-related subjects. What cons are coming up and where—everything the eager "Trek" fan wants to and should know.

Well, you have just been taken around the world with "Star Trek" conventions. In the coming years, there will be conventions held in Australia, Germany, Japan, and other countries, as well as all over the United States. Some of them will be held to make money—some will, some won't. But the majority are held by fans to get together with other fans to trade ideas, addresses, and maybe film clips.

I remember one mother telling me about her son. He was bright, almost brilliant, but a recluse closed off from the rest of the world. Then he got interested in "Star Trek" and went to our 1973 con. Now he visits and is visited by fans (here a synonym for friends) from all over the world.

His mother is delighted. His father, who doesn't understand it all, shakes his head and says, "Well, it's better than stealing hubcaps."

A lot better! So if you've never been to a convention and you find one sprouting in your area, why don't you spend a day or so there? Find out what I've been talking about. Go and have a good time, and most of all, find a new friend.

For that's what fandom is all about: friendship, love, hope, and understanding. May you find them all, as I did.

Take care.

APPENDIX: *Answers to Trivia Contests*

THE 1972 "STAR TREK" TRIVIA CONTEST ANSWERS

1. B	6. C	11. C	16. C	21. B
2. A	7. B	12. B	17. B	22. B
3. C	8. C	13. A	18. A	23. A
4. A	9. B	14. C	19. C	24. A
5. B	10. B	15. A	20. A	25. B

THE 1973 "STAR TREK" TRIVIA CONTEST ANSWERS

1. B	21. B	41. A	61. A	81. B
2. C	22. C	42. C	62. C	82. A
3. B	23. C	43. A	63. C	83. C
4. A	24. B	44. B	64. A	84. C
5. A*	25. C	45. C	65. B	85. A
6. C	26. A	46. B	66. C	86. C
7. A	27. B	47. A	67. B	87. C
8. C	28. A	48. B	68. C	88. A
9. B	29. A	49. B	69. A	89. C
10. A	30. C	50. C	70. A	90. A
11. B	31. A	51. A	71. B	91. I
12. C	32. B	52. B	72. B	92. E
13. A	33. A	53. B	73. B	93. K
14. B	34. B	54. A	74. C	94. C
15. A	35. C	55. C	75. A	95. D
16. C	36. A	56. B	76. C	96. O
17. C	37. C	57. A	77. B	97. S
18. A	38. A	58. C	78. A	98. F
19. B	39. B	59. C	79. B	99. H
20. A	40. B	60. A	80. A	100. G

* According to Miss D. C. Fontana, the part of Mr. Spock was written for Leonard Nimoy, and no one else was ever offered the role. This question was given free to all entries in the contest. The answer provided was the intended answer.

THE 1974 "STAR TREK" TRIVIA CONTEST ANSWERS

1. C	21. B	41. A	61. B	81. B
2. C	22. B	42. A	62. B	82. A
3. A	23. C	43. B	63. C	83. B
4. B	24. C	44. A	64. A	84. A
5. A	25. C	45. A	65. B	85. C
6. A	26. B	46. C	66. A	86. C
7. C	27. A	47. B	67. C	87. A
8. B	28. A	48. A	68. A	88. A
9. A	29. B	49. B	69. B	89. B
10. C	30. A	50. A	70. A	90. C
11. A	31. C	51. A	71. C	91. C
12. B	32. C	52. C	72. B	92. B
13. C	33. A	53. B	73. A	93. A
14. B	34. B	54. A	74. B	94. B
15. A	35. B	55. C	75. C	95. C
16. B	36. A	56. C	76. A	96. A
17. C	37. C	57. A	77. B	97. A
18. C	38. B	58. B	78. A	98. A
19. B	39. C	59. A	79. C	99. B
20. A	40. C	60. C	80. C	100. C

THE 1975 "STAR TREK" TRIVIA CONTEST ANSWERS

1. B	21. A	41. B	61. B	81. C
2. C	22. B	42. A	62. B	82. B
3. B	23. B	43. B	63. A	83. C
4. A	24. A	44. A	64. B	84. A
5. B	25. A	45. B	65. C	85. B
6. C	26. B	46. A	66. B	86. A
7. B	27. A	47. A	67. C	87. B
8. A	28. B	48. B	68. B	88. C
9. C	29. C	49. C	69. B	89. B
10. C	30. B	50. B	70. A	90. A
11. B	31. C	51. A	71. A	91. B
12. A	32. A	52. B	72. B	92. L
13. B	33. C	53. A	73. B	93. G
14. C	34. C	54. C	74. A	94. C
15. C	35. B	55. C	75. B	95. B
16. B	36. C	56. B	76. C	96. H

17. C	37. A	57. A	77. B	97. I
18. B	38. C	58. A	78. A	98. K
19. A	39. A	59. B	79. B	99. A
20. C	40. B	60. C	80. A	100. F

THE 1976 "STAR TREK" TRIVIA CONTEST ANSWERS

1. B	21. B	41. A	61. G	81. I
2. C	22. B	42. B	62. J	82. A
3. B	23. A	43. C	63. F	83. H
4. A	24. C	44. C	64. H	84. B
5. C	25. B	45. A	65. A	85. BB
6. B	26. C	46. B	66. I	86. W
7. A	27. A	47. B	67. D	87. S
8. B	28. B	48. C	68. A	88. C
9. A	29. A	49. A	69. C	89. N
10. C	30. B	50. A	70. D	90. I
11. C	31. C	51. B	71. P	91. K
12. B	32. C	52. A	72. C	92. M
13. B	33. C	53. B	73. CC	93. D
14. C	34. B	54. A	74. E	94. T
15. B	35. B	55. B	75. X	95. G
16. A	36. A	56. B	76. Z	96. V
17. A	37. B	57. C	77. U	97. W
18. B	38. A	58. C	78. G	98. Q
19. A	39. C	59. A	79. L	99. AA
20. A	40. B	60. A	80. F	100. T

THE LAST "STAR TREK" TRIVIA CONTEST ANSWERS

1. B	21. A	41. D
2. A	22. B	42. F
3. A	23. C	43. I
4. C	24. A	44. L
5. A	25. A	45. G
6. A	26. B	46. U
7. B	27. A	47. D
8. B	28. B	48. B
9. B	29. C	49. A
10. A	30. B	50. F
11. C	31. B	51. G
12. B	32. A	52. J

13. A	33. B	53. N
14. A	34. C	54. M
15. B	35. A	55. I
16. B	36. A	56. P
17. A	37. C	57. R
18. C	38. B	58. S
19. C	39. A	59. D
20. C	40. C	60. H